101 Ways to Market Your Books

For Publishers and Authors

Other Books by John Kremer

Book Marketing Opportunities: A Directory
Book Marketing Opportunities: A Database
Book Marketing Made Easier
Directory of Short-Run Book Printers, Third Edition
The Independent Publisher's Bookshelf
    (formerly *The Self-Publishing Book Review*)
FormAides for Direct Response Marketing:
    Mail Order Made Easy
70 Full-Color Printers: A Report
Kinetic Optical Illusions

Coming soon:

Publicity Database: Magazines
Publicity Database: Newspapers
Publicity Database: Radio and TV
PrintBase: A National Printing Database
Sources and Resources: A Business Database

101 Ways to Market Your Books

For Publishers and Authors

Includes two special chapters showing writers how to take a more active role in marketing their books and how to capitalize on the increased recognition a book gives their work

John Kremer

Ad-Lib Publications
Fairfield, Iowa

Published by Ad-Lib Publications
51 N. Fifth Street
P. O. Box 1102
Fairfield, Iowa 52556-1102
(515) 472-6617

Printed and bound in the United States of America

Library of Congress Cataloging in Publication Data

Kremer, John, 1949-
101 ways to market your books.

   Bibliography: p.
   Includes index.
   1. Books—Marketing. 2. Publishers and publishing. 3. Authorship. 4.
Self-publishing. I. Title. II. Title: One hundred one ways to market your
books. III. Title: One hundred and one ways to market your books.
Z278.K72   1986   070.5   86-7995
ISBN 0-912411-08-2
ISBN 0-912411-09-0 (pbk.)

Table of Contents

Dedication

To lovers of books—

I hope this book helps you to get your own word out, to stir the appropriate people with your message, to reach the widest possible audience for your ideas, and—most of all—to enlarge the vision of all people everywhere for all time to come.

That's a great challenge, and maybe it's not possible to achieve. But it is certainly worth an attempt. Even several attempts.

Take your time. Do it right. And enjoy. That's the best advice I can give you.

INTRODUCTION

How to Get the Most Out of This Book

Let's make one thing clear right at the beginning: This book is not intended to be a textbook on how to market books. Rather, it is designed to be an organized potpourri of ideas, examples, tips, and suggestions to stimulate your creativity and to encourage you to explore new ways to market your books.

To be quite honest, the title of this book is a lie because there are far more than 101 ways to market your books listed here. I haven't stopped to count the actual number, nor would I encourage you to do so. It's not important.

Here's what is important:

1) Once you have reviewed the ideas in this book, make them your own. Don't just copy someone else's approach; adapt it to your own needs, make it better, and then use it.

2) Remember the old 80/20 rule. Generally speaking, 80% of your business comes from 20% of your customers. So focus your efforts on your prime markets first. Don't scatter your attention by trying to apply all 101 ways to market your books on each book you publish. Be selective. And maintain your focus on those markets and advertising methods which offer the best possible return for your time and money.

3) Again, I repeat, maintain your focus. Take the best ideas from this book and use them. Don't go overboard and dilute your efforts by trying to do everything at once. I've seen too many marketing efforts fail because the companies had no plan, no focus, and no clear conception of what in the world they were doing in the first place (or the second place, or the third place). That's why I devote an entire chapter to planning your marketing strategy. Planning is the first and most crucial step in marketing any book, so be sure you do it justice.

4). Study, study, study. That means, come back to this book after you've spent some time in marketing your books. Read this book more than once. Read other books on publishing and marketing, especially the companion titles to this book, *Book Marketing Made Easier* and *Book Marketing Opportunities: A Directory*. Other superb titles are listed in the short bibliography to this book and in my extended review of books about publishing, *The Independent Publisher's Bookshelf*.

5) Most important, review your own marketing efforts. And do it with a critical eye. Where can you make your program better? What more can you do? Test, test, test.

Don't be afraid to mark up this book unless, of course, you've borrowed this copy from a friend or library—in which case, turn to the back of this book to find out how you can get your own personal copy of this invaluable reference guide. You know you're going to want to refer to this book again and again anyway, so why not order your copy now. Then you can be free to mark up the copy all you want.

As you read this book, make notes to yourself. Use a marker to highlight those sections or ideas which have the greatest potential for your own marketing program. Use this book as you would a dictionary or workbook. Keep it handy. Mark it up. Scribble notes to yourself.

Above all, don't just glance through this book once and then toss it aside. If you do, you'll miss many opportunities to sell more books.

I have my own philosophy about publishing. I am dedicated to selling my books—not just for the money, or the prestige, or whatever—but because I don't believe in wasting my time. If I'm going to publish a book, then I'm going to do my best to make sure that anyone and everyone who might at all benefit from the book gets a chance to read the book. I believe that every publisher should be as committed to marketing their own books. And that's why I've written and published this book—to make it easier for you to meet that commitment. I hope it helps.

CHAPTER 1

Some Basic Fundamentals of Marketing

The following points are basic to any marketing strategy. Read them and get to understand them before you go on to read the more practical points covered in the other chapters of this book.

1:01 Selling is Your Responsibility

No matter how you choose to sell your books—whether through bookstores, to libraries, via mail order direct to the reader, or however else—one thing you will always have to do: You will have to sell your books. No one else can do that for you.

Even if you sell exclusively through bookstores, it will still be up to you to see that potential readers know about your books and where to buy them. Don't expect anyone else to do your selling for you. That's your job. At best, others can only provide channels. It will always be up to you to provide the motivation for readers to buy your books.

1:02 The Two Fundamentals

There are two fundamental activities in marketing any product: 1) promotion and 2) distribution. In other words, you must get the word out and then you must make sure that your product is available. One does not follow the other. Both must be done simultaneously, or neither will be effective. Promotion will not be effective unless readers can readily buy your books, and distribution will be disappointing and full of headaches (and returns) unless your promotions help to move your books out of the stores.

1:03 Look Before You Leap

But even before you begin to promote and distribute your books, you must be engaged in a great number of other marketing functions. You must decide what you are going to sell (editorial). You must package your books (design and production). You must decide who your customers are and how you are going to position your book (market planning). You must set a price (accounting). And much, much more.

1:04 Publishing as Marketing

If you haven't noticed by now, I consider every function of a publisher to be an integral part of book marketing. And, because I do, this book will cover more than just promotion and distribution. As far as I'm concerned, no detail is too small to consider if it will make a difference in how many readers get to know about and read a book.

So, if you happen to be with the marketing department, I encourage you to share this book with the other departments in your company. Not only will it make your job easier, but it will also, I believe, foster better cooperation among the people in your company. Indeed, if you are very wise (and very kind), you will buy a copy of this book for every employee (and every employer) in your company. I'd certainly like that.

Now, with the commercial out of the way, I want to repeat the point I've been making: Marketing is a company-wide activity. It cannot be, and should not be, restricted to one department. Too many things enter into the making of a successful book (and a successful book publishing company) to allow parochial interests to limit your possibilities.

Even the least recognized department of most publishing companies, the fulfillment division, has a crucial marketing impact. Many companies rise and fall based on their customer service (fast delivery, ease of ordering, cordial service reps, customer confidence, and more). Any company which does not regard its fulfillment division as an integral part of its marketing will certainly fail.

1:05 Marketing Requires Commitment

It takes time to build a company (even longer to build a reputation). You must be prepared to spend years developing a list, making contacts, testing various advertising methods, establishing a network of sales representatives or distributors, and doing all the other jobs that go into building a company that will be around for years to come. Don't give up. If you can make it through the first few years, you'll be well on your way to success.

Of course, this same advice applies to each book you publish. Never give up your marketing efforts as long as the book is still in print.

Too many publishers have failed because they ignored this fundamental of marketing: You must be committed to what you are selling. You must believe in it. How can you sell anything if you don't believe in it, and if you're not willing to back it up with time and effort? Why publish a book if you're not going to commit your resources to marketing the book so it reaches the people who can use it and enjoy it?

1:06 Marketing as an Investment

Especially when you are just starting out, you must think of your marketing program as an investment. You cannot approach marketing as a sporadic activity—either it flies or it doesn't. If you do, you'll just get caught up in one fad after another. That's no way to build a business.

1:07 For Most Effective Marketing, Be Consistent

Though consistency may be, as Emerson said, the hobgoblin of fools, it is also the basis for developing a stable business. A marketing plan is essential to any success. And that marketing plan should include a clear picture of the face you want your company to present to the public. Once you've set your goals and your means to those goals, stick to them as long as they still serve your needs.

1:08 Marketing Is the Means, Not the Goal

The last three points of this chapter have, in essence, been making the same point. Effective marketing requires commitment. It requires a stable base. It requires a long-term point of view.

I have reiterated these points because I want to ensure that as you read about the wide variety of ways to market your books, you don't lose sight of your major purpose in being a publisher. Remember: Marketing is the means, not the goal.

CHAPTER 2

Book Publishing: A Statistical Overview

To help put the business of book publishing into perspective, here are some statistics, facts, figures, and assorted tidbits of information:

- According to a 1978 study, 45% of Americans do not read books at all. 95% of all Americans listen to at least one hour of radio each day.

- The average number of books read per year by those people who read regularly is 16 books. On the average, Americans spend $35.00 per year on books.

- According to Tom Parker, in his book *In One Day* Americans buy five million books every day—and over 35 million paper clips.

- U.S. book publishers produce over 45,000 titles per year. Of those titles, as many as 30,000 don't make a profit.

- In 1984, over $9 billion worth of books were sold in the United States. The 15 largest U.S. publishers accounted for $5.3 billion of those sales (or 57.7%). The 5 largest accounted for 35% of all trade sales. 70% of all hardcover sales were made by the top 11 trade hardcover publishers. 95% of all mass-market paperback sales were made by the top 13 mass-market publishers.

- To put these annual sales into greater perspective, U.S. retail liquor sales for 1984 were over $20 billion; drug store sales were over $40 billion. Meanwhile, over 30 American companies had greater annual sales than the entire book publishing industry. Exxon, with sales 10 times greater than the entire book industry, had profits equal to 50% of all book sales.

- School textbooks account for approximately 30% of all book sales. Technical and professional books account for another 20% of sales. Religious books, another 5%. Reference books, another 5%. Trade books account for the other 40% (about 20% for trade paperback and hardcover retail sales, another 15%

for book club and mail order sales, and the other 5% in mass-market paper-back sales).

* The average price for a hardcover book in 1985 was $26.50 (with the average for non-genre fiction being $16.95). Trade paperbacks averaged $13.50 and mass-market paperbacks $3.60.

If you need more statistics on the book publishing industry, contact Alfred Lane, Director of the Crouse Library for the Publishing Arts. This Library has 2000 volumes about book publishing, 65 periodical titles, and a large reference collection of directories, dictionaries, publishers' catalogs, bibliographies, and more. Mr. Lane is very willing to answer any questions.

The Library's hours are from 2:00 to 6:30 p.m., Monday through Thursday. For telephone inquiries, call (212) 764-6338. Or write to The Crouse Library, CUNY Graduate Center, 33 West 42nd Street, New York, NY 10036.

CHAPTER 3

Planning: The Basis of Successful Marketing

No company can be successful without some sort of marketing plan. Whether it be written on the back of a matchbook, carried in the mind of the company president, or formalized in a 200-page bound report, a marketing plan is a must. Without it, you might as well be gambling—the effect would be the same.

3:01 Preparing Your Marketing Plan

What should a marketing plan include? At the very minimum, it should list the following items:

- the books or lines to be offered,
- the packaging, display, and pricing,
- how the books will be positioned,
- the audience or market, and
- a program for reaching that market.

In other words, at the very least, you should have some idea of what you plan to sell, how you plan to package it, how you will create a desire for your books, who will buy the book, and how you intend to let those buyers know about the book (and where they can obtain it).

Other points you should consider when preparing a marketing plan include: market research, competitive titles, budgets, schedules, and how the proposed product promotion fits in with major company objectives and on-going projects.

For more help with the details of organizing your marketing plan, see my book, *Book Marketing Made Easier.*

3:02 Positioning to Sell

No book manuscript or proposal should be given the go ahead until you have a firm idea how you will position the book. That means, that before you make any editorial decisions, you should always ask yourself the question: "Who will buy this book, and why?" The last part of that question is crucial. You should always be able to describe what needs and/or desires your new books fulfill.

David Ogilvy, author of *Confessions of an Advertising Man*, once listed thirty-two things he had learned during all his years as an advertising man. Of the items on that list, he said the most important was how you positioned your product. Results, he claimed, were based not so much on how the advertising was written as on how the product itself was positioned.

Positioning is vital when your book is not the first one published about the topic. For example, if you are publishing a new diet book, the first question a reader will ask is, "'Why should I buy another diet book? The other four I've bought didn't work. Why will this one work any better?" If you expect readers to buy your diet book, you need to answer that question. And you will need to have answered that question long before you even begin to typeset the book. Because your answer to that question will not only affect how you market the book, it will also affect how you edit, design, and package the book.

3:03 Scheduling the Publication of Your Books

The date of publication should not be a production decision; it must be a marketing decision. The timing of a book can be a crucial part of any marketing plan.

- For example, college textbooks must be presented to academics before March for fall adoption. Summer is too late.
- Instruction books for golf and tennis sell better in the winter when the readers are not actively playing.
- Diet books do well after the winter holidays and before the summer bathing season.
- Prima Publishing designed special Valentine's displays for their new book, *How to Find the Love of Your Life*, and made sure the book was widely available early enough to encourage sales.
- To tie-in with special days, you need to let retail stores know about your books at least five to six months in advance. Christmas gift books should be promoted in July and August (the major gift industry trade shows for Christmas

are held in July and August). Calendars need to be promoted in May and June (August is too late, since most stores have already bought their supply of calendars which they then put on display in September).

- Smaller publishers can often gain more notice and reviews during January and February and in late summer before the major publishers announce their spring and fall lists. So consider setting your publication dates for those times.

- Random House required Tip O'Neill to have his memoirs ready so they could be published within three months from the time he retired as Speaker of the U.S. House of Representatives because once he was out of office his memoirs would not be as promotable.

3:04 Prepare a Marketing Budget

Set your marketing budget well in advance of publication. Be sure to have a clear plan of how you intend to spend your advertising dollars, reserving the major portion for your prime markets and media. Because word of mouth is still the most cost-effective way to advertise your books, set aside at least one-third of your marketing budget to be used for promotion and publicity.

Again, there are several forms in my book, *Book Marketing Made Easier*, which should help you to organize your budget.

3:05 Repeat, Repeat, Repeat

When planning your marketing budget, be sure to include enough money to allow you to advertise to your major prospects at least several times. Repetition is a key to gaining audience recognition.

3:06 Research Your Market

If you are approaching a new market, do what you can to get to know more about that market. Ask questions, conduct surveys, read the major trade and consumer magazines for that area, attend shows and exhibits, poll retailers, and do test markets with your potential audience.

- For example, if you decide to publish books on fishing, you might want to do a survey of the managers of sports shops to find out what kind of discount they expect to receive, how they normally obtain the products they sell, who the major wholesalers/distributors are for their field, and what kind of packaging/display would be most appropriate for their market. Show them copies of any cover designs and book titles you propose to publish and get their comments on how the books can be improved to appeal more directly to their market.

- Meanwhile, you could also conduct focus groups, survey fishing associations, do informal polls at several favorite fishing holes, and test market trial runs of the books to targeted lists.

3:07 Spotting New Markets

Here are some statistics to spur you into thinking about new markets that are developing. Watch for these kinds of statistics in your daily paper and trade magazines so you can spot new trends and markets before they become over-saturated with new book offerings from other publishers.

- For example, while many publishers are now pursuing the yuppie market, you could be going after two new growing markets: those over 65 and those under 10.

- Ten percent of all Americans are now over the age of 65. And, while senior citizens tend to be more conservative and discriminating in their buying habits, they represent a large, virtually untapped market. Their 1983 total household income was $263 billion.

- Children, on the other side of the age line, now number 20% of all Americans. Although they have little income of their own, they do represent an estimated $300 billion per year of spending power. TV is the most effective medium for reaching them. If you want to sell books to this market, the books must have strong child appeal (play value or high interest) as well as value (since parents or grandparents make the final decision in most cases). Children are loyal to brands they are familiar with, so once you have sold to them your chances of selling to them again are much improved.

- 55% of all Americans are women. And women are said to control 80% of every dollar spent on consumer goods. Women are also more likely to buy books than men. Now that more women are working, they also value convenience; hence, the more readily they can obtain your books, the more likely they will be to buy them.

- 90% of all teenage girls have bought something by mail (70% have bought magazines, 25% books and records). Their average annual spendable income is $900.

- Hispanics, with 10% of the American population, now represent a $55 billion annual market. 45% are not fluent in English, but 90% do listen to a Spanish-language radio station. The top Hispanic markets are Los Angeles (3.4 million), New York (2.4 million), Texas (2.3 million), Miami (.8 million), Chicago (.7 million), and San Francisco (.7 million). Note, however, that Hispanics in Texas have a different cultural background from those in Miami or those in New York, so you cannot treat the Hispanic market as one homogeneous mass.

- According to the Evangelical Christian Publishers Association, 37 million people bought at least one Christian book during 1983. 48% of those sales were through Christian bookstores.

- The average American woman owns 15 cookbooks. Three out of ten women and one out of ten men collect cookbooks. As cookbook collecting has increased over the past ten years, so has publishers' output (from 365 new cookbooks in 1973 to 833 in 1984). $285 million were spent on cookbooks in 1984. Bookstores sold 42% of all hardcover cookbooks sold and 31% of the softcover; supermarkets sold 9% of the hardcover and 19% of the softcover.

3:08 Spotting Trends

Besides watching the changing statistics, you should also be watching for new trends in society. The first company to spot a trend has the best chance of capturing the largest share of the market.

- Trivial Pursuit, for example, was the first game to exploit people's fascination with trivia. As a result, it became one of the hottest selling games of the century.

- Mabel Hoffman's *Crockery Cookery* was the first major book published describing how to use crockpots. It has sold over three million copies since 1975.

- Tom Clancy, with his *The Hunt for Red October*, captured a new trend in militaria and helped to put the Naval Institute Press on the map.

- Travel guides and regional titles are on the upswing again. With lower gas prices and cut-rate airline tickets, people are travelling more.

- As more members of the baby boom generation decide to have kids of their own, childrearing books have also taken off. So have children's books in general. An indication of the growing interest in this area (and the greater opportunity for sales) is the number of new bookstores specializing in children's titles and the recent formation of the Association of Booksellers for Children.

3:09 The Benefits of Specialization

When planning your book list, you should carefully consider how each new title fits into your current publishing program. The more you can specialize in certain areas, the greater your chances of success in those areas. Do what you do best, and do it better than anyone else.

Here are just a few of the advantages of focusing on only a few areas:

1. Your company gains recognition for its expertise in your areas of specialization (for example, McGraw-Hill and Que in computer books).

2. You create a readership that avidly awaits your next offerings. This creates a marketing momentum that makes each new book much easier to sell to bookstores. This becomes readily apparent in category fiction and continuing sagas such as Jean Auel's Earth Children series (whose first book in the series, *The Clan of the Cave Bear*, sold 119,000 hardcover copies its first year; while the next book, *The Valley of Horses*, sold 289,000 hardcover copies its first year out; and the third in the series, *The Mammoth Hunters*, sold 1,470,000 hardcover copies within three months of publication).

3. You can make greater use of your house list to sell new titles since your previous buyers will naturally be interested in new titles along the same lines as the books they previously bought. For example, the three titles in Ad-Lib's own book marketing series will naturally attract the same audience as our previous *Directory of Short-Run Book Printers*.

4. As you publish more books in the same field, people in that field will become more and more familiar with your company name and reputation. Even if they don't buy your first or second or third book, they will buy eventually.

5. Specialization will strengthen your acquisitions program as well. Major writers/experts in your area of specialization will begin offering you first look at their new manuscripts. Hence, the quality of your offerings will only get better as you continue to specialize.

6. Finally, specialization allows you to market books together as a package, to display them together, to offer special discounts for ordering three or more different titles, to offer bouncebacks for the entire range of titles, to publish special interest catalogs, and much, much more.

3:10 Develop Series for Continuing Sales

A variation on specializing is to develop a series of titles on the same topic. The advantages are the same as for specializing in general.

- Modern Publishing publishes 30 to 40 different series of children's books each year and then packages them as a display unit. As Lawrence Steinberg, Modern's president, points out: One book gets lost in the midst of many other books, but six books make a display and, hence, are much more visible.

- Dover Publications publishes a whole collection of Ready-to-Use Alphabets and Cut & Assemble books along with many other series which they then sell by mail to regular customers.

- East Woods Press offers a series of Bed & Breakfast guide books for different parts of the country. Each book, I'm sure, helps to sell the others, just as Fodor, Fielding, Frommer, Baedeker, and other travel guides continue to sell year after year.

- Bantam has sold almost thirty million copies of their two series aimed at teenage girls, Sweet Dreams and Sweet Valley High. New titles in these series regularly hit the best seller lists for young adult titles.

- Writers, of course, often develop series when one of their books hits big. It'a a natural follow-up, and once you've written one book on the subject, the second is that much easier to write (and to sell). Spencer Johnson and Kenneth Blanchard have written a good number of other One Minute books since their first (originally self-published) *One Minute Manager* became a best seller. Now there's *The One Minute Father*, *The One Minute Mother*, *The One Minute Salesperson*, *Putting the One Minute Manager to Work*, *Leadership and the One Minute Manager*, *The One Minute Manager Gets Fit*, and *One Minute for Myself*. Similarly, Laurence Peters has come out with *The Peter Plan* and *The Peter Pyramid* since hitting it big with *The Peter Principle*.

3:11 Category Books: Sales after Sales after Sales

Category or genre books can be viewed as a combination of a book series and a magazine. They tend to develop a regular following just as any magazine does. Hence, if you publish a line of romances or science fiction or westerns (such as Silhouette romances or DAW science fiction), you begin to establish an expectation in your readers. They begin to look for your new releases. This repeat readership allows you to forecast sales much more readily than for non-category fiction (which is always a gamble at best). This consistency of sales also makes it easier to convince booksellers to carry your books.

Category books, of course, need not just be fiction. Nonfiction categories such as cartoon books, automobile repair books, and computer books among others have also developed a regular and predictable customer base.

3:12 Annuals and Perennials

Another form of series that can ensure consistent sales and income for your company is to develop an annual directory or guide. These directories can form the foundation for an entire line of related books.

- As mentioned before, Ad-Lib's own *Directory of Short-Run Book Printers* (an annual directory) has generated the customer base for our new book marketing trilogy of which this book is a part.

- R. R. Bowker, Gale Research, and a good number of other companies have established a strong sales base from their annual directories and guides.

- And, of course, annuals can become perennial best sellers such as the J. K. Lasser and H & R Block tax books.

3:13 Develop Standing Orders

Another benefit of developing a specialty, series, or annual directory is that you can solicit standing orders from libraries and customers who require the latest information.

- Third Sector Press has established a standing order policy whereby their customers are sent each new title for a free 60-day examination. Only customers who have prepaid or paid previous invoices within five weeks are offered this review privilege. The customers benefit from this standing review policy because they get to see each new title at least five to six months before publication date (at the same time that reviewers are sent copies). And Third Sector benefits because they thereby establish a strong continuing customer base.

3:14 Develop Continuity Series

Continuity series are a variation on the standing order idea mixed with the negative option of the book club. In a continuity series, customers sign up for the first title in a series and are sent all further titles until they either cancel their participation or the series is completed. In such series it is not unusual to have as many as 50% of the initial customers drop out by the fourth book in the series. Nevertheless, the series can still be a success if you start with a large enough customer base.

- Time-Life Books has run such continuity series for years with remarkable success. Their revenues for 1985 were over $550 million. Of course, not all that revenue came from their continuity series.

3:15 The Value of Best Sellers

When planning your lists, always be on the lookout for any title that has the possibility of becoming a best seller. Then do everything you can to make it a best seller. Why? Because a best seller can put your company on the map.

- The Naval Institute Press had that happen to them when they published *The Hunt for Red October*. Not only did booksellers and librarians look more carefully at the Institute's new titles, but they also began buying more of their backlist titles as well. Book reviewers also began giving more serious consideration to new titles produced by the Press.

- North Point Press reported similar results after Evan Connell's *Son of The Morning Star* hit the best-seller lists.

- Another side effect of publishing a best seller is that you begin receiving many more submissions from freelance writers and, more important, from established writers who can provide you with more best-selling titles.

- Acropolis Books has developed a line of books from their best seller by Carole Jackson, *Color Me Beautiful*. They now offer *Your Colors at Home* and *Always in Style with Color Me Beautiful*, both written by other authors.

One word of caution, though: If you are serious about promoting a book to best-selling status, be sure you are prepared to deal with all the accompanying headaches: reprintings, distribution, fulfillment, returns, collections, and the cash flow crunch. More than one small company has found themselves in bankruptcy because they weren't prepared to handle the demand, either materially or psychologically.

3:16 Develop a Perennial Best Seller

Developing a perennial best seller is often more a function of luck and happenstance rather than careful planning, but when it does happen it sure can put a small company on solid ground.

- Ten Speed Press has become a well-recognized press because of Richard Bollen's *What Color Is Your Parachute*, which has been a perennial best seller for years.

- Other perennial best sellers include *The Joy of Cooking*, *Elements of Style*, *The One Minute Manager*, *Color Me Beautiful*, *Think and Grow Rich*, and *The Elements of Style*.

- Of course, many annual guides have also become perennial best sellers, such as the *World Almanac*, the various tax and travel guides, the *Rand McNally Road Atlas*, the *Guinness Book of World Records*, and *Kovel's Antiques & Collectibles Price List*.

3:17 Develop Brand Names

Even book publishers can develop brand names that help to promote their titles. Brand names can be developed not only from company names (to be discussed in greater detail in the next chapter), but also from series titles, authors, and individual books. Brand names, if they represent quality or consistency, can help to build a loyal customer base.

- It wouldn't be an exaggeration to say that the One Minute series has become a brand name. Personally, I'm still waiting to read the *One Minute Lover*. It's only a matter of time before it comes out.

- Publishers' imprints such as Laurel, Dolphin, Plume, Torchbooks, Vintage Contemporaries, and Linden Press have also established strong reputations for quality. As a book reviewer in the *Philadelphia Inquirer* noted, "If I had to pick a line of paperbacks I would buy sight unseen, title unknown, it would be the Laurel series."

- Annual directories can often develop brand name qualities as well. How many of you would not recognize the LMP and the PTLA? Almost anyone who has been in the book industry for a few years would recognize those two books as Bowker's *Literary Market Place* and *Publishers' Trade List Annual*. We at Ad-Lib are looking forward to the time when our new *Book Marketing Opportunities* directory and database develop such recognition. In the years to come, you'll be looking to the BMO for information on new marketing opportunities. Just you wait and see.

- Simon and Schuster's new series, Harold Robbins Presents, is selling more because of the headline name than because of the contents of the titles themselves. International rights guarantees for the series have by themselves exceeded $225,000. Here's an example where one author's reputation is carrying an entire line of books, none of which are written by him.

- Other brand name authors (whose new books are almost sure best sellers) include: James Michener, Danielle Steel, John Jakes, Kathleen Woodiwiss, Barbara Taylor Bradford, John le Carre, Stephen King, Robert Ludlum, John D. MacDonald, Dick Francis, Robert Heinlein, Judy Blume, Toni Morrison, Dr. Seuss, and Isaac Asimov (who even has a magazine named after him). These names are in no particular order, just off the top of my head. The list is obviously incomplete.

- *Timescape*, a Nebula award winning book by Gregory Benford, became the brand name for a superb series of science fiction books from Pocket Books.

- Price/Stern/Sloan's Wee Sing series of activity books and cassettes have consistently been in the top ten of B. Dalton's juvenile best-seller list.

- The *World Almanac* has given rise to a number of subsidiary titles like the *Kids' World Almanac of Records and Facts*, *World Almanac Book of Inventions*, *World Almanac Book of the Strange*, *World Almanac Book of World War II*, *World Almanac Consumer Information Kit*, *World Almanac Dictionary of Dates*, and the *World Almanac Guide to Natural Foods*.

3:18 The Importance of a Lead Title

Even if you don't develop any best sellers or brand names, you should set priorities for your new titles. Usually this means that you'll feature one or more lead titles each season. And, although these lead titles will take most of your time and money in promoting them, they do not need to detract from your other titles. Indeed, if chosen carefully and promoted well, lead titles can actually help to attract attention to your other titles.

• One way lead titles can help is by opening doors to reviewers and booksellers who would not otherwise look at any of your titles. One of the lead titles for New Society Publishers in 1985 was a wall calendar featuring *Cat Lovers Against the Bomb*. The calendar, of course, appealed to many general readers (especially cat lovers) who would not otherwise have been immediately attracted to New Society's line of political and social justice books. Once readers bought and enjoyed the calendar, they would be much more likely to look into the other books published by New Society (many of which were listed on the back page of the calendar).

• Para Publishing's lead title for the fall of 1985, *Is There a Book Inside You?*, is a natural lead-in to Para's other books on self-publishing. Hence, lead titles can attract attention not only to your current list, but also to your backlist.

3:19 Whatever You Do, Build a List

Good list building is the only way to ensure steady income over a number of years. If you rely solely on your new titles, your company will always be on a boom or bust cycle. So when selecting new titles, be sure to look for titles that will have a lasting value—books on health rather than fad diets, books with real content rather than instant non-books, books written with style and depth rather than by formula.

3:20 Build a Superb and Deep Backlist

As a corollary of the above dictum, when you prepare your marketing plans you should be thinking ahead to how new titles will fit into and contribute to your current backlist. Think backlist. It truly forms the solid backbone of any successful book publisher.

• Bantam's backlist now includes well over 2000 titles, of which over 250 sell more than 10,000 copies per month.

• According to a recent Huenefeld survey, 65% of all sales for book publishers comes from titles more than a year old. College textbook publishers obtained over 80% of their sales from backlist.

• Cookbooks are perennial backlist sellers. At one time, six of the ten top backlist sellers for Harper and Row were cookbooks. 80% of Walden Book's sales of cookbooks are backlist titles.

• A strong backlist title rarely gets returned—one very good reason for developing a quality backlist.

- Backlist titles will sometimes come back to the forefront due to new promotions. *Out of Africa and Shadows on the Grass* by Isak Dinesen became a new best seller as a result of the release of the Robert Redford/Meryl Streep movie, *Out of Africa*.

- Independent booksellers welcome any publisher with a strong backlist. Backlist titles allow independent booksellers to compete with the discounters, chains, and supermarkets which usually feature only frontlist titles.

3:21 Plan for the Long Term

The main point of much of the above chapter has been to encourage you to develop a long-term marketing plan rather than focus only on short-term seasonal marketing plans. Your publishing company will become much stronger if you do so. Ideally, your long-term and short-term plans should mesh in such a way that each contributes to the other. If done well, your frontlist will then merge into your backlist making it even better and better as the years go on.

CHAPTER 4

Establishing and Marketing Your Company

An integral part of marketing your books is marketing your company name and image. If booksellers, librarians, and readers do not have a strong awareness of your company, you will have a difficult time selling your books. So you must, as HumptyDumpty pointed out to Alice, begin at the beginning.

4:01 Do the Obvious

Although it may not be necessary to point out the obvious, in the interest of being complete, I will mention that you should start your company out on the right foot. That means you should acquire all the proper permits, rent or arrange a separate workspace, print up official stationery and business cards, and get down to business.

While you're at it, learn how to use business cards. And be sure your employees, sales people, and authors also know how to make best use of them. Here's some hints:

- Carry your cards with you wherever you go. Hand them out to everyone you talk to (on the street, in an airplane, at the market, wherever). More often than not, these people will be interested in your books and what you do—and will contact you again later. This is especially effective for authors.

- When visiting key contacts, give out two cards—one for them and one for their secretary (for the Rolodex).

- Exchange cards. Don't just give your card away. Be sure to get the other person's card as well. In fact, an easy way to make sure the other person gets your card is to ask for theirs. Once you have their card, write a note on the back reminding you of the conversation and any follow-up you want to do.

- When giving out your card, write your home phone number on the card before you give it to the other person. Do this only for people you really want to mark as being special.

- Have your office hours printed on the card, or note when you are commonly available. This will make it easier for the other person to contact you.

- Business cards are an absolute must at conventions, exhibits, meetings, and conferences. Don't leave home without yours.

4:02 Choose a Company Name

Give careful thought to what you call your company. Here's a few hints:

- Avoid names that are hard to pronounce or whose spelling is not immediately obvious. I often have cause to regret my own decision to name the company, Ad-Lib Publications. It's not an easy name to catch over the phone. Plus, people have come up with innumerable ways of spelling it (not quite as many ways as with my own last name—but I didn't have a choice in that matter).

- Peggy Glenn, in her book on *Publicity for Books and Authors*, describes how she came to change her company name from Pigi Publishing (P.G. from her initials, but often pronounced "piggy") to Aames-Allen. First, borrowing an old trick from the telephone book, she began her company name with two a's. That way her company would always be first in the various trade listings. It's a small quibble, and I certainly wouldn't recommend that anyone else follow suit because then the LMP would begin to look like the yellow pages of any major city. As publishers, we must remember that there are twenty-six letters in the English alphabet.

- Peggy's second reason for naming her company Aames-Allen, however, is superb. It sounds very English. Plus it has the hyphenated name associated with many established publishers, such as Addison-Wesley, McGraw-Hill, Prentice-Hall, and others. Hence, it not only sounds like proper English, but it also sounds familiar, as if it had been around for a long time. I remember when I first saw the name in print; I was sure I'd seen the name before and I took several minutes trying to remember where.

- Don't use the word, enterprises, at the end of your company name. It usually marks the amateur in the business world. Don't ask me why that is the case, but when I was working in the gift and toy industry, any such company name was always suspect. The situation may have improved in the past seven years, but I wouldn't bet on it.

- Many smaller presses have wonderful names like The Lunchroom Press, The Green Hut Press, Bear Tribe Publishing, The Spirit That Moves Us, Devil

Mountain Books, and Peanut Butter Publishing. The disadvantage with such names is that they sound like small presses, and some booksellers still hesitate to order from smaller presses because of past problems getting orders or receiving credit for returns. On the other hand, these names project an alternative image that many presses want to promote—and which many readers find appealing.

• In the final analysis, you must pick a name that appeals to you and projects the image you want to project. Whatever you do, choose a company name that helps you to reach your ultimate audience. Your company name should be—and is—part of your company image. Make sure it fits.

4:03 Create a Brand Name

One of your first goals as a publisher should be to establish your company name as a brand name—one that will be immediately recognized by readers. A brand name can be worth thousands, even millions of dollars, in advertising every year.

• One scholarly publisher with an established imprint tested a new imprint name in a direct mailing to its regular audience. The mailing under its established imprint outpulled the new mailing by over 200%.

• The Bantam sales and marketing directors both asserted in a *Publishers Weekly* article that they sell the Bantam name as much as any individual titles when they sell to bookstores.

• Because both the Penguin name and logo are familiar to most English-speaking readers, Penguin has begun to promote Penguin boutiques (separate sections devoted solely to Penguin titles) in various bookstores. And the bookstores are buying the idea.

• Repetition is the key to creating a brand name. If you decide to try to establish your company name as a brand name, be sure to repeat it in all your ads and to feature it on the covers of all your books.

• Harlequin has done such a thorough job of establishing its company name as a brand name that it comes close to being a generic term for romances.

4:04 Become a Joiner

To help establish your company name, you should join the standard trade associations for the book industry. Besides giving you more visibility in the industry, membership in a trade association can help to foster working relationships with other publishers, provide you with the latest news and resources, enable members of your company to attend informative seminars, and provide a number of other educational and marketing opportunities.

- The Association of American Publishers (AAP) is the major trade association for book publishers in the United States. It functions mainly as a networking and lobbying association for major publishers. (AAP, 220 East 23rd Street, New York, NY 10010.)

- Smaller companies and start-ups may find it more useful to join one of the smaller trade associations such as COSMEP (the International Association of Independent Publishers) and PMA (Publishers Marketing Association). Both offer excellent newsletters, seminars, conferences, and co-op marketing opportunities. (COSMEP, P. O. Box 703, San Francisco, CA 94101 and PMA, P. O. Box 299, Hermosa Beach, CA 90254.)

- For a list of over 50 other publishers associations in the U.S. and Canada (many of which are superb regional or topical resource associations), see my article in the January-February, 1986 issue of *Small Press* magazine or the full listing in my 80-page bibliography, *The Independent Publisher's Bookshelf.*

- While you are at it, don't overlook the booksellers associations. Membership in the American Booksellers Association can benefit your company in a number of ways: You receive the monthly *American Bookseller* magazine and the weekly *Newswire* which both keep you informed of other publisher's activities as well as the major concerns of booksellers. Meanwhile, you are helping to support an association that can only strengthen independent booksellers—which, in turn, means that you are helping to strengthen one of the main outlets for your books. (ABA, 122 East 42nd Street, New York, NY 10168.)

- There are many worthwhile regional booksellers associations as well, such as the Upper Midwest Booksellers Association, to which Ad-Lib belongs. (UMBA, P. O. Box 40034, St. Paul, MN 55104.)

- If you are a specialty publishers, you should join the specialty booksellers associations such as the Christian Booksellers Association (CBA) and the Association of Booksellers for Children (ABC). (CBA, 2620 Venetucci Boulevard, Colorado Springs, CO 80901 and ABC, c/o Hicklebee's, 1345 Lincoln Avenue, San Jose, CA 95125.)

- Finally, if you publish books of interest to specific trade and professional associations, you should also join those associations. Since you are publishing in that area, you probably already know which associations are most active. Join those.

4:05 Become a Reader

If you are serious about marketing your books, you should read everything you can to keep you up to date on current events in the industry. Plus, you should never stop learning. Continue to read new books such as this one on book marketing, publicity, advertising, publishing, printing, graphics, and anything else that applies to the fields in which you publish.

* Above all, you should subscribe to at least one trade magazine such as *Publishers Weekly* or *Small Press*. Plus look into subscribing to various newsletters such as the *Information Marketing Letter*, the Huenefeld newsletter, *Inside Bookselling* and others. Again, refer to *The Independent Publisher's Bookshelf* for reviews of the major trade magazines and newsletters.

* Subscribe to trade magazines for the fields in which you publish. For example, both the *Science Fiction Chronicle* and *Locus* are superb newsletters for any publisher of science fiction and fantasy (of the two, I prefer SFC because it is better designed, more readable, and more informative). If you are publishing children's books, you should subscribe to *Toy and Hobby World* and *Playthings*.

* Finally, don't overlook the consumer magazines published in your areas of interest. Again, for science fiction and fantasy, that means reading *Omni*, *Fantasy and Science Fiction*, *Analog*, *Isaac Asimov's Science Fiction Magazine* and others. If you publish for women, you can selectively read any number of magazines, from *Vogue* and *Self* to *Good Housekeeping* and *Family Circle* from *Crafts* and *Soap Opera Digest* to *Ms* and *Working Woman*. Read those which are most applicable to your current line of books.

4:06 Get the Notice Out

Once you've established your company, don't hide under a bucket. Get the word out. Let the key people in the industry know that you are in business.

* Send notices to all the trade journals. *Publishers Weekly*, *Small Press* and *Small Press Review* all list new ventures as a regular feature. Don't forget the library and bookseller journals as well. And the appropriate specialized trade magazines.

* Also send notices to key contacts in the industry: wholesalers and distributors such as Baker & Taylor and Ingram, book store chains such as B. Dalton and Walden Books, book clubs, catalogs, and any other businesses who you think might be interested in what you are doing (and can help you to do it).

4:07 Get Listed Wherever Possible

As part of your publicity, be sure to have your company listed in all the appropriate industry reference books. Not only will such listings help get you orders from booksellers and librarians, but they will also add legitimacy to your company.

* Certainly the most important listings for your company and its books are the Library of Congress Cataloging in Publication office, the ISBN office, and the Bowker Books In Print series. For details on how to get listed in these places as well as dozens of other places, see the companion book in this Ad-Lib marketing series, *Book Marketing Made Easier.*

4:08 Continuing Publicity

Don't be shy about announcing other achievements as your company continues to grow. Anniversaries, new book publications, author signings, new discount and return policies, changes in employees—these are all news and should be announced to any key contacts and trade magazines which would be interested.

4:09 Get Involved, Become a Sponsor

When you join associations, don't just fade away into the woodwork; become an active member. Get to know other publishers, booksellers, librarians, and others involved in the industry. Get to know their concerns, their needs, their desires—and let them know yours.

* As part of your active participation in the industry, sponsor awards or contests or scholarships to give others recognition and to help them grow in their profession. Or, work with your associations when they sponsor such awards and scholarships. Any such activity may not immediately show on your balance sheet, but they do help your company to gain recognition in the industry and further the image you want for your company—as long as the activities you sponsor are compatible with the image you want to project).

* I don't know of any publishers who are currently sponsoring marathons, bake-offs, and other such events (though several did help sponsor the 1984 LA Olympics). Such sponsorships have certainly helped gain recognition for Budweiser, Miller Light, Pepsi, and Pillsbury. If your company's line of books would lend itself to such sponsorship, you should give it serious consideration. For example, why couldn't a publisher of auto books help sponsor the Indy 500 or the Daytona 500? Or a publisher of cookbooks sponsor its own bake-off? Such sponsorships take time and commitment, but they can pay off in the long run.

4:10 Create a Unique Selling Proposition

When you are considering how to build up your company image, try to create a unique selling proposition that can set your company apart from others. To be honest, I'm not aware of any publishing companies that have a recognizable unique selling proposition, such as Seven-Up's Uncola or Avis's "We Try Harder". Wouldn't it be nice to position your company the way Perrier positioned itself? After all, it is just water, isn't it?

Can you name the companies or products associated with the following slogans?

• Let your fingers do the walking.

• A _____ is forever.

• When _____ talks, people listen.

• Reach out and touch someone.

• Look, mom, no cavities!

• Snap, crackle, pop!

• We build excitement—_____!

• Ring around the collar.

• Don't leave home without it.

Of course, gaining such name recognition usually requires quite a bit of mass market advertising. But your company name need not be recognized by everyone; it only needs to be recognized by your prime prospects. So even a publisher with a limited audience can promote its unique selling proposition to that audience— and make them remember it.

• Dan Poynter of Para Publishing has done that with the slogan for his *Self-Publishing Manual*—the book that's launched a 1000 books!

• Dustbooks calls itself, with justification, "the information source for the small press world."

4:11 Persistence Pays

Follow the rules. Ignore the rules. But whatever you do, stick it out. Persist. And you will win out. One of the basic secrets of marketing is persistence. Marketing takes time. If you can persist long enough, your company will eventually get the recognition it deserves. You must give that great book marketing tool, word of mouth, a chance to operate.

• For example, it has taken us three years and three editions of our *Directory of Short-Run Book Printers* to gain the recognition it deserved. Libraries have finally discovered the directory, with the third edition selling ten times faster than the second. Moreover, Walden Books and B. Dalton have finally started carrying the book. Even then, we still get people calling us to ask, "Where have you been all these years?" Right here, folks.

- May-Murdock, a self-publisher in Marin County, has been quietly publishing books about railroading for a number of years. Finally the word has gotten around. Just recently a leading San Francisco television personality asked them to publish his collection of commentaries. Not only, then, will your books sell better as you gain experience and exposure over the years, but you will also begin to receive more proposals and ideas that have greater commercial potential as writers and other contacts discover your existence.

- Penguin Books just celebrated their 50th anniversary on July 30, 1985, and gained an incredible amount of publicity as a result. So another advantage of persistence is that someday you, too, will be able to celebrate your golden anniversary. Please invite me when you do. I love parties.

CHAPTER 5

The Customer Is Always Right

This short chapter is here to remind you that your customers are almost always right. Make it a point to develop a loyal customer base. Treat your customers with respect. Listen to them. Serve them well, and they will continue to buy from you.

5:01 Accept Credit Cards

One way to develop a steady customer base is to accept credit cards. Why? Here's a number of good reasons:

- Credit card holders have better credit histories, greater household income, and more disposable income than others.
- Credit card customers tend to spend more on each order.
- Credit card holders are more likely to buy by mail.
- Accepting credit cards makes it easier for your customer to order from you—and to pay you.

How do you go about accepting credit cards? For VISA and MasterCard, check with your local bank. You may have to check more than one before you find one that will allow you to process credit card orders through their system. Optionally, you can join the ABA and process orders through their connection with the Merchants Discount Service Association.

If you are selling to businesses, you should also accept American Express cards since many businesses provide employees with this card for travel and miscellaneous expenses. To contact American Express, call (800) 526-7443, Ext. 575. If you are located in New Jersey, call (800) 522-4503.

For Sear's Discover card, call (800) 624-6673. For Carte Blanche and Diners Club, call (800) 525-7376.

5:02 Install an 800 Number

If you are serious about providing customer support and service, you should install an 800 number to make it easier for your customers to call and order from you. Such 800 numbers are so inexpensive nowadays that you really cannot afford to offer anything less.

If you do install an 800 number, be sure to let your key customers and contacts know that you have such a number. Have it printed on all your sales literature, catalogs, news releases, and other out-going mail. Above all, be sure it's on your order forms.

Here's just a small list of the advantages of having an 800 number:

- An 800 number makes it more convenient for your customers to order from you.
- It speeds response to your mail offers.
- It can triple the response to such offers.
- It produces larger orders because it allows you to interact with your customer. If your telephone order takers are alert, they can increase sales by letting customers know about other books you publish that are similar to the ones the caller ordered.
- People buying by telephone have a better payment record and tend to be better credit risks.
- Toll-free phones encourage impulse buying.

Here's the number to call to set up your toll-free 800 number: (800) 222-0400.

Oh, by the way, after all this promotional talk about 800 numbers, you're probably wondering what our 800 number is. Well, by the time you read this, Ad-Lib should have its own 800 number. Call (800) 555-1212 to get our number. We are currently delaying installation until we are sure whether we are moving or not (just down the street, folks, so our P. O. Box 1102, Fairfield, IA 52556-1102 is still a valid address).

5:03 Create a Customer

Don't just make a sale, create a customer. Satisfied customers are repeat buyers. So do whatever you have to do to make your customers happy. The following points go into more detail.

5:04 Fast, Friendly Service (with a Smile)

Never delay any response to your customers. Always respond to any orders, inquiries, or complaints with fast, friendly service.

- Process orders as fast as possible. One reason so many independent booksellers shop with Ingram is because Ingram fulfills orders the same day and ships right away. If you process your orders the same day you receive them, you'll begin to pick up orders that would otherwise go to wholesalers (at a higher discount). Plus, since booksellers will be able to obtain books while the books are still hot, faster order processing will mean increased sales and less returns.

- Respond to inquiries the same day you receive them. The faster you respond (whether by phone, mail, or a sales representative), the greater your chances will be that the inquirer will order from you.

- Acknowledge immediately any back orders, out of print titles, or other books that cannot be shipped right away. Be as specific as possible about the date you will ship the order.

- Answer complaints right away. In fact, don't just answer the complaints, resolve them. Remember, no matter how petty or ill-conceived the complaint, the customer is always right. Don't take that statement as just another platitude; make it a working philosophy that all your personnel adhere to without question.

- Send refunds as soon as they are requested. Stand by your guarantee, and your customers will stand by you.

- Ship by UPS rather than book rate when the order needs to be shipped quickly or when you need to make sure it gets there at all.

5:05 Answer Your Phone

Keep your phone lines open for customer service and orders. If you are a small one- or two-person company and no one is available to answer the phone, then install an answering machine (and then make sure you get back to callers right away). If you are a larger company with telephone operator and three tiers of secretaries, make sure they know when a call should come through to you rather than terminated somewhere along the chain of command. As Tom Peters noted in his audiotape, *The Excellence Challenge*, "the only magic of the $40 billion giant IBM is that in a $500 billion industry they happen to be the only company that answers the phone."

5:06 Don't Run Out of Stock

Always try to keep all your titles in stock, readily available for any orders that may come in. Plan ahead so you don't run out at the last minute right before a big promotion. Work with your various printers so that you always have good turnaround on reprintings. And, finally, keep track of your inventory so you don't have any costly surprises.

5:07 Everyone Wins

One of the key rules of marketing is to structure your product, prices, and services so that everyone wins. Give your customers good product (contents, style, design, and promotion). Offer it at a fair price. And give them fast service. Then they win by getting what they want, when they want, at a price they can afford. You win because you've gotten your books into the hands of the people who can use them—and you got paid for doing it.

5:08 Go for the Additional Sale

Never fulfill an order without going for the additional sale. Include bounceback offers in your shipping package. Or put order/inquiry cards describing related titles in the books you ship out. Don't feel shy about letting your customers know about other books that might interest them. Such notices should be an integral part of your service to them.

5:09 Do What You Do Best

Create the best books you can, offer the friendliest and fastest service in the West, and always let your customers know that they are important to you. Then you need not fear competition from any other source.

5:10 Offer Satisfaction Guaranteed

Offer a firm guarantee of satisfaction, and then stand by it. Sears, the largest retailer in the world, built its business on its unconditional guarantee of satisfaction. Why should you offer less?

5:11 Give a Little Extra

Always give your customers more than they expect. Make your books the best available. Add bonus reports or little gifts (bookmarks, cards, whatever) when you ship their orders. And, especially with your key customers, send them something special around the winter holidays, or for Valentine's, or some other appropriate occasion.

5:12 Keep in Touch

Keep in touch with your key customers and contacts. Let them know you appreciate their business. Send them advance announcements and pre-publication specials for your most important titles. Send them complimentary advance review copies of attractive titles. Whatever you do, don't let them get a chance to forget you.

5:13 Always Say Thank You

Whether you overtly say thank you with every order, or you choose to say thank you by demonstrating to your customers their importance to you (by responding to them quickly and courteously), you should always let your customers know that you appreciate their business.

5:14 Satisfied Customers Spread the Word

Not only are satisfied customers repeat buyers, but they are also your best advertisements. When you create satisfied customers, you are also creating walking/talking billboards for your books. So when planning your fulfillment and customer service systems, remember that word of mouth is the most productive advertising available to book publishers—and that the best word of mouth advertising comes from satisfied customers.

CHAPTER 6

Editorial: The First Step

The first step in marketing any product is to produce something worthwhile, something people want or need, something people will buy. As products, books involve a combination of content, author, title, design, packaging, and price. All these elements must work together to create a best selling book.

6:01 Strive for Excellence

Regardless of what kind of books you publish, the books must have some sort of content. Yes, it is possible to sell books with no content at all (witness the Anything Books and diaries), but that is a limited market. Most publishers must give priority to content. And rightly so. Indeed, the reason most of us are in publishing is because of the content. We want to create books with lasting value, with significance, with substance.

Excellence of content does not come out of thin air. You must seek it out. And the first step in finding what you want is to define as clearly as possible what it is that you are seeking. Set a firm objective, make it clear to your editorial staff, and then let them go to work.

Here's a few guidelines your editors should have:

- Seek the best available.

- Make sure it fits into the company's current and projected lines of books.

- Always be aware of the marketing implications. (As an extension of this responsibility, your editors should participate in your major marketing meetings and decisions.)

- When reviewing a proposal, consider not only its potential for direct sales but also for subsidiary rights, international and special sales.
- Think big. (Not that all books have to be bestsellers, but rather that all books should have grand possibilities, either for sales, or for the enlightenment of the world, or for both.)

6:02 Edit for Clarity and Simplicity

Don't let a book out your door which has not been edited carefully by an experienced editor. Edit for clarity. Edit for a readable style. Edit for ease of use. The more accessible you make the contents of a book, the more likely readers will be to finish the book. . . and recommend it to their friends and associates.

- *Mail Order Know-How* by Cecil Hoge, Sr. could have sold many more copies if it had only been edited more thoroughly. It could have been cut by thirty per cent without detracting from its content. It would have made an outstanding 300-page book. As it is, the superb content is lost in the rambling, unedited nature of the book.

6:03 Edit for Promotional Clout

When editing a manuscript, consider ways to insert material into the book to make it more promotable.

- For example, if you are editing a book on gardening, why not list specific seed and tool companies as resources in the appendix? Not only will such lists benefit the reader, but they will also provide you with potential premium sales. Any company with marketing savvy would jump at the chance to use your book as a premium to give away or sell to its customers—especially if it is mentioned in the book as a prime resource.
- Another way to increase the promotional value of a book is to expand a special chapter or section so the book attracts a wider audience. While editing the third edition of my *Directory of Short-Run Book Printers*, I decided to also feature those book printers who were capable of doing annual reports, catalogs, and other commercial work. I was thus able to expand the potential audience for the directory from just publishers and self-publishers to businesses and organizations as well. This slight change in editorial matter has significantly increased the bookstore sales of the directory.

6:04 Look for Tie-In Possibilities

Your editors should be on the lookout for any manuscripts which could tie in with current television programs, movies, or other products already being promoted. The resulting book can then hitch a ride on an already rolling promotional wagon. As Ralph Waldo Emerson recommended, "Hitch your wagon to a star."

- Television—Avon sold over ten million copies of *The Thorn Birds*, many after the TV mini-series. *Shogun* also sold well after its release as a TV mini-series.

- Television—Already two Sniglets books have hit the best sellers lists. Certainly it hasn't hurt their sales to be indirectly promoted on *Not Necessarily the News* every week.

- Television—The Muppets shows and movies have given rise to a great variety of licensed products including books by Holt, Rinehart & Winston, Random House, and Fenmore Associates and software by Simon & Schuster. Many gift stores have included these books in the Muppet Boutiques they have organized.

- Radio—*Lake Wobegon Days* would not be the best seller it is now without the prior exposure of Garrison Keillor and Lake Wobegon on the weekly National Public Radio series, *Prairie Home Companion*.

- Movies and Television—Pocket Books has sold over two million copies of the book tie-in to the movie, *Star Trek: The Motion Picture* and over a million for the tie-in to the third Star Trek movie,*The Search for Spock*. Their Star Trek series of original novels regularly sell over 300,000 copies each. It's a continuing gold mine for them.

- Movies—Avon has sold over 2,800,000 copies of their *Gremlins* movie tie-in book. Ballantine has sold over 1,500,000 copies of their movie tie-in, *Indiana Jones and the Temple of Doom*.

- Movies—A number of companies brought out books to tie-in with the recent movie biography of Isak Dinesen, *Out of Africa*. Two of these titles became bestsellers, Vintage's combined edition of Dinesen's *Out of Africa and Shadows on the Grass* and St. Martin's biography of *Isak Dinesen: The Life of a Storyteller* by Judith Thurman.

- Movies—Alice Walker's *The Color Purple* stayed on the top of the mass-market best-seller lists for months after the release of the movie by same name.

- Magazines—Consumer Guide and many other magazine publishers regularly publish books that draw upon their editorial expertise. Rodale Press has built its catalog of titles from its magazine base and its sales from the subscriber lists of those same magazines.

- Catalogs—Addison-Wesley has published an entire series of Eddie Bauer sporting guides. And, of course, the take-off on the L. L. Bean catalog, *Items from Our Catalog* became a best seller.

* Sports—Too many to mention, but most are steady sellers.
* Food Products—*Campbell's Creative Cooking with Soup* cookbook is the only one that comes readily to my mind, but many other product tie-ins including at least one for Hershey's chocolate have been published.
* Other Products—Computers (in all models), automobiles (including the classic, *How to Keep Your Volkswagon Alive*), and many other products have been featured successfully in books.
* Cities and Regions—Everybody loves their own hometown, so regional and city-specific titles almost always sell well. Not only the usual tourist coffee-table books with plenty of pictures, but also other titles such as *The Boston Ice Cream Lover's Guide, How to Live (Fairly) Elegantly on (Virtually) Nothing in Los Angeles*, and *The Washington Driver's Handbook: A Guide to Capital Cruising* have all found a strong audience, both local and tourist.

6:05 Get the Best Authors You Can Afford

When selecting possible books for publication, look to the author's qualifications, experience, and promotability. Here are a few pointers:

* Select authors on the basis of past performance. Obviously, authors who have written and published books before are more reliable, less likely to cause problems, and clearly more promotable. If they are also a "big name," so much the better. As mentioned previously, there are a number of authors whose new books are almost guaranteed best sellers.
* If you have a choice between a celebrity author and an unknown, choose the celebrity (as long as the books are fairly equal in content and quality). Again, someone who is better known is more promotable—even if they've never authored a book before. Movie stars, sports heroes, political figures, company presidents are all promotable authors (provided that, in many cases, they have help from ghost writers).
* When selecting celebrity authors, it is best if you can publish the book while the celebrities are at the peak of their fame. As mentioned before, Random House required Speaker of the House Tip O'Neill to have his memoirs ready in time for the book to be published within three months of his retirement—before he disappeared from the limelight. In another case, Pergamon Press began to re-advertise their collection of Deng Xiaoping's speeches and writings within weeks after *Time* magazine named the Chinese leader Man of the Year for 1985.
* If the author is an authority on the subject, again so much the better. And if the author is an authority, don't keep it a secret. Play up the expertise in your promotions. For example, a diet book by a doctor, a book on early

childhood learning by a teacher or a psychologist, or a book on the science of hitting by Mickey Mantle or Pete Rose—all are more promotable because of the acknowledged expertise of their authors.

- If you have the choice between an author with adequate style, such as myself, and someone with superb style, choose the author with superb style. Well-written books will tend to sell better, provided the style fits the subject.
- While focusing on celebrities and established authors, don't forget the unknowns. Do what you can to develop new writers as well. Remember: All established writers had to begin somewhere—and that was as unknowns. If that is not enough to convince you to develop new writers, note that first time novelists are often more promotable than second or third time novelists whose first books were only mid-list sellers. Finally, there is nothing really as exciting in the book world as discovering a new talent and sharing that talent with others.

6:06 Editors as Stars

When publishing an anthology, textbook, or other compilation, choose an established author to head the editorial effort. The name quality of the author will help to sell the compilation.

- Houghton Mifflin's anthology series, *The Best American Short Stories*, sold only 6000 to 7000 copies a year until they began using a different celebrity author as guest editor each year. Sales now total close to 35,000 copies per year, a fivefold increase.
- A great number of science fiction anthologies have been produced by the team of Isaac Asimov, Charles G. Waugh, and Martin Harry Greenburg. The sales of these anthologies, of course, were not hurt by the fact that Isaac Asimov was associated with them, though by now both Waugh and Greenburg are probably as well known by the readers of these anthologies.

6:07 Using Celebrity Forewords and Blurbs

If you can't sign celebrities or established authors, the next best thing is to obtain a foreword or blurb from such people. Anyone with visibility or name recognition is a good candidate for writing forewords for books by unknown authors.

- Sales of Robert Miller's *Most of My Patients Are Animals* were given a big boost by James Herriot's rave introduction to the book. The book, published by Paul S. Eriksson, was also chosen as a featured alternate by both the Literary Guild and Doubleday Book Club.

- Don Dible's *Up Your Own Organization* received such favorable advance comments that he decided to make use of them to help promote his book. In the end, three known business leaders, Robert Townsend of Avis, William Lear of Lear Motors Corporation, and John Komives of the Center for Venture Management, wrote an introduction and foreword to his book. Of course, he made sure their well-known names were featured on the front cover of his book.

6:08 Titles: The First Impression

A good title alone can make the difference between a mediocre seller and a best seller. The title of a book, like the headline of an advertisement or news story, often makes the difference between a reader passing the book by or picking it up and giving it more careful consideration. More often than not, the reader gives less than a moment's attention to any book title; if you don't capture the reader's imagination or curiosity or desire in that short moment, you will have lost the sale.

Perhaps more important, however, is that many distributors, bookstore buyers, reviewers, and subsidiary rights buyers also judge a book by its title (and its cover). They know from experience that a good title sells more books. As Gloria Norris of the Book-of-the-Month Club once noted, "We can break out good writers—especially if their books have good titles."

Here's a few suggestions on how you can make your titles sell more books:

- Test your titles beforehand, either by using focus groups, your key contacts, or small test markets. Classified ads are a cheap and effective way to test the effectiveness of titles, since in such a case the title alone either sells the book or it doesn't. In one such case, a publisher tested two different titles for two books by advertising the books in full page ads in leading newspapers across the country. Which of the following titles do you think did best?

1. The Art of Courtship vs. The Art of Kissing
2. Care of Skin and Hair vs. Eating for Health

Here's the actual results: *The Art of Kissing* sold over 60,000 copies in one year while *The Art of Courtship* sold only a little over 17,000 copies. *Care of Skin and Health* outsold *Eating for Health* by 52,000 copies to 36,000. In each case, both titles had the same number of exposures to the same number of readers.

- The example above points out one other factor in titling your books: Be specific. Let the readers know what they can expect to get from the book. Specific benefits are usually more effective than general benefits in appealing to book buyers.

- Use subtitles to provide further explanation or description of the book's contents or benefits. Here's two examples of superb benefit subtitles: Herb Cohen's *You Can Negotiate Anything: How to Get What You Want* and Callan Pinckney's *Callanetics: 10 Years Younger in 10 Hours*. Here's the rather long subtitle of one of the other books in Ad-Lib's book marketing trilogy: *Book Marketing Opportunities: A Directory of Book Wholesalers, Distributors, Chain Stores, Clubs, Catalogs, Reviewers, and Other Book Marketing Channels*. It's rather long, perhaps even too long, but it does describe the contents of the book more thoroughly than the title alone.

- Choose titles that play off the titles of other well-known books. Melvin Powers of Wilshire Book Company wrote a parody of Jim Everood's best-selling book, *How to Flatten Your Stomach*, which he titled, *How to Flatten Your Tush*. His parody made several best-seller lists. Charlotte Peche titled her book on gynecology, *The One-Minute Gynecologist*, thus drawing on reader's familiarity with the other One-Minute books. The subtitle for her book helped to clarify what it was all about: *One Woman's Search for the Quick and Painless Visit*.

- Choose familiar leads to your titles. For example, *The Joy of Sex, The Joy of Lex, The Joy of Cooking, The Joy of Photography*, and so on. Or, *Mail Order Made Easy, Astrology Made Easy, Tennis Made Easy, Book Marketing Made Easier*, and other such titles. Or, that classic book title lead-in: *How to. . .*do just about anything. Or, finally, how about *101 Ways to. . .*do just about anything?

- Use the subject of your book as the lead-in to the title. In that way your book will be listed in the title index of any reference work just where inexperienced readers would look for a book on that subject. That is one reason we changed the title of BMO from *The Directory of Book Marketing Opportunities* to *Book Marketing Opportunities: A Directory*. It's also a good argument for such titles such as *Book Marketing Made Easier* and *Iacocca: An Autobiography*.

- If you expect your authors to tour or do interviews, make sure the title is one they can pronounce. I wrote one book about kinetic optical illusions (illusions created when you spin a pattern on a record turntable) with a working title of *Dizzy Discs and Other Kinetic Illusions*. However, I would never use that title for the book, because I have an impossible time pronouncing the word "discs"—that "c" between the two "s's" is incredibly awkward.

6:09 Choose Uniquely Wonderful Titles

This suggestion for titling your books is the most important of all: choose new titles, wonderful titles, titles that speak of romance, glory, wonder, or delight. This advice is absolutely important when titling novels. Non-fiction books can get away with being prosaic, but novels must be enticing, or startling, or daring, or warm.

*   As I was writing an earlier chapter of this book, I reviewed the catalog offerings of New Society Publishers. One of their book titles immediately attracted me: *Heart Politics*. What a wonderful title, full of contradiction, conflict, warmth and promise. I was so attracted to the title that I stopped writing this book long enough to write a check and send for the book.

Here are a few of my other favorite book titles (not in any particular order and certainly not complete):

Cold Sassy Tree
The Unbearable Lightness of Being
Parachutes and Kisses
Stolen Ecstasy
Ancient Evenings
The Lonely Silver Rain
Bus 9 to Paradise
Zen and the Art of Motorcycle Maintenance
The Hunt for Red October
The Little Drummer Girl
A Confederacy of Dunces
Outrageous Acts and Everyday Rebellions
The Winds of War
The Lonesome Gods
Silk Lady
Angels of September
Gone with the Wind

And here are a few titles that work well, that do a good job of selling the book (again, in no particular order):

Color Me Beautiful
In Search of Excellence
How to Be Your Own Best Friend
Think and Grow Rich
Dress for Success
*Everything You Always Wanted to Know about Sex But Were
    Afraid to Ask*
Thin Thighs in 30 Days
Chocolate: The Consuming Passion
The Dieter's Guide to Weight Loss During Sex
Eat to Win
The One Minute Manager
The Beverly Hills Diet

6:10 A Rose by Any Other Name

Don't be afraid to change a title if you can make it better. Never stop playing with the title. Even after the book has been published, it is still possible to change a title. It's been done more than once. And successfully.

- One paperback publisher changed the title of a book from *Five Days* to *Five Nights*. The second title sold much, much better than the first.

- One of the first books I published was titled *FormAides for Direct Response Marketing*. What a horrible title! The book has been well-reviewed, but its sales have been anything but spectacular. It's a superb book, with a poor title and poor cover design. I can't wait until this current edition sells out so I can change both the title and the cover. Indeed, I may not wait. They're that bad. Wouldn't the title *Mail Order Selling Made Easy* be a better title for the book? It precisely describes the the book's major benefit.

Here are some other title changes, all of which I feel were made for the better:

- *The Pineapple Diet Book* to *The Beverly Hills Diet Book*—much more glamorous and enticing. Pineapples pucker my mind.

- *Catch 18* to *Catch 22*—better rhythm and assonance.

- *Notes from a Teacher's Wastebasket* to *Up the Down Staircase*—the first has the flavor of an old maid teacher, the second catches the chaos and joy of teaching.

- *Chapters in the Life of a Young Man* to *The Portrait of the Artist as a Young Man*—more romance in being an artist. Plus the vibrant "portrait" enlivens the title much more than does the rather stale "chapters."

- *John Thomas and Lady Jane* to *Lady Chatterley's Lover*—the first could be a simple tale of married live between a commoner and a noble; the second clearly suggests an illicit romance which is far more exciting.

- *Cain Mark* to *East of Eden*—the first title is ambiguous; the second hints of oriental romance.

- *The PRE-Reading Experience* to *Developing the Early Learner* to *The IQ Booster Kit*—note how the title becomes more specific while at the same time offering greater benefits. Which would you buy?

- *Trimalchio in West Egg* to *The Great Gatsby*—which would you rather recommend to a friend? I can't even pronounce the first title, but, oh, the second title! Look out, Tony the Tiger, here I come!

- *Hunting Caleb* to *Searching for Caleb*—the first suggests morbid violence, while the second suggests longing and desire.

6:11 Titles as Point of Purchase Advertising

Whatever you title your book, remember that the title of your book must serve at least three purposes:

1. It must attract the attention of the book buyer.
2. It must indicate what the book is about. For non-fiction, the title should be as clearly descriptive as possible; for fiction, the title should be appropriate for the specific genre.
3. It must, if possible, create the desire to buy.

The best titles, like all good advertising headlines, serve all three functions at the same time. Remember that the title (and cover) of your book is often the only advertising message any buyer ever sees. Make sure the message is clear and effective.

CHAPTER 7

Designing Your Books as Sales Aids

As mentioned in the previous chapter, the marketability of a book is determined not only by its editorial content and the qualifications and fame of the author but also by the design, packaging, and price of the book. In this chapter, we'll discuss the last three elements in greater detail.

7:01 You Can Judge a Book by Its Cover

It's an old maxim that you can't judge a book by its cover, but this maxim does not hold true in the real world of commercial bookselling. People do judge a book by its cover—not only readers but also bookstore buyers, reviewers, and distributors.

Here's just a few reasons why you should place major attention on the cover design of your books:

- The cover or jacket is used by your sales representatives and distributors to sell your book to bookstore buyers. Often the cover is the only thing the buyers see—the only thing that can either make the sale or lose the sale. At Falker-Verlag, a German trade publisher, cover designs originate with the marketing and sales department. No book is sent out whose cover has not been approved by the sales representatives.

- The cover is featured in your advertisements, catalogs, and reviews. If it is well-done, it will increase your sales. If it is boring or unconvincing, it will detract from your sales.

- For bookstores, the cover is important for a number of reasons: 1) it must fit into the atmosphere the bookstore is attempting to create, 2) it must fit into (and yet stand out from) other titles in the same category, and 3) it must attract the casual browser.

- The cover is often the only advertising a book buyer sees. It is the ultimate in point of purchase advertisements. It either works, or it doesn't. And it only has about 8 seconds to do so, since the average bookstore browser, according to the *Wall Street Journal*, spends only 8 seconds on the front cover of a book—and then only if the reader is attracted enough to the book to pick it up in the first place.

- Book covers are very important for advance sales at exhibits or with key wholesale, chain store, and book club buyers. Again, it is often the only part of the book that they see first hand before the book is produced. And many of these buyers must make their purchase commitments months in advance of any book's publication date. At the 1983 ABA Convention, Alan Gadney of Festival Publications took many large orders for three computer books based solely on the sample covers he had produced. The sales could not have come from the contents of the books, because Alan hadn't written the books yet.

- To many buyers and reviewers, the cover design reflects the attention the publisher has put into the book (and will continue to put into the book by way of continued promotions). Hence, your books will get far more reviewer attention if you yourself put more attention into designing an effective cover. As the book editor of *Newsday*, Leslie Hanscom, has commented, "I know when I see a really attractive jacket that the publisher is behind the book and, of course, I pay attention to it."

- For some kinds of books, a well-illustrated cover increases the value of the book. For example, in the science fiction and fantasy fields, the cover illustration is often the number one criteria by which book collectors in that genre judge a book. Indeed, the annual Hugo awards granted by the fans has separate categories for both fan artist and professional artist. And the art shows at the various SF conventions are often better attended than the seminars and speeches.

- Design is crucial, of course, with non-books such as diaries, the Anything book series from Crown, and personalized recipe books like Nancy Edwards's *With Love From My Kitchen*, published by Paint Box Studio. In such cases, the design is the book.

7:02 Elements of Good Cover Design

The basic rule of cover design is that the cover should match the contents of the book. That means that the style, format, and message of the cover should be compatible with the style, format, and message of the book itself.

An effective cover design should have at least some of the following elements:

- Use a standard format. The book should look like a book, and especially like other books with similar contents. If you want to attract the attention of buyers of a specific genre, your books must look like other books within the genre. Just as all oatmeal boxes look alike, so must all romance novels that hope to sell to repeat buyers. In the case of romance novels, this means a cover with a feminine typeface combined with an illustration of a man and woman caught in a wild embrace (the woman with long wind-blown hair and at least one naked shoulder revealed).

- At the same time the book must look different. It must be able to stand out in the crowd. That is one reason Zebra Books has begun putting holograms on the covers of its romance novels. It hopes to distinguish its line of books so the books stand out on the paperback racks and thereby attract more attention from potential buyers.

- The front cover of a book should be bold and simple, more like a billboard (which it is) than a full-page display ad. The cover should be uncluttered, easy to read (with highly readable type), and simple enough that the casual browser can catch the title and author without searching for either.

- If the author is well-known, feature the author's name in bold type at the top of the cover. If the title is more important, then feature it at the top.

- The typography should match the style of the book. For example, a simple typeface is more appropriate for a serious book while a fancy script typeface might be more appropriate for a romance novel. Novelty books, on the other hand, might use a casual typeface such as Hobo (one of my favorites). Typefaces come in all sorts of characters from simple to complex, from feminine to masculine, from strong and bold to light and airy, from romantic to businesslike. Be sure that your graphic designer selects a typeface that matches the style and subject of the book.

- Fiction should almost always have some illustrative element on the cover while non-fiction can easily do without any illustration or graphic elements at all. Indeed, serious nonfiction books may be better served by a simple bold headline and little else. Again, the design of the cover depends on the style and subject of the book as well as the intended audience.

- Full-color covers are almost a requirement for coffee-table books, high-priced cookbooks, pictorial travel guides, and most fiction. Full-color covers also encourage impulse sales for almost any book.

- If you are publishing a series, there should be some continuity in the cover design so that bookstore browsers can readily see the connection. For example, Wei-chuan's Cooking uses the same format for all four covers of their line of Chinese cookbooks. The two complimentary titles from Advocacy Press, *Choices* and *Challenges*, both had similar overall cover design though one was feminine in style and the other masculine—thereby, matching the audience for each book.

- Try different sizes of books. 101 Productions was the first cookbook publisher to use an 8″ × 8″ format for trade cookbooks, a format that allows for more flexibility in the layout of pages while enabling the book to lie open more easily without breaking the spine. In the past fifteen years, 101 has sold more than four million copies of their cookbooks.

- Finally, remember that besides being your major point of purchase advertising for the book, the cover must also protect the book. If it is a paperback book, have the cover varnished, film laminated, or coated with a UV plastic. If it is hardcover, use a jacket (which also allows for more promotional copy than a cover by itself).

7:03 Don't Forget the Spine

More than once in my own publishing career I have forgotten to add copy for the spine before sending the materials to the printer. Thus I had to rely on the printer to set the type and place it appropriately—a procedure that is not recommended if you like to sleep at night. Anyway, the spine of your books should always have at least the following elements: the full title of the book, the name of the author and, if there is room, your company name and logo.

Remember: most books in libraries and bookstores are displayed spine out, so make sure the title is large enough to read.

7:04 What to Put on the Back Cover

While the front cover should act as a billboard to attract potential buyers, the back cover should serve as a display ad to encourage the buyer to get the book. Hence, the back cover can be more complex, more wordy, more detailed. For example, the average book now has about 10 to 15 words on its front cover and from about 70 to 100 on its back.

What should the back cover contain?

- First and foremost, it should have more details about the book, anything about the book that will encourage the reader to buy the book. List an abbreviated form of the table of contents, or use a section from the author's introduction, or, in the case of a novel, write a short synopsis of the crisis/setting/characters of the story.

- Second, it may contain blurbs from reviewers and experts—blurbs, of course, that praise the book. Testimonials or endorsements help to instill confidence in the book.

- Third, include some details about the author, anything that will establish his or her credentials to write the book. If the author is a celebrity, be sure to include a recent photo of the author, either at work or at play depending on the nature of the book.

- Fourth, list the price of the book. For the convenience of the bookseller, the price must appear somewhere on the cover. For most mass-market paperbacks the price is listed on the front cover, most trade paperbacks on the back cover, and most hardcovers on the inside front flap.

- Fifth, print the ISBN number and Universal Product Code (if sold in food stores and drugstores). Your company may sign up to participate in the UPC code by writing to the Uniform Product Code Council, 7051 Corporate Way #201, Dayton, OH 45459. Or by calling (513) 435-3870.

Remember that whatever you put on the back cover should serve one purpose: to inspire the reader to buy the book. Few browsers look beyond the front and back covers; hence, the covers have to be so designed that they encourage the browser to buy the book right away or else open the book to learn more about its contents.

7:05 Jacket Flaps

The jackets of hardcover books usually include a short synopsis of the book on the front flap and a short biography of the author on the back flap. This arrangement usually allows the back cover to be used primarily for testimonials and advance reviews. Since a hardcover book is usually higher priced, use this extra space to include more copy that will overcome the casual browser's price resistance.

7:06 Selecting the Right Binding

There are five basic binding options currently available: hardcover, perfect-bound paperback, saddle-stitched paperback, comb or spiral bound, and loose-leaf binders. How do you choose which ones to use with your new titles? Here's a few guidelines:

1) **Hardcovers**—Use for gift books, library editions, permanent collections, major works of fiction and non-fiction, and professional reference titles.

- Since hardcovers are still taken more seriously by booksellers, reviewers, and subsidiary rights buyers, publish hardcover editions of your books if you want to reach a wide general market through book reviews and author tours.

- Libraries still prefer hardcover editions because they wear better under heavy use. For the same reason, professionals prefer hardcovers for their expensive reference manuals.

- Most higher priced books are published in hardcovers because such covers are viewed as being more expensive. An exception to this rule are many annual directories (such as the LMP) which are expected to wear out quickly and be replaced with a new edition each year.

- Cookbooks often sell better in trade paperback editions except around Christmas time when many people are buying the cookbooks as gifts for others; then the hardcover edition has a much higher perceived value.

- Hardcover editions are also indispensable for books which are destined to be collector's items—anything from a cookbook to a limited edition.

2) **Perfectbound paperbacks**—Use for most mass-market titles, inexpensive editions, novelty books, pocket travel guides, and any book with an ephemeral topic.

- As mentioned above, many annual directories are published in perfectbound paperback format because they are expected to only last a year until the next edition comes out.

- Most genre novels are published in this format because, again, they tend to reflect changing tastes and aren't likely to be read again and again.

- The main reason to use this format is to keep the retail price down so more readers can afford to buy the book. It also cuts your upfront costs in publishing a book, leaving you more money to put into advertising and promoting the book.

- Of course, you could publish both a hardcover and a paperback edition (either simultaneously or, as is more common, the hardcover first followed by the paperback). Publishing two editions opens the potential audience of the book. The book can then be promoted to both library and food store markets.

- Publishing two editions also allows you to sell each edition to a different book club without endangering the exclusivity of either club. Festival Publications did this with one of their titles, selling the $15.95 paperback to one book club and the $23.95 hardcover edition to another.

3) **Saddle-stitched paperbacks**—Use mainly for school workbooks and some manuals.

- Because saddle-stitched books have no spine and thus cannot be shelved with the spine out, they are hard to sell to libraries and booksellers. Don't use such binding if these are your major markets.

- The main value of saddle-stitched books is that they are cheap to produce. Hence, they make excellent workbooks, lab manuals, and atlases.

- They also lie flat more easily than perfectbound books—another reason they make good workbooks and atlases.

4) **Comb-bound and spiral-bound books**—Use primarily for cookbooks, computer manuals, and other books where there is a great need for the book to lie flat while allowing the reader's hands to remain free.

- A survey by the Benjamin Company showed that 54% of cookbook buyers consider it essential that a cookbook lie flat. An additional 32% considered it nice but not essential.

5) **Loose-leaf binders**—Use primarily for subscription services and any other books which require periodic updating or removal of the pages.

- A collection of forms may either be published as a perfectbound book with perforated pages (which does not allow the pages to remain together in a neat way) or as a loose-leaf binder (which allows for the pages to be removed, copied, and then returned for safe keeping).

- Loose-leaf binders are usually sold only by mail to end users because librarians and booksellers do not like stocking books whose pages can be removed easily. In addition, binders do not sit neatly on most bookstore and library shelves.

7:07 Good Books Come in Unusual Packages

While in most cases your books should look like books, there are arguments for packaging your book in unusual ways to reach a new market. In many such cases, it's a good policy to publish two editions, one for the standard book market, the other for the special market.

- Unusual packaging can allow you to reach other markets, just as L'eggs's unique packaging allowed it to reach into the food store market to sell nylons. Para Publishing die-cut its *Frisbee Player's Handbook* into a circular shape and then packaged it inside a frisbee, thus encouraging sales to toy and sports shops that might not otherwise have carried the standard edition of the book (which sold better to bookstores and libraries).

- Unusual packaging can set your book apart from other books. The Pet Rock, for instance, was really just a short book, *The Care and Feeding of Your Pet Rock*, packaged with a plain rock in a fancy box. It wasn't the rock or the fancy box that really caught the imagination of the public; it was the book with its humorous approach to something as commonplace as a little rock.

- Even small format changes can make a difference in sales. Dial added a fancy ribbon marker to Paula Wolfert's *The Cooking of Southwest France* thereby setting the book apart from other cookbooks. So, even though the book had few illustrations and a high price, it still sold well because of that little touch of class.

- Richard Scary's *Biggest Word Book Ever!* from Random House is two feet high—almost taller than many of its intended users (ages 3 to 5). But its size sets it apart from other books—and fits the title. The size also allows Random House to justify the high price tag of $29.95.

- You can use unusual packaging to adapt your books to particular seasons, celebrations, or events. Little Simon, the juvenile publishing division of Simon & Schuster, has repackaged its Hatchling line of small board books into see-through Easter eggs which are then nestled on top of green paper grass inside a large counter-top display. These books are sure to sell well during the Easter season.

- Unusual book packages such as pop-ups, die-cuts, sticker books, and board books are often used in creating books for children. Such books combine play-value with content to help attract and keep the attention of children. Hence, they sell almost as well as toys.

7:08 Combine Books with Other Items

One way to expand the market for your books is to repackage them with other media, from audio tapes to frisbees, and then sell the package as a kit.

- As noted above, Para Publishing packaged its *Frisbee Player's Handbook* with a frisbee. This combined package actually sold better than the book alone and helped to get the book into several catalogs.

- Many children's books are now packaged with an audio tape so that the children can listen to the audio tape as they read the story or look at the pictures.

- Harper & Row has just published a new novel by Ursula LeGuin, *Always Coming Home*, which is accompanied by an audio tape. The book tells the story of a future Amerindian society while the audio tape contains songs and poems from this fictional future.

- Computer software is almost always packaged with a manual or manuals explaining how to use the software. Certainly the software sells better because it has the printed documentation. Of course, the documentation is often inadequate; otherwise, there wouldn't be the large market that now exists for computer books explaining how to use the software.

- Midwest Financial Publications, a subsidiary of the Beckley Group, packages courses that contain several books, a collection of cassette tapes, and other information which they then sell via hour-long television shows. The packages are priced at almost $300—well over the total price that could be charged if each item were sold separately.

7:09 Designing the Inside

When designing a book, take some time designing the inside as well as the outside of the book. Here's a few inside design elements that can affect the marketability of books:

- Use acid-free paper for books that must last a long time: library editions, limited editions, professional texts, and any other books worth preserving. If one of the main markets for the book will be libraries, acid-free paper could double the sales of the book.

- Be sure that the typeface you use for the text of the book is readable. And, if the book is to be used by many older people, make sure the type size is large enough. New England Press once published a superb cookbook (practical content, great reviews, attractive design, and reasonable price), but the book did not sell well. Only by watching browsers in a bookstore pick up the book and page through it did they discover that the typeface was too small for use in a kitchen.

- Use color inside high-priced books, pictorial books, and children's books. Few coffee-table books, pictorial travel guides, or expensive cookbooks will sell without full-color photos. Even fewer children's books will sell if they are not colorful and attractive. In the cookbook buyers survey conducted by the Benjamin Company, 48% of the respondents said that color photographs accompanying the text were essential for cookbooks.

- Illustrations help to sell books. Photographs, line drawings, tables, graphs, charts, sidebars, and other illustrations all make a book more attractive and more useful. Especially in this visual age where many new readers have grown up watching TV, graphic elements help to sell books. Certainly this book could have benefited from having at least a few illustrations. The only reason it doesn't have any illustrations is that I did not have the time to obtain the reprint permissions which would have been required.

- Give a sense of spaciousness to your books. Now, here again I have not always practiced my own advice (certainly my *Book Marketing Made Easier* and *Directory of Short-Run Book Printers* are both crowded to the gills). Nevertheless, if your major distribution outlet is bookstores, your books should be as attractive and as inviting as possible, both inside and out. Remember: As many as two-thirds of all bookstore sales are impulse purchases. The more attractive you make your books, the more likely they are to sell.

7:10 Front and Back Matter

The front and back matter of your books can be used to help market the books. Front matter such as forewords and dedications can help to promote the purpose of your books, while back matter such as appendices and bibliographies can increase the resource value of the books and, hence, their marketability. Here's a list of front and back matter which can be used to increase the promotability of a book:

- Inside front cover (or end papers)—These may be used for maps, family trees, or other illustrations which add to the reader's understanding of a book.

Illustrations printed on the inside covers or end papers are easier to refer to while reading.

- **Half-title page**—If included at all, this page is most often used to list only the title of the book. It may, however, also be used to print additional testimonials and endorsements or an enticing lead-in paragraph to the story itself.

- **Verso of half-title page**—If you include a half-title page in your books, use the opposite side to list other books by the author (especially those published by you). It's an inexpensive and unobtrusive way to let readers know about other books by the author.

- **Title page**—List the title of the book, including any subtitle or explanation; the author, authors, or editor; and the name and logo of your company. Listing your company's address and phone number on this page will make it easier for them to order more books from you.

- **Copyright page**—List the copyright notice, ISBN number, CIP information, and company name and address (if not listed on the previous page). The copyright notice, of course, is required to secure the fullest protection of the copyright law. The ISBN number allows booksellers and librarians to reorder copies more easily. The CIP information makes it easier for librarians to catalog your books; hence, librarians are more likely to order your books if this information is included.

- **Dedication**—Encourage your writers to include some human interest in their dedications, anything that will speak to the readers and make the dedication more memorable. Robert Holt included the following dedication in his self-published book, *Hemorrhoids: A Cure and Preventative*: "To the silent sufferers." His dedication was picked up by several reviewers who used it as the lead to their reviews.

- **Foreword**—Forewords to your books should be written by celebrities or by experts in the subject of the book—someone, in short, who will add legitimacy or interest to the book. As mentioned in the previous chapter, that's why Don Dible got Robert Townsend, president of Avis Rent-a-Car, to write the foreword to his book, *Up the Organization*.

- **Preface**—Note to authors: Take this opportunity to establish a rapport with readers of your book. Use the preface not only to establish your authority or expertise, but also to reveal why you chose to write the book. Many bookstore browsers read the preface before anything else, because the preface can reveal your motivation for writing the book, give them insight into your style and approach to the subject, and provide them with background on your background and research for the book.

- **Acknowledgements**—Acknowledgements are a great place to thank those who helped you in writing the book, especially the experts and other resource people who provided the necessary background facts and examples. Such acknowledgements help to establish the reliability of your information.

- **Table of contents**—After the front and back covers, the first thing most bookstore browsers look at is the table of contents. In preparing a table of contents, be as specific as possible. Let the reader see at a glance what your book offers. Include not only the chapter titles, but also major subheads. (Here's one reason why your chapter titles and subheads should be lively, interesting, and informative.)

Nat Bodian, in his two volumes of the *Book Marketing Handbook*, included not one but two tables of contents. The first was a short two-page table of contents listing only the major chapter titles; the second was fifteen pages long listing the major chapter titles and all the subheads. The first provided the reader with a brief summary of the book's contents, while the second provided a complete and detailed overview.

When preparing the table of contents, consider the possibility of using the table as part of the advertising brochure for the book. Many professional and how-to books use this approach very successfully, since most readers of such books are most interested in what the book offers, and a well-prepared table of contents provides the best overall summary of the book's contents.

- **Lists of illustrations/tables/charts**—If your book includes many illustrations, charts or maps, you should include a list of illustrations. Such a list makes it easier for the reader to locate a specific illustration. (Such a list also makes the book more attractive to librarians, because it makes the book easier to use as a reference source.)

- **Introduction**—Use the introduction to lead the reader into the rest of the book. After the table of contents, most bookstore buyers will look at the introduction. The introduction must be so written that the reader is enticed to read on (and, in most cases, that means buying the book).

With fiction, the first chapter often serves the same function as an introduction in a non-fiction book. The first chapter, indeed the first sentence, must entice the reader into the book. Earlier today I picked up one of the Fletch mystery novels by Gregory Mcdonald. Well, say no more. Honest, I was just going to glance at it, but the first chapter was so delightful that I had to keep reading. I just finished the book a few minutes ago. Sorry for the interruption (Did you notice it?).

- **Back Matter**—Most of the traditional back matter (appendix, glossary, bibliographies, footnotes, and index) serve one major purpose: They provide readers with access to more information, to additional resources. For that reason, they are considered essential by many librarians. At the very minimum, a book should contain an index and bibliography.

The real bibliography for this book was so long I had to publish it as a separate book, *The Independent Publisher's Bookshelf.*

The index for the first volume of Nat Bodian's *Book Marketing Handbook* was 50 pages. The second volume not only reprinted the index from the first volume but also included its own index of 58 pages. That's 108 pages of indices—about ⅕ of the book. Yet those indices are worth every extra page, because they make all the detailed tidbits of Bodian's books far more accessible.

In more than one case I've recommended books solely because of their appendices which provide access to so many resources. A complete and detailed appendix may also allow your book to be listed in such resource bibliographies as *Directory of Directories* which can lead to extra sales. Tom and Marilyn Ross's *Encyclopedia of Self-Publishing* was listed in the *Directory of Directories* because of its extensive resource list.

It's also possible to so expand an appendix that you actually begin the writing of another book. Our *Book Marketing Opportunities* directory grew out of the appendix we were planning for this book. The list of resources got to be so large that it would have made this book cumbersome to use. So we broke the book down into two parts. Now the directory is over 300 pages itself—and has grown into a significant database.

7:11 Ask for the Order

Placing an order form in every book you produce is an inexpensive way to increase the sales of all your titles, especially those related to the book. This order form can be designed in a number of formats, from a gift certificate for friends...to a listing of your related titles...to a coupon requesting your catalog...to an order blank headed by the question, "Did you borrow this copy?"

Order blanks will encourage orders from customers who first saw the book in a library or at a friend's house or on an associate's desk. Other orders will come from repeat buyers who are buying extra copies as gifts for friends. Still more orders will come for other titles in your line that are related to the book from which the order form was taken.

- Such order forms are now quite common in most mass-market paperbacks, especially in the genre titles such as science fiction, western, and mystery novels. For example, in the mystery novel by Gregory Mcdonald that I read today, Warner Books had two pages of advertisements for other books, one page listing four other Fletch titles by Mcdonald, the other page listing ten titles by P. D. James.

- Dover Publications routinely includes listings of other related titles in their various lines of books. I've bought a good number of books from them in this way.
- Janet Martin of Redbird Productions reports that most of the orders for their *Cream and Bread* book are placed via the order blanks in the back of the book.
- To build interest in forthcoming titles, Bantam has begun printing 16-page previews of upcoming titles in related books. For example, they printed a 16-page preview of a new Nero Wolfe adventure written by Robert Goldsborough in the reprint editions of Rex Stout's original Nero Wolfe series.

7:12 And Ask Again

Rather than print the order form in the book itself, many publishers slip an order card in each book they send out. A separate order card makes it easier for the reader to send in an order.

- Barron's includes comment cards in most of their new cookbook titles. These comment cards serve at least four functions: 1) they get feedback from the users of the book, 2) they find out where the readers bought the book, 3) they elicit opinions from readers on what other titles they'd like to see produced, and 4) they allow readers to request Barron's complete catalog of cookbook titles. Barron's has added 15,000 names to their mailing list in this way.
- Writer's Digest Books includes similar comment cards in all their new titles as well. They encourage readers to use the cards as bookmarks while reading the book and then to write down their reactions to the book after they've completed reading it. When the readers send in the card, they may also request information regarding five of Writer's Digest services: newly published titles, the Writer's Digest School, the Writer's Digest Book Club, the Writer's Digest magazine, and the Photographer's Market Newsletter.

CHAPTER 8

How Authors Can Help Promote Their Books

Many publishers are quite hesitant about having authors get involved in the marketing of their own books. Publishers often have good reasons for such reluctance: Many authors get a little too enthusiastic and demanding. Nevertheless, an author's help is indispensable to the active promotion of any book. If you make it clear to your authors right from the beginning where you need and expect their help (and where you don't), you will gain invaluable marketing assistance. Use it. It can make the difference between a poor seller and a best seller.

8:01 Authors, Please Note!

Although you have a right and duty to help market your books, don't get in the way of your publishers. Remember, above all, that the publishers have had more experience in editing, designing, producing, promoting, and marketing books than you have had. Let the publishers do their job; you do yours.

Here's some suggestions on how you can help your publishers do their job more effectively:

- Work with your editor. Your editor should be your main contact with your publishers. If you have any suggestions for different ways to market your books, channel those suggestions through your editor. Your editor, in turn, should pass those suggestions on to the appropriate departments within the publishing company.

- Listen to your editor when he or she makes suggestions on ways to improve the style, content, or approach of your book. That doesn't mean that you shouldn't give your editor feedback based on your own knowledge and experience, but it does mean that you should listen very carefully to his or her suggestions and, in most cases, follow those suggestions.

- Consider ways to change your book's contents so the book becomes more marketable. For details on how you can improve the contents of your book, reread the two preceding chapters.

- Answer all questionnaires and other requests for information from the publisher promptly and completely. Use these requests as an opportunity to suggest other ways to market your books—especially those ways which draw on your own experience, associations, and expertise.

- Provide your publisher with a detailed biography of your life, including your activities and interests. The publisher may have contacts or knowledge that can turn some of your activities or interests into promotions for your book.

- Never stop thinking of ways to market your books. Pass on those suggestions which would be most appropriate for the publisher to carry out. Also consider ways you yourself can market your books. More suggestions along this line are listed below.

8:02 Use Your Authors's Connections

Although many authors are famous for their love of seclusion, most authors do have associations, connections, contacts, and friends who can be of assistance in promoting the author's book. Use those connections. They are a prime audience for the book.

- Ask your authors to compile at least four separate lists of such contacts: 1) those who might be interested in personally buying the book, 2) those who might purchase the book in quantity (for associations, businesses, etc.), 3) those who can provide their expertise in reviewing, commenting on, and perhaps writing a promotional blurb or foreword for the book and, finally, 4) those in the media who might review the book or provide other media exposure for the author and/or the book.

- Other lists the author might be able to provide include: 1) the names of individuals involved in the subject area of the book, 2) buyers of products or services described in the book, 3) companies or other organizations that might be interested in the book (either for resale to their members or for use as premiums), 4) membership directories of clubs and associations in which the author is an active member, 5) a list of media for the city in which the author lives (or has lived previously), and 6) names of individuals who have expressed an interest in the author's previous books, articles, or other activities.

- Your authors can also arrange to have announcements of the publication of their books place in the newsletters of any associations to which they belong, in their company's in-house magazines or newsletters, in appropriate alumni publications, and other club bulletins.

- If your authors work for a company or other institution, encourage them to ask the company's public relations department to issue its own news release.

- If the author is a regular contributor to a magazine or newspaper, that periodical might be interested in doing a review or special advertising promotion for the author's current book, especially if the book fits its editorial profile. Because Robert Miller was a regular contributor to their magazines and because his book, *Most of My Patients Are Animals*, fit into their editorial focus, *Veterinary Medicine* and *Western Horseman* together took 8000 copies of the book to sell to their subscribers.

8:03 Provide Authors with Sales Material

Since your authors's friends, colleagues, and other connections are prime prospects for their books, provide your authors with any promotional material which might help stimulate sales to these special audiences.

- One suggestion made by John Huenefeld in his newsletter is to print your regular news release on legal-size paper with a tearoff order coupon at the bottom of the page. These announcements can then be sent by your authors to all their friends and . This procedure not only allows your authors to announce the publication of their books, but also relieves them of having to let each individual acquaintance know where to obtain their books.

- Let your authors know that you'll supply similar announcements, advertising copy, or more formal brochures to any organization or individual acquaintance wanting to promote the author's book in their newsletter, membership mailings, or other promotions. The orders may come direct to you, or may go direct to the organization or individual (who will then order the books from you in quantity).

8:04 Keep Your Sales Force Informed

Your authors are your best sales force for their own books. Encourage them always to carry a copy of the book with them wherever they go, to talk up the book with any individuals or organizations they encounter, and to always let you know what they are doing in the way of personal promotions.

The last point in the above paragraph is perhaps the most important of all: Make sure your authors keeps you informed of any of their activities, speeches, or other events that might have an impact on the sales of their books. In turn, you should let your sales representatives and distributors know of all such activities so they, in turn, can take advantage of any such promotions.

8:05 Authors as Self-Promoters

Your authors can do many things on their own to increase the sales of their books. Give them room to act. Indeed, encourage them to do their own promotions. But, of course, make sure they also keep you informed so you can tie their promotions into your own.

The following comments will be address directly to authors; see that your authors know about these ways to promote their books during their day to day activity.

- Become a Speaker—There are a good number of ways to use speaking engagements to sell books. Here's just a few of them:

1. Simply mention your books in any talks you give, whether to the Lady's Auxiliary, Rotary Club, or an association meeting. Integrate the subject of your books into the subject of your talk so that mentioning your books is a natural part of the talk. Then let the audience know they can buy copies of your book in the back of the room after the talk (these sales are known in the speaking trade as back-of-room sales). One speaker earns over $1000 per talk from sales of his books. Sir Edmond Hillary used to sell at least two books to every person who attended his lectures.

2. Here's a few other places you might want to give a talk: libraries (especially meetings of the Friends of the Library), bookstores, churches, clubs, civic groups, chambers of commerce, schools, colleges, PTA's, writer's clubs, garden parties, businessmen luncheons, workshops, seminars, professional meetings, cruise ships, museum shows, conferences, ski lodges, and anywhere else that welcomes speakers and entertainers.

3. Give something free to everyone who attends your lectures. Art Fettig of Growth Unlimited offers everyone a free copy of one of his verses, illustrated and ready for framing. Each verse has his name, address, and phone number. He gets many bookings and book sales through this means alone.

4. Give everyone a brochure and order blank. Hand them out free during the lecture, or just afterwards.

5. Offer to accept MasterCard and VISA orders (if you are set up to do so). Again, when Art Fettig offers one of his higher priced book/tape combos, he tells members of the audience to just write their charge card number on the back of their business card. In this way, he often gets over $1000 in orders each lecture.

6. If you are giving a seminar to a corporation or a talk to a professional association, you might try preselling your books to the program planner so that each attendee receives a free copy of your book as part of the program. If your books will make the meeting that much more effective, the corporation will probably jump at the chance.

7. Have the toastmaster announce that you will be available after your talk to autograph books and to speak to anyone with any additional questions.

8. If you are speaking at a significant or otherwise newsworthy event, let the media know about your speech. Send them an advance copy of your talk so they might quote accurately from your talk if they decide to cover the event.

9. Remember, as a professional you should also charge for speaking to any major seminars, conferences, clubs, and so on. These fees will help to pay your way to other speaking engagements and help to keep your promotional show on the road. On the other hand, Bruce Sievers does not charge for his poetry readings, but he does insist on his right to sell his books after the readings. And does he sell! In one year alone he sold over 25,000 books just as a result of his poetry readings.

10. If the topic of your book is of interest to a specific national association with local chapters, why not set up a speaking tour with these local chapters? Linda Salzer, author of *Infertility: How Couples Can Cope*, set up such a lecture tour, visiting local chapters of Resolve, the national support group for infertile couples.

11. As you travel, plan ahead. Try to arrange speaking engagements wherever you travel. Beverly Nye, author/publisher of *A Family Raised on Sunshine*, bought a 30-day bus pass to toured five cities where she had previously lived. In each city she arranged with Mormon church groups and homemaking classes to give lectures, where she talked about her own methods of homemaking. Not only did she make money on the admission fees charged for the lectures, but she also sold over 1500 copies in those 30 days.

12. Finally, remember that it was through such speaking engagements that Wayne Dyer, Leo Buscaglia, and Robert Allen all became best-selling authors. Robert Allen used to travel to different cities, offer "A Free Evening with Robert Allen" seminars, get people excited about his ideas for creating wealth, and sell loads of books.

• Become a Teacher—A good number of self-publishers and writers have found that lecturing at colleges and adult education classes is a superb way to market books. Melvin Powers, publisher of Wilshire Books and author of *How to Get Rich in Mail Order*, has been doing this for many years in the California college system. Not only does a description of his course get mailed to over a million potential students, but in the course description he recommends that his own book be bought and read ahead of time. He suggest that students buy the book at a local bookstore or check it out of their library. As he notes, "The result was phenomenal from a standpoint of sales."

• Write Articles—Besides selling first or second serial rights to your books, you might also consider adapting chapters of your book or writing related articles for magazines. Tom and Marilyn Ross did this for their *Encyclopedia of Self-Publishing*, selling short articles about self-publishing to such diverse magazines as *Southwest Airlines Magazine*, *Toastmaster Magazine*, *Pro-Comm Newsletter*, and others. In each case, they insisted that the magazine include an endnote telling readers where they could order the book. If you can sell these articles, all the better; but even if you don't, you should try to place articles in any magazine where readers might be interested in the topic of your book. Be sure to coordinate any such freelancing with your publisher (who may already have approached the magazine about second serial rights).

- Write a Column—To gain greater visibility, write a regular column for the appropriate trade journal or newsletter. Luther Brock, a direct mail copywriter, currently writes regular columns for *Direct Marketing Magazine*, *Mail Order Connection*, and *Information Marketing Newsletter*. He does no advertising because these columns bring him all the business he can handle.

I currently write a regular column for the COSMEP newsletter. Not only does the column help members of the association, but it also provides additional visibility for my publishing activities. Moreover, many of the columns are taken straight from my forthcoming books. Currently I am running a series of four columns taken from my book, *Book Marketing Made Easier.* Of course, I mention the book at the end of each article. It's a perfect way to give potential buyers a sampling of my book without hurting sales of the book.

- Become a Joiner—Do anything you can to become visible. This means joining appropriate trade and social associations related to your topic (if you don't already belong). But don't just join; become active in the association's activities. If you were interested enough to write a book about the subject, you should be interested enough to become active in working with a related association. That's why I'm a member of COSMEP and also why I am currently a member of its board of directors—not just because it's good for business, but because I really am concerned about the problems and possibilities of smaller book publishers.

- Become an Expert—As a published author, you automatically become an expert in the subject area of your book. To become recognized, however, as an expert, you must also establish yourself as a reliable source of news or information. Hence, do not respond to a reporter's question if you do not know the answer. Admit the limits of your expertise if you want to become quoted as "a reliable source."

As an author of a number of books about publishing, I am often called upon to consult with smaller publishers and non-profit associations about book production and marketing. I help where I can, and when I don't know the answer I send them to people who can help them. In the same way, many editors and publishers have sent people my way because they knew I could answer the questions from their readers.

While you're at it, you can even sign up as an official expert with the Library of Congress's National Referral Center. The Center has a subject-indexed, computerized file of over 13,000 individuals and organizations who will provide answers to almost any question. If you don't mind fielding some unusual queries, you can let the Center know that you're available to answer questions within the subject area covered by your book. To sign up, just call (202) 287-5670, or write the Library of Congress, National Referral Center, Washington, DC 20540.

- Become a Talker—That means just what it says. Talk to anyone and everyone you meet. As a self-promoting author, you should not hesitate to talk about your book and your writing. Let people know you are an author. Naturally, they will then ask what you've written. Don't just tell them; show them the book (especially when your book is first published, be sure to carry a copy around with you at all times so you can show people the actual book). Be sure to let them know where they can order the book. One author of a guidebook for handicapped travellers happened to sit next to Abigail van Buren on an airplane flight. Of course, in the course of their talk, she happened to mention her book. Some time later, van Buren found an opportunity to mention the book in her syndicated column, "Dear Abby." Over two sackfuls of mail—all orders—resulted from that one little mention.

- Sell Your Books Door-to-Door—Don't laugh. It's one of the most effective ways to sell your books. People love to meet and talk with authors—and they love reading books by people they've met personally. Who wouldn't buy and cherish a personally autographed copy?

  Gary Provost, author/publisher of *The Dorchester Gas Tank*, began his career this way. He'd take a suitcase of books to downtown Boston every day, settle down at some busy corner (around City Hall, the public library, a subway entrance, or plaza), and begin peddling his books to anyone who'd listen. He'd sell 20 to 25 books a day. That's more sales than most books make per day.

  Another author sold his novel, *A War Ends*, door to door. While knocking on doors one day, he met a reporter for a Los Angeles newspaper. The reporter was so taken by the author's approach to selling books that he featured him in a story. That story not only brought the author many local sales, but it also inspired a number of other feature stories nationwide, thus bringing more attention to the novel. . .and more sales.

- Set a Record—One way to get publicity for your book is to set a world record (a record that can somehow be related to your book). Note that you don't have to set a world record to gain publicity, you only have to attempt it. Actually, if you're not into setting world records, you could sponsor an attempt or announce a contest and prize for such an attempt—anything at all that associates you and your book with the world record. For more details on how to go about getting in the record books, read Clint Kelly's self-published book, *The Fame Game*, available from Performance Press, P. O. Box 7307, Everett, WA 98201.

- Do It for Charity—While you're attempting the world record or, for that matter, while you doing other promotions for your book, do them for a charitable cause. Not only will this help you in getting publicity for your book, but at the same time you'll be doing a good turn for the charitable cause by bringing publicity (and money) to it as well.

8:06 How to Help Your Authors

Not only can your authors help you with the promotion of their books, but you can also help them. It's a two-way street where both of you can benefit if you're willing to work together. Don't be afraid to ask for your authors's cooperation in your marketing plans.

Here's a few suggestions on how they can help you and how you can help them:

- Have your authors autograph several hundred copies of their books. When sending complimentary review copies to major reviewers and other key contacts, send these autographed copies. Indeed, if your authors are willing, have them personalize the autographs for each key reviewer and contact. These personalized copies will get more attention than ordinary copies.

- Support your authors with material for doing bookstore appearances and media interviews. For major titles and other books that lend themselves to a national tour, help to organize such a tour and pay the author's expenses. National tours are one of the best ways to establish a nationwide demand for a book, and such widespread demand can often propel a book to the best-sellers list.

- Allow your authors a little freedom to do the unusual. Not only was Jacqueline Susann a superb interview subject for TV shows, but she was also a tireless self-promoter, going so far as to get up at six in the morning just to meet the drivers for mass-market paperback jobbers and encourage them to place her books in the prime spots. And they responded to her personal attention. Wouldn't you?

- Encourage the formation of fan clubs for your regular authors by providing special membership cards, posters, and other promotional material for any fans who request help in forming such a club. Janet Dailey, author of *The Great Alone* and *The Glory Game*, has such a fan club, and Pocket Books sends regular mailings to club members announcing new titles. It's a great way to establish a stronger bond between authors and their most ardent fans (who are also their strongest word-of-mouth supporters).

- Promote tie-ins with other authors, books, or events wherever possible. For example, be on the lookout for promotions such as the one run by the Village Green bookstore in Rochester, New York. One of their staff members happened to read in one of Alice Walker's books that Zorah Neil Hurston was her favorite author. So the Village Green, building on the publicity from the current movie and Walker's best-selling book, *The Color Purple*, ran a promotion for Hurston's book, *Their Eyes Were Watching God*. The store sold 365 copies of Hurston's book during the Christmas season alone.

- Be sure your authors are listed in Gale's *Contemporary Authors* and other directories of writers. These listings not only help to bring greater immediate recognition to the writers, but they also make it easier for media, librarians, and other researchers to find out more about the authors.

8:07 The Value of Awards and Honors

When one of your authors or books wins an award, make sure everyone knows about it. Send out press releases. Prepare new brochures announcing the award. When reprinting the book, add the announcement to the cover of the book. Also, when publishing new books by the author, let people know that the author is an award-winning author.

Also, don't forget to submit your best designed books for consideration in many of the annual graphics or design competitions, such as the Boston Bookbuilder's and AIGA awards. These give added prestige to your company and will also result in many orders from libraries.

Some literary awards which have a major impact on sales include the following (obviously, not an all-inclusive list):

American Book Awards (fiction, first fiction, nonfiction)
Caldecott Medal (illustrators of children's books)
Golden Medallion (romance)
Golden Spur (westerns)
Hugo and Nebula awards (science fiction and fantasy)
National Book Critics Circle Book Awards (biography, criticism, fiction, nonfiction, poetry)
Newbery Medal (authors of children's books)
Nobel Prize (literature)
Poe Award (mysteries)
Pulitzer Prize (biography, fiction, nonfiction, poetry)
R. T. French Tastemaker Awards (cookbooks)

- It has been estimated that the annual Hugo awards in science fiction are worth over $50,000 to the winners in increased sales of their books, higher advances and royalties, and greater subsidiary rights sales. Although the winners do not receive a cash award with the Hugo, they become instant celebrities within the genre and each following book is heralded with the legend, "by the Hugo Award-winning author." That legend along sells thousands of extra books each year.

- In 1985 the trade paperback edition of Harriet Doerr's *Stones for Ibarra* sold over 100,000 copies. Sales were undoubtedly helped by the fact that the book had won the 1984 American Book Award for First Work of Fiction.

- Again, in 1985 William Kennedy's 1984 Pulitzer-winning book, *Ironweed*, sold over 180,000 copies in trade paperback. If you'd like your books to be considered for the Pulitzer Prize, send four copies of each book, a photo of the author, a short biography of the author, and a $20.00 entry fee to the Pulitzer Committee, Graduate School of Journalism, 706 Journalism Hall, Columbia University, 116th Street and Broadway, New York, NY 10027. Even if your books don't win the Pulitzer, a nomination will still boost sales by a wide margin. Of course, only a few books which are submitted are actually nominated for the award, and only one is selected. This weeding out process is one reason awards and honors boost sales, because readers are then alerted to a book which has passed inspection more than once.

- Awards can also help sell subsidiary rights. Just recently, Dick Lochte's *Sleeping Dog*, winner of the 1985 Nero Wolfe Award for Best Mystery Novel, was optioned for a movie and also obtained $41,250 for paperback reprint rights. Similarly, the winner of the Jonathan Cape Young Writer's Award, Joseph Olshan, just had his book *Clara's Heart* optioned by Warner Brothers for a movie, plus sold paperback rights for $14,300.

- When the Czechoslovakian author Jaroslav Seifert won the 1983 Nobel Prize for Literature, the only English translation of any of his books published in the United States was a poetry book, *The Casting of Bells*, published by the Spirit That Moves Us Press. As a result, the small publisher was swamped with orders for the book and had to return to press for another printing.

- Similarly, when Bishop Desmond Tuto won the 1984 Nobel Peace Prize, Eerdman's Publishing became swamped with orders for his book, *Hope and Suffering*. Here's one example where a nonliterary award had a great impact on the sales of a book.

- Macmillan recently had one of its book covers (for *Unknown California*) win an Award of Distinction in the 1985 Andy Awards competition sponsored by the Advertising Club of New York.

8:08 Sponsor an Award Yourself

One way to draw attention to your books is to sponsor award competitions which are in some way connected with the book. For example, if you were publishing a book on cooking with woks, you might sponsor a wok recipe contest.

• Addison-Wesley is currently sponsoring a national Best Teacher Award competition in connection with their new book by Marty and Barbara Nemko, *How to Get Your Child a Private School Education in a Public School*, which emphasizes the value of committed teachers.

8:09 Encourage Interaction

Note that authors can do much more than just a few media interviews and bookstore signings if you work with them and allow them to work with you. To get the most help from your authors, you should have a procedure in place by which your authors can interact not only with their editors but also with your marketing and public relations people. This procedure should have some safeguards so your marketing people are not continuously bombarded with suggestions or wild phone calls from your authors. If you can set up such a procedure, I believe you'll find that your authors are quite willing to work more closely with you in the promotion of their books—and that this closer cooperation will lead to greater sales.

8:10 A Dramatic Example of Persistence

Here's one recent example of how an author, through persistence and a little bit of luck, promoted her book into the best-seller lists—a year after the book was given up as dead by her publishers! The book: *Callanetics*. The author: Callan Pinckney.

The book was first launched by Morrow in September 1984 and, after a first round of publicity and 10,000 copies sold, went into a second printing of 5000 copies. But there the book died. Because Callan Pinckney was not a celebrity and because the book was competing against another exercise book by Victoria Principal, Morrow was not able to get any more media interviews for Pinckney.

On her own, Pinckney continued to promote the book but with little effect until a fan in Chicago called her to ask if she would be coming to Chicago any time soon. Pinckney, of course, said she would be able to come if she could do a TV show in the area. Well, the fan was determined to have Pinckney come so she arranged for the producers of *A. M. Chicago* to contact Pinckney. And the rest is history.

Within hours of Pinckney's appearance on the show, Kroch's & Brentano's had taken over 400 orders. That was in August, 1985. From there Pinckney went on to do other shows in many other smaller cities, and each time she created another spurt of sales for her book. During this time she also personally called the major chains to let them know that Morrow still had books in print, stored in their New York warehouse. Finally, after about three more months of such promotion, her book reached the bestseller lists and, as of this writing, is still on the lists. Furthermore, Morrow has arranged for a new author tour of the major cities, and Pinckney finally got on a major TV show, the Phil Donahue show. The book has now sold over 180,000 copies, and paperback reprint rights just went for almost $200,000.

CHAPTER 9

Tips on Publicizing Your Books

There is an old definition of publicity that still applies today as it did years ago: Publicity is doing good, and then telling the world about it. Here, then, is the essence of getting good publicity: 1) Produce a good book, and 2) let people know about it. It really is that simple. But both steps do require patience, and persistence, and attention to detail.

Never think that publicity is free. It is not. You must pay your dues. If you're going to invest your time and money in promotions, make sure much of it is committed to your publicity efforts. Remember: Publicity does sell books, more books that any other means of promotion.

9:01 The Three Basics of Gaining Publicity

The three basics of gaining publicity are: 1) You must create real news about your book, something worth publicizing, 2) You must locate and cultivate the appropriate media contacts, and 3) You must be persistent; you must follow through.

1. A book with solid content and style will help immensely in fulfilling the first basic requirement for gaining publicity. Of course, a highly promotable author also helps.

2. For help you in locating appropriate media contacts, refer to our *Book Marketing Opportunities* directory. It includes the names of editors at all major newspapers and magazines, plus the program directors and producers at all major radio and TV stations.

3. Ron Gold, author of *The Personal Computer Publicity Book*, asserts that the three most important PR jobs are: 1) followup calls, 2) followup letters, and 3) followup calls. In other words, you must be persistent and follow through. Any PR professional will tell you the same thing: Persistence pays. If you knock on enough doors enough times, you're bound to get through.

9:02 Dealing with the Major Book Reviewers

Of all the book review media, there are about ten that are most important for establishing your books as critical and commercial successes right from the beginning. These include the trade magazines for booksellers (*Publishers Weekly, Kirkus Reviews*, and *West Coast Review of Books*), the major library review media (*Library Journal, School Library Journal, Booklist, Choice*, and *Horn Book Magazine*), and the book review sections of the large city newspapers (*New York Times Book Review, Los Angeles Times Book Review, San Francisco Chronicle, Washington Post Book World*, and *New York Review of Books*)

Of course, not all would be appropriate for every book you publish since *Choice* only reviews books appropriate for college and high school libraries, *Horn Book* only reviews children's books, and *School Library Journal* only reviews books that might be acquired by school libraries.

Here's some guidelines on getting your books reviewed by some of the major review media:

- *Publishers Weekly*—Published weekly as a trade magazine for booksellers, librarians, and publishers, this magazine reviews about 5000 books per year. They review almost any sort of book except reference books. Send galley copies at least two to three months before publication date to the appropriate editor, as follows: Sybil Steinberg, fiction; Genevieve Stuttaford, nonfiction; John Mutter, paperbacks; Diane Roback, children's books; Penny Kaganoff, how-to books. Send to PW Forecasts, Publishers Weekly, 205 East 42nd Street, New York, NY 10017; (212) 916-1600.

- *Kirkus Reviews*—Published biweekly as a prepublication review journal for booksellers, libraries, periodicals, agents, and publishers, this newsletter reviews from 80 to 100 books per issue, about 2500 per year. They review almost any fiction or non-fiction book, except poetry, mass-market paperbacks, and children's books for toddlers. Because they are a prepublication review service and usually try to run reviews at least two months prior to publication date, they like to see review copies at least three to four months in advance, the sooner the better. Ron de Paolo is nonfiction editor; Ann Larsen is fiction editor. Send review copies to Kirkus Reviews, 200 Park Avenue South, New York, NY 10003; (212) 777-4554.

- *West Coast Review of Books*—Published bimonthly for booksellers and the general public, this magazine reviews about 600 books per year. They review almost any sort of book, with special topical review sections each issue. Send review copies to D. David Dreis, Editor, West Coast Review of Books, Rapport Publishing, 1501 N. Hobart Boulevard, Los Angeles, CA 90027; (213) 464-2662.

• *Booklist*—Published biweekly by the American Library Association for librarians, this magazine reviews about 7000 books per year. They review almost any book that would be of interest to a general public library, including fiction, nonfiction, children's and young adult books, and reference. Send books or galley copies as soon as they are available. Bill Ott is the editor of adult books, Barbara Duree of young adult books, Barbara Elleman of children's books, and Sandy Whiteley of reference books. Write to Booklist, American Library Association, 50 E. Huron Street, Chicago, IL 60611; (312) 9446780.

• *Library Journal*—Published monthly for public librarians, this magazine reviews about 5000 books per year. Again, they will review almost any book that is appropriate for a general public library. Send the finished book or galley copy three to four months before publication date to Janet Fletcher, Book Review Editor, Library Journal, 205 East 42nd Street, New York, NY 10017; (212) 916-1927.

• *School Library Journal*—Published ten times per year for school librarians, this magazine reviews about 2500 books per year. They will review any book appropriate for school library use. Send galley copies or finished books to Trevelyn Jones, Book Review Editor, School Library Journal, 205 East 42nd Street, New York, NY 10017; 212- 916-1907.

• *Horn Book Magazine*—Published bimonthly for anyone interested in children's literature, this magazine reviews about 500 books per year. They review only children's and young adult books. Send review copies to Anita Silvey, Editor, Horn Book Magazine, 31 St. James Avenue, Boston, MA 02116; (617-482-5198).

• *Choice*—Published monthly by the Association of College and Research Libraries, this magazine reviews over 6000 books per year. They will review any books appropriate for college and high school libraries. Send finished books only. Write to Book Review Editor, Choice, 100 Riverview Center, Middletown, CT 06457; (203) 347-6933.

• *New York Times Book Review*—Published every week as part of the *New York Times* Sunday edition, this review does about 3000 book reviews each year. They do not review how-to books (cookbooks, diet books, etc.) except at Christmas time. They prefer that you send galleys as soon as available and then send books when printed. The best times to send them books for review are in time for January, February, July or August reviews, before the announcements of the major publishers's spring and fall lists. According to Rebecca Sinklar, deputy editor of the Review, they welcome phone calls or visits to discuss your upcoming book list even if you only publish one book per year. After you've sent them review copies of your books, you may call (212) 566-1466 and talk to Arlene Youngman, who will be able to tell you if your book has been assigned to a reviewer. Mitchel Levitas is editor of hardcover book reviews, Gerald Fraser of paperback reviews, and Ross Lipson of children's books. Send review copies to the New York Times Book Review, 229 West 43rd Street, New York, NY 10036; (212) 5561234.

- *San Francisco Chronicle Book Review*—Published weekly as part of the Sunday *Chronicle*, this review does about 1000 book reviews per year. They are open to almost any books and are especially interested in books produced by California publishers (even self-publishers). Send review copies to Patricia Holt, Book Review Editor, San Francisco Chronicle Book Review, 901 Mission Street, San Francisco, CA 94119; (415) 7777042.

- *Washington Post Book World*—Published weekly as part of the Sunday *Post*, this supplement reviews about 2000 books per year. They review general fiction and non-fiction books. Send review copies to Brigette Weeks, Editor, Washington Post Book World, 1150 15th Street N.W., Washington, DC 20071; (202) 334-7882.

- *Los Angeles Times Book Review*—Published weekly as part of the Sunday *Times*, this supplement reviews about 2000 books per year. Like most other newspapers, they review general fiction and non-fiction books. They do not welcome visits to the newspaper offices and also prefer that you do not follow up with phone calls. Jack Miles is book review editor; Jonathan Kirsch writes a special column, "Paperback Originals." Send review copies to Jack Miles, Book Review Editor, Los Angeles Times Book Review, Times Mirror Square, Los Angeles, CA 90053; (213) 972-5000.

- *New York Review of Books*—Published biweekly for the general public, this magazine reviews about 1000 books per year. They not only review books but also use excerpts from books and buy serial rights. Send review copies to Barbara Epstein or Robert B. Silvers, Editors, New York Review of Books, 250 West 57th Street, New York, NY 10107; (212) 757-8070.

- *USA Today*—Published daily for the general public, this newspaper will often review books under special subject areas such sports, money, lifestyle, or arts and entertainment. Send review copies to the appropriate subject editor, Attn: Books for Review, USA Today, P. O. Box 500, Washington, D.C. 20044; (202) 872-8329 or (703) 276-3400.

As you may have noticed, one of the most important things to do if you want reviews from these major review media is to send books as early as possible—preferably four months in advance of the book's publication date. Send galley copies if finished books are not yet available at that time; then send the finished books when they do become available.

If you have any questions about their review policies, don't hesitate to call them and ask. All the book review editors I've ever talked with have been very willing to answer questions and make suggestions.

9:03 The Importance of Book Reviews

Book reviews are critically important to any hardcover book that is targeted at a general audience. No publisher can afford to advertise in all the general newspapers and magazines which reach a wide audience, so the only major way to reach the most people with the least money is to obtain reviews in newspapers across the country. Almost any general trade publisher who relies on bookstore sales will tell you that reviews are a key factor in generating word-of-mouth and, hence, sales.

* For example, the Mexican writer Carlos Fuentes has written many books in the past twenty years, all of which received critical acclaim. However, in almost every case the reviews came too late to have a great impact on the sales of his books. Just last year, though, his new novel *The Old Gringo* received top billing in almost every major book review supplement (including front cover stories in the review sections of the *New York Times*, *Los Angeles Times*, *San Francisco Chronicle*, and *Chicago Tribune*). All these reviews appeared within three weeks of the book's publication date. As a result, the book hit the *New York Times* bestseller list within six weeks of its publication date.

* Melvin Power's book, *How to Get Rich in Mail Order*, was reviewed by Og Mangino in *Success* magazine. That one review brought in over 1600 orders for the book.

9:04 How to Get Reviews: Rule #1

Send out review copies. Send out lots of them. Send out more than you think you should. Hit every major newspaper and magazine which you think might be at all interested in the subject of your book. In most cases this means sending out somewhere between 300 and 500 review copies.

Don't be stingy about sending out review copies. For every hundred copies you sent out, you'll maybe get ten reviews. And those ten reviews will bring you anywhere from twenty to one hundred direct sales and many more indirect sales. Even at a conservative estimate, you'll receive 200 orders for every 100 copies you sent out. That's very cheap advertising. And if your list of media is selective and your book appeals to a wide potential audience, that rate of return will be even higher. (Note that the above estimate is based on sending your review copies to media which regularly review books similar to the book you send them.)

For other possibilities on your media list (that is, those media which are not prime prospects for reviewing your book), send them a news release, brochure, and reply card offering to send a review copy upon request.

• Here's one example of the impact of giving away sufficient review copies. When Epson came out with their first dot matrix printer, they sent 500 printers to the major opinion makers in the computer industry. They did not say, "Use this printer for 90 days and then send it back." No, instead, they said, "It's yours. Keep it. Use it any way you want. Enjoy." As a result, by the time other dot matrix printers got their promotional campaigns underway, Epson had already established itself as the standard among the movers and shakers in the industry. So, of course, when these people wrote about computer printers, they naturally talked about Epson—simply because that was the printer they used.

Note, however, that this giveaway policy would not have worked if Epson had not produced a solid, reliable printer. Similarly, sending out review copies will not help you unless your book is actually worthy of review.

• A major literary agent for some of the best-known cookbook authors says that one of the most effective ways to promote cookbooks is to send out plenty of review copies to anyone involved with food—from newspaper and magazine food editors to teachers at cooking schools and owners of gourmet cooking shops. The word-of-mouth these people create is worth any amount of regular advertising.

9:05 How to Get Reviews: More Tips

Here are some general tips on how to go about getting reviews for your books. Use those tips which make the most sense to you within your own procedures for sending out review copies.

• Don't just send review copies to book review editors. In many cases, especially with cookbooks and how-to books, you'd be better off sending your books to the food or lifestyle editors. Indeed, many book review supplements at major newspapers do not review how-to books or cookbooks except around Christmas time or other special occasions. So, watch for other opportunities for reviews: newsletter editors, specialty shop owners, in-house magazines, trade magazines, freelance writers, and other authors writing books in the same subject area.

• Some magazines and newspapers have special sections or theme issues where they review certain types of books. Have your advertising manager let you know about any such special themes or issues (note: more often than not, your advertising manager is the one who will be sent notices of these special issues). For example, *Scientific American* does an annual review of science books for children in their December issue. Also, as noted above, the *New York Times Book Review* only reviews cookbooks and how-to books at Christmas time.

• Have several hundred copies of your book's cover overprinted with the heading, "Advance Reading Copy—Not for Sale." Also include the publication date and retail price. Send these copies out to the potential reviewers. Such ARC's (advance review copies) offer several advantages: 1) The heading clearly indicates to the reviewers that they are receiving advance copies, 2) Such exclusive review copies tend to receive greater attention than ordinary copies, and 3) The other printed information (publication date and price) provide the essential data that any reviewer requires.

• Alternatively, you may print labels that provide the same information and attach them to the outside of the cover or the inside front cover.

• The basic information every reviewer needs to have at hand when reviewing a book includes the following:

1) Title of book (including the subtitle),
2) Author(s) of book,
3) Publication date,
4) ISBN number,
5) whether the book is available in both hardcover and paper,
6) the price(s) of available editions,
7) the name and address of the publisher,
8) the address where individuals orders should be sent, and
9) any handling charges for individual orders.

• Send a cover letter or press release with the book. These may never be read (and may well be thrown out when the receiving clerk unwraps the book), but they are indispensable for media which do have a policy of saving such enclosures. The press release or cover letter should contain the following information:

1) the basic facts about the book (what does the book do?),
2) the significance of the book (what benefits does it offer?),
3) the intended audience (who will the book help?),
4) a biography of the author (how is the author qualified?),
5) a list of the author's previous books.

The first three points of the press release should provide a quick summary of why readers would be interested in the book. The last two points clarify the author's credentials and background, the final point indicating any previous publishing history.

• Note the final point in the above suggestion: If the author has been published before, be sure to indicate that. Reviewers are more likely to review a book by an author who has already had several other books published. Why?

Because an author who has been published more than once has demonstrated that he or she can write books that readers will be interested in reading. The reasoning here is that publishers would not continue to publish an author whose books have not performed well or at least broken even.

- For special reviewers, you might want to write a personal letter to accompany the review copy. You might also want to have the author autograph the review copy. Some book reviewers will notice these little touches, and some will even appreciate the extra attention.

- If you have a book that appeals to a number of different audiences, you might print up special press releases focusing on the benefits of the book for each particular audience. For example, with our own *Directory of Short-Run Book Printers*, we sent one news release to magazines for writers and publishers, another release to business magazines, and still another to association and club magazines. And, for media which seem to fit no particular category but whose readers would still be interested in our Directory, we sent a personal letter to the editor outlining the benefits of the Directory for his or her readers. We've done this for school journalism newsletters and genealogy magazines,

- Do something special to draw attention to your book. When Crown published Elizabeth Alston's *Muffins* cookbook, they accompanied review copies with a basket of homemade muffins. When Morrow published Paul Prudhomme's *Louisiana Kitchen*, they invited a group of key wholesalers and booksellers to New York to sample a dinner cooked by Prudhomme.

9:06 Any Review Is a Good Review

Don't worry about the kind of reviews your books get. Any review is a good review, whether the reviewer like the book or not. Even a bad review helps to bring attention to the book and and to fix the book's title in the mind of the reader. Many readers will buy a book despite a bad review—if for no other reason than to prove the reviewer wrong. Others buy out of curiosity. Still others buy because they remember reading about the book but do not remember whether the review was good or bad.

- *The One Minute Manager* by Spencer Johnson and Keith Blanchard did not receive good reviews from most of the critics. Nonetheless, readers loved it. So, although good reviews can help put a book on the best-sellers list, they are not absolutely necessary.

9:07 What to Do After the Reviews

To make your book review program really effective, you must follow up your efforts. Here's a few suggestions on how to make the most of your books's reviews:

- Write a thank you note to the reviewer. Moreover, if you have gotten a good response from the review, let the reviewer know what the response was. Any review media is interested in what their readers respond to, and if your book received a good response and you let them know about that response, they will be more likely to review similar books in the future (and if your list is specialized, those books will be yours).

- If your books are hardcover, print only a limited number of book jackets in the beginning. Then, when the reviews start coming in, print additional dust jackets featuring the best reviews. This procedure is more costly than printing all the jackets at once, but if the reviews are good, the extra expense will be well worth it.

- Make copies of the best reviews and include them with news releases and review copies you send out after the first big wave of publicity. These reviews will help to convince later reviewers that the book is important, worthy of review, and of interest to their readers. (When making copies of reviews, underline the most favorable and important comments. Also, be sure to include a tag line identifying the name of the periodical and the date the review appeared.)

- Also send copies of major reviews to your key bookselling contacts (your sales reps and distributors, chain store buyers, wholesalers, book clubs, mass-market reprinters, foreign rights buyers, periodicals that buy second serial rights, etc.). Keep these key contacts informed of your books's publicity.

- You might also feature copies of reviews in the bounceback offers you send to direct mail customers.

- Quote the best reviews in all your continuing advertisements, brochures, catalogs, and other promotional materials.

- When you get a large response from a review, consider advertising your book in that magazine or newspaper. Obviously, if readers were interested in the book as a result of a review, other readers will probably order the book if they see another notice of the book. And since you are not likely to get two reviews in the same periodical, the only way you can get additional notices of your book in the periodical is to advertise. After receiving a favorable review and response to that review in *Entrepreneur's Magazine*, Wilshire Book continued to advertise their book *How to Get Rich in Mail Order* every month for the next year. Their ads continued to produce superb results for the whole year.

- Advertise in a periodical after a review rather than in the same issue as the review. That way, if the review is favorable, you can quote from the review in your ad. Plus the repeated exposure of the book in the periodical will produce better results than two exposures (one ad and one review) in the same issue.

- Subscribe to a press clipping service so you can keep tabs on all reviews and other features that appear in any print media. Note that few media will automatically send you copies of reviews or other features that they publish; hence, the only way you will know about these reviews is to subscribe to a clipping service. You cannot count on reader inquiries and orders to alert you to all reviews and features that appear, and you certainly cannot expect them to send you copies of the reviews when they order. (Some services will also provide you with tapes of any reviews or mentions on radio and TV stations as well as copies of print reviews.)

- Send copies of any reviews to the author. Not only does this notify the author that you are promoting the book, but it also provides important feedback which the author can use in revising the book (or writing a new book which covers material left out of the current book). Some of the reviews might also cause the author to think of other possible review media or promotions.

- Keep copies of all reviews in your files, along with copies of any other promotions. Each book should have its own file.

- Also place a copy of the review in your media file for that particular newspaper or magazine. If you don't already have one, you should begin one. The file should include a record of that medium's name, address, phone number, book reviewer, other important contacts (editors, producers, etc.), category of books they review, and other important notes. File a copy of every book review, notice, features, or other publicity which that medium publishes about your company or its books.

9:08 The Importance of Author Interviews

Author interviews are perhaps even more important than book reviews in propelling a book to best-seller status. Few radio and television shows actually review books; most only interview authors. And despite what you might think, radio and television shows are not incompatible with either selling or reading books. There is research showing that not only are book sales helped by television exposure (via talk shows and interviews), but that people who watch a lot of TV also read a lot of books. Indeed, it might be fair to say that key television shows sell more books than reviews in such major media as the *New York Times Book Review*.

Interviews, of course, can appear in print as well. Both print and audio/video interviews have certain advantages over book reviews.

1. They tend to be more personal and intimate. They give the reader a better feeling for the author's intent in writing the book as well as the author's qualifications.
2. More people watch radio and TV talk shows than read book review sections of newspapers.

3. The author has greater control over what will be covered in the interview; hence, the author can be sure to include more promotional comments about the book.

4. Most interviews are longer than reviews and, in general, the greater the length, the greater the impact.

9:09 Tips on Obtaining Interviews

The basic guideline for obtaining interviews is the same as obtaining any publicity. You must be persistent, and you must follow through. Of course, you'll have an easier time arranging interviews if your authors are interesting and entertaining speakers and if your books appeal to the personal interests of a wide audience.

Here are a few tips on how to arrange interviews in the various media:

• Know your media. Don't try to get interviews on a show or in a newspaper section where your book doesn't fit.

• Demonstrate to editors or producers that your author will be a good interview subject and that the book will interest and benefit their audience.

• Prepare a professional press kit which includes a copy of the book, a biography of the author, a news release or brochure describing the book, a list of questions that will produce a good interview, and a list of previous author interviews (where and when), including copies of any print interviews.

• Telephone the stations or newspapers and make a contact with someone who can make decisions on interview subjects. Then mail your press kit to them. A week or two later, follow up with another phone call to your contact. At this time, see if he or she is interested in setting up an interview.

• Call well ahead of time. Major TV and radio interviews must be set up four to six weeks ahead of time.

• Don't give up. If the first person you contact is not interested in an interview, try someone else at the same media. While arranging interviews for Peter McWilliams, author of the *Personal Computer in Business Book*, Ron Gold was rudely turned down by the business editor of a major Southern newspaper. But he didn't give up. His next call was to the computer editor at the same paper. As it happened, that editor had been wondering how to get in touch with McWilliams; hence, he was only too glad to set up an interview.

• For more help in researching the media, setting up interviews, and booking author tours, see *Book Marketing Made Easier*.

9:10 The Value of Print Interviews

Don't neglect press interviews when you are arranging author tours and interviews. Press interviews have several advantages over radio and TV interviews: 1) They are more concrete, 2) They tend to linger longer in the readers's minds, 3) Readers can read them at their leisure, 4) You can collect and copy press clippings more easily and send them to key contacts, 5) Print features are more likely to be syndicated, which can result in features being published in as many as 100 other newspapers, and 6) Print articles are more likely to inspire other feature stories.

* Peter Workman, who published *The Silver Palate Cookbook* (which has sold over 800,000 copies), believes that newspapers features are the best way to promote a cookbook. People try the recipes, then buy the book and, if the book is good, then word-of-mouth does the rest.

* William Zimmerman, author/publisher of *How to Tape Instant Biographies*, is also a firm believer in the power of the press. He's had feature spreads in *Business Week*, the *Washington Post*, and the *New York Times*. The *Times* feature story alone brought in over 2000 inquiries for his book.

* One mention in "Dear Abby" of *The Read-Aloud Handbook* by Jim Trelease boosted sales of that book to over 200,000 copies.

9:11 Radio Interviews Via Telephone

Radio interviews are an easy and effective way to promote your authors and books. In many cases, radio stations will handle interviews with the author over the phone. It is possible to organize a "national author tour" without your author ever leaving his or her home. Such telephone interviews are becoming more and more commonplace.

Radio stations like the idea because it means that any author, no matter how famous or how busy, can be accessible to them even if they broadcast from Missoula, Montana. Besides, authors usually make superb guests; they are articulate, intelligent, know a lot about their special areas of interest, and are usually better prepared to answer impromptu questions.

Authors, of course, love the idea because they do not have to bear the long hours of travel (though it may be difficult sometimes to have a real conversation with a disembodied voice). Publishers love the idea even more because such interviews are far less expensive than full author tours. Plus they are easier to arrange. There need not be any time conflicts or tight schedules to fit.

For those publishers with limited funds, here are a few ways to get the name of your books and authors in front of the people who schedule such interviews:

* You can get a free listing in *Broadcast Interview Source*, which lists individuals and organizations willing to speak on just about any topic. For more

impact, you can buy advertising space as well to promote your major authors. This sourcebook is sent to all the top radio talk show producers and hosts. For more information, write to Broadcast Interview Source, Mitchell Davis, Editor, 2500 Wisconsin Avenue N.W., Suite 930, Washington, DC 20007.

- You can pay to be listed in *Spotlight*, a co-op brochure advertising only books and authors. Three issues are prepared each year. Two issues are sent only to the top 400 radio and TV stations; the other issue is sent to 5000 media decision makers. For more information, write Spotlight, P. O. Box 51103, Seattle, WA 98113; (206) 527-2900.

- Dan Poynter, author/publisher of *The Self-Publishing Manual*, has just started a new co-op mailing service to 800 of the top radio stations which do telephone interviews. This mailing currently goes out twice a year. For more information, write to Radio Interviews Mailing, Para Publishing, P. O. Box 4232, Santa Barbara, CA 93140-4232; (805) 968-7277.

- If you'd like to reach the largest radio audience on earth, then contact Bonnie Mullins of the Armed Forces Radio Network. Bonnie is always looking for interesting authors to interview over the phone. She'll interview any author who can speak of some subject that will benefit her listeners all over the world. For further information, write to Bonnie Mullins, AFSINC-IIBE, Kelly Air Force Base, TX 78241-5000; (512) 925-6261.

- Finally, you can organize your own mail or telephone campaign by using *Book Marketing Opportunities: A Directory*, which lists over 400 radio and TV stations. The listings include addresses, names of contacts, shows that feature books or authors, topics of interest, phone numbers, and other details.

9:12 How to Do TV Talk Shows

One appearance on a major network or syndicated TV talk show such as *Good Morning America* or the *Phil Donahue Show* can sell thousands of books. Even local TV talk shows can produce dramatic sales (note Callan Pinckney's success in Chicago and other cities). Again, don't ignore TV shows just because you think TV viewers do not read. As noted above, that is not the case. TV viewers do read, and they do respond to reviews and interviews they see on TV.

For example, Bill Sand's book about his life while in prison and after his release, *My Shadow Ran Fast*, did not sell well when first published. However, during an appearance on the *Tonight Show*, he so captivated the audience that he was invited back for second show. Those two appearances alone were enough to put the book on the *New York Times* best-seller list.

Here, then, are a few more tips on how to arrange TV appearances for your authors (these tips supplement the general suggestions for obtaining interviews outlined in section 9:09 above):

- Allow four to six weeks lead time for TV talk shows. That means you must begin contacting the show producers at least four weeks ahead of the date your author will be available.

- When you call, first talk to the receptionist at the station to confirm the name of your contact. In this business people change jobs often so even if you use the most up-to-date directory, chances are that some of your major contacts will have moved on.

- Once you've confirmed the name of the booking agent (producer, talent coordinator, or whatever their title might be), have the receptionist transfer your call to that person. At this time you simply want to introduce the subject of your book and/or the credentials of your author and to encourage the person to watch for more information in the mail. This pre-call can save you time and money because often the person will either tell you that the show does not do such interviews or will refer you to someone else at the station who would be more likely to be interested in your particular author or subject.

- Once you've alerted the person that you will be sending him or her something in the mail, mail your press kit that same day by first class mail. You should not send it by express mail unless you're under a tight deadline. Express mail is simply expensive and a bit ostentatious. Other gimmicky deliveries are also rarely appropriate.

- Within five days of the day you expect the person to receive your press kit, follow up with a phone call. Don't wait for anyone to call you. They're not about to. In this follow-up call, you must make your best pitch. The pitch should be well rehearsed and short (no more than 30 seconds). If you cannot get your pitch down to three or four sentences, then you are not likely to get anyone's attention. Remember that the attention span of a person while watching TV is very short, so your description of why anyone would be interested in what your author has to say must be equally short. Don't become pushy; such tactics rarely work. If someone says no, go on to call the next person on your list. If the person indicates they will think about it, then suggest that you'll call them back again in a few days. Then do so.

- When you do receive a booking, send a letter out to the person right away thanking him or her for the booking and confirming the exact time and place. This confirmation letter will prevent any later misunderstandings or mishaps.

- The real secret, of course, in obtaining interviews is to keep on calling. If the first person rejects your pitch, call the second; if the second also rejects your pitch, call the third. Continue calling until you get a booking. If your author or the subject of the book is at all interesting, you should not have trouble obtaining a good number of interviews.

- It's best to start your new authors out with appearances on local shows so they can get more experience dealing with the hectic environment of a TV studio during the taping of a show.

- You might find it easier to book the national network shows by working through your local network affiliate. If your author makes a good impression on their talk show, then the local affiliate might be willing to help you book the author on a national show.

- When sending out your press kit to major local and national shows, you might want to include a videotape of your author in action. This videotape could be taken from a previous interview where the author performed well, or it could be a demo tape of the author during a simulated interview taped especially for the press kit. In either case, the tape should give program directors a great opportunity to see how well your author comes over on TV.

- Here's two things you should bring to a TV interview: 1) any visual aids or props that will help to make the interview more interesting (for example, fire extinguishers or alarms for a book on fire safety), and 2) an index card with the author's name typed on one line and the title of the book on another (just in case the show's production crew needs this information so they can flash the information on the screen while the author is talking).

- When booking shows, don't overlook the cable TV stations and networks. Also, when sending out review copies, send not only to talk show hosts but to anyone who might be interested in the book. When Warner Books published Stephen Davis's story of the rock group Led Zeppelin, *Hammer of the Gods*, not only did *Rolling Stone* magazine serialize the book, but MTV somehow got wind of the book and began plugging the book (free of charge). As a result, this hardcover book sold over 70,000 copies.

9:13 Organizing Effective Author Tours

Author tours can be expensive, a hassle to put together, and very wearing on the author, but for some books they can make a great difference for sales. In general, author tours are not productive unless the author is a celebrity or the subject of the book has a wide appeal or is somehow connected to a current issue of interest to many people.

Author tours are not easy to arrange. Not only do you have the additional expense of long-distance phone calls, but you must also fit interviews into a tighter schedule since you cannot afford to pay for the author to stay more than a day or two in any one city. Nevertheless, for certain authors and books you will want to arrange such tours.

My book, *Book Marketing Made Easier*, includes a number of forms and procedures to help you organize such author tours with a minimum amount of effort. Plus, here are a few additional suggestions to make the tour more effective:

- Consider doing several short tours rather than one long one. Not only would this be easier on your author, but it could also save you money (especially if you can organize the mini-tours around your author's normal business or vacation travel).

- Arrange for a local contact in each city, someone who can pick the author up at the airport and take care of any other driving during the author's stay in the city. This local contact could be one of your sales representatives, a friend or relative (yours or the author's), or a professional escort service.

- When booking interviews, don't forget other possible events or appearances that could boost sales for the author's book. Check to see if any bookstores would be willing to host an autograph session. Try to schedule a speaking engagement for the author with a local club, association, or business. Have the author visit any key wholesalers, distributors, or other sales outlets. How about any local festivities, celebrations, or other events?

- Give a copy of Peggy Glenn's book, *Publicity for Books and Authors*, to each of your authors you send on tour. In this book, Peggy describes how to prepare for interviews, how to dress for travel, what to pack and, in general, how to survive the wear and tear of an author tour. The list of what to pack is by itself worth the price of the entire book.

- Pay for a listing in *Publicity Circuit Monthly*. For $65.00 per month you can list the tour schedule for one author along with your company name and phone number; for another $29.00 each you can list additional authors. This monthly newsletter is mailed free to 600 radio and TV producers and newspaper feature writers in the top 15 markets. This listing could help to get your author a few additional interviews. For additional information, write to Bill Harrison, Bradley Communications, P. O. Box 299, Haverford, PA 19041; (215) 8966146.

- Call the regional offices of Associated Press and United Press International and ask that your author's appearances be listed in their Day Book. The Day Book is a calendar of events which is checked every day by media sources which subscribe the AP or UPI services. This could, again, result in additional interviews or other coverage of your author's tour.

9:14 Distribution Is Everything

Make sure you have distribution before arranging an extensive author tour or major media interviews. If there are not enough books in the stores to cover the anticipated demand, the entire effort can be wasted. This means, at the very minimum, that you should give advance notice to the booksellers in each city the author will be touring. Even better, you should have your sales representatives or distributors make sales calls just prior to your author's appearances.

Here's a few other things you can do:

• Pay for a short listing of your author's tour in the weekly *Newswire* newsletter published by the American Booksellers Association. For more information and advertising rates, write to Dan Cullen, Editor, Newswire, American Booksellers Association, 122 East 42nd Street, New York, NY 10168; (212) 867-9060.

• Arrange for distribution yourself. When Beverly Nye organized her own author tour, as she arrived in each city she checked the yellow pages for retail bookstores. She called each store to let them know that she would be doing interviews and to confirm how many of her book they had in stock. She then drove around to each store peddling her books and confirming that each store would have sufficient stock to cover the demand.

• Work with one of the major book chains to ensure that your books are carried in each city your authors will be visiting. Then have your authors mention that the books are definitely available at that chain if the viewer cannot find them elsewhere. Waldenbooks worked with the Fairfield Press to ensure that the Press's reissue of *The TM Book* was in stock when TV shows promoting the Transcendental Meditation program were aired in different cities.

9:15 Making Waves by Making News

Besides being featured in reviews and interviews, your authors and books can also be publicized via regular news or feature stories. Indeed, some of the best publicity for books and authors comes outside the normal review/interview channels. Don't overlook any chance for publicity. Make news. Find a news hook. Connect your books or authors with news that's already happening or about to happen. Here's just a short list of ways you can hitchhike publicity for your books with other news (in no particular order):

• **Anniversaries**—Schedule the publication of your book to coincide with an appropriate anniversary. Anything from the anniversary of a state (Putnam's *Make Way for Sam Houston* tied in with the Texas Sesquicentennial celebration), to the anniversary of a TV show (the CBS/Library of Congress "Read More About It" book promotion project featuring a number of books about soap operas on the 30th anniversary broadcast of "As the World Turns"), to the anniversary of a college (Globe Pequot Press's promotional tie-in of *The Illustrated Harvard* with that university's 350th anniversary), to the anniversary of current events (Congdon & Weed's publication of the book *One American Must Die* to commemorate the anniversary of the terrorist hijacking of a TWA jetliner).

• **TV series**—Publicize books that are tied in to continuing TV series such as the various soap operas or to miniseries such as "Roots" or "Shogun."

Genealogy books, for example, would sell better after each showing of "Roots." "Dream West," a new miniseries, is part of the CBS/Library of Congress "Read More About It" book promotion project. The project, in connection with this new miniseries, is promoting books about America's westward expansion.

- **Book anniversaries**—Celebrate the anniversaries of book classics by republishing the classics and by publishing new related titles. For example, a number of publishing companies are bringing out new titles related to the 50th anniversary of the publication of Margaret Mitchell's *Gone with the Wind*. Macmillan is publishing a golden anniversary facsimile of the original edition of the novel, while Outlet Books is excerpting part of Ronald Haver's *David O. Selznick's Hollywood* for release as *David O. Selznick's Gone with the Wind*. Meanwhile, Dutton is celebrating the 60th anniversary of the publication of A. A. Milne's *Winnie-the-Pooh* by publishing *The Winnie-the-Pooh Journal*.

- **Local interests**—Make special note of any local angles when sending out press releases or review copies. For example, if the author has lived or still lives in the region, note that fact (perhaps by placing a label on the cover of the book announcing that the author is a local resident).

- **Retailing promotional tie-ins**—Whenever you can associate your book with a retail promotion, whether local or national, do so. Fredrick Warne is publishing several Beatrix Potter books to tie in with "The World of Beatrix Potter" department store promotion currently touring eleven major cities.

- **Holidays**—Many books are already published to coincide with Christmas, Hanukkah, Easter, Thanksgiving, Valentines, and other holidays. Dolphin has scheduled the publication of Bill Cosby's new book *Fatherhood* for Father's Day, 1986.

- **Special months**—September is back to school month; June is dairy month; April is school media month. Time your book's publication date with a month that suits your book's subject. Learning Publications found out the hard way. They sent out press releases in June for their book called *Joyful Learning— Learning Games for Children Ages 4 to 12*, but they did not receive any reviews for the book until September because that is the time when people's interest again returns to educational issues.

- **Special weeks**—April has Library Week and Secretary's Week; October has Children's Book Week and Fire Safety Week; and August has National Scuba Diving Week. For almost any subject, there's a week that fits. Try to arrange your book's publication date or big promotions to fall within weeks (or months) that tie in with the subject of the book. Peggy Glenn arranged for major publicity during Secretary's Week for her book on *How to Start and Run a Successful Home Typing Business*; as a result the book received feature stories in a number of major newspapers and magazines.

- **Special days or celebrations**—As there are weeks and months for almost everything, there are also special days and/or celebrations as well. Look in *Chase's Annual Events* to discover any days that might fit in well with your books. For its new book *Tall Ships of the World*, Globe Pequot Press planned a promotional tie-in with the Fourth of July Tall Ships Parade in New York City.

- **Current events**—Scan the daily newspapers for any current news that you might use to further publicize your books. Be on the lookout for the offbeat as well as the headline news. For example, the author of a book on how to stop snoring noticed a short item about a wife filing for a divorce because she could no longer stand her husband's loud snoring. The author quickly sent off a copy of his book to the judge hearing the case. The judge, in turn, announced in court that he felt the book could save the couple's marriage. Of course, that statement made the local news and was later picked up by the wire services. Soon there were feature articles all over the country, every one of the stories spreading the word about the book. As a result, the book went into four printings.

- **Natural events**—Associate your book with a natural event, anything from eruptions like Mt. St. Helens to regular events such as the coming of Halley's Comet. The predictable events obviously work best because you can plan your publishing calendar around the events. For example, a number of publishers have brought out books to coincide with the return of Halley's Comet, including Hunter House's *Tales of the Comet* and Polestar-Nexus's *Mr. Halley and His Comet* (which is also the premier book in a new series of children's books about men and women of science).

- **Conferences and conventions**—Set your publication date to coincide with an important conference or convention. That's what we did when we scheduled the publication date of *Book Marketing Made Easy* for the Saturday of the 1986 American Booksellers Convention in New Orleans. Similarly, Princeton University Press scheduled their main publicity campaign for the book *Makers of Modern Strategy from Machiavelli to the Nuclear Age* to coincide with a major conference on "War in History and War Today."

- **Charity events**—Contribute your books as prizes for a charity event, anything from the semiannual public television fundraisers to special campaigns such as the recent Statue of Liberty renovation. For an auction to benefit the Mercantile Library in New York City, Isaac Asimov offered to include the name and occupation of the highest bidder in his next short story. B. Dalton has given $3 million to fund a four-year program to improve literacy; this program now involves over 16,000 volunteers in over one hundred cities.

- **Local book fairs and other festivals**—Tie-in the publication of your book with a local book fair or ethnic festival. For example, if your book is aimed at an Hispanic audience, one of your best promotions would be to give away sample chapters of your book to people attending a festival celebrating one of their holidays such as the Cinco de Mayo. Redbird Productions promoted their book on growing up in a Scandinavian community *Cream and Bread* at any festival or event where people of Scandinavian descent might attend. As a result, in less than two years they have sold over 27,000 copies of their self-published book.

9:16 32 Other Publicity Ideas

Here's a checklist of 32 more ways to obtain more promotional exposure for your books and authors:

- Send out announcements of any major author appearances (at local bookstores, national conferences, or other events).

- Announce any major author signings, subsidiary rights sales, premium sales, reprintings, new editions, or other newsworthy sales news.

- Send out unusual news releases. Ballantine, as part of its promotion for Robert Shea's *All Things Are Lights*, sent out postcard releases featuring the cover of the book. They also sent out custom-made candles tied into the book's title.

- When you send out a news release, include the basic bibliographic information for the book at the bottom of the news release: title of book, author, ISBN #, LCCN #, publication date, size and binding, and retail price. This information is especially important when you are sending a release to a library trade journal or newsletter.

- Janet Martin and Allen Todnem of Redbird Productions developed a funny skit to help promote their book *Cream and Bread* on local radio shows.

- They also developed a slide show based on the book to present at meetings of Scandinavian-related organizations.

- Simon & Schuster produced a 90-minute cassette of one-minute tax tips to help promote its perennial best seller *J. K. Lasser's Your Income Tax 1986*. They sent this tape to radio stations in thirty major cities with a request that one tip be featured each day for three months. As an added incentive, they also sent each station 90 copies of the book to be given away as prizes over the three-month period.

- To promote their *The Book of Inventions*, World Almanac produced a one-minute videotape, "History of Inventions in 60 Seconds," which they sent to televisions stations nationwide.

- World Almanac also sponsored a contest for the best invention by a reader of the book. As a prize, the winner of the contest will be featured in a later edition of the book.

- Conduct a poll or survey related to one of your books. Then announce the results. Indeed, many books are nothing more than a summary and comment upon a poll or survey (such as *The Hite Report*).

- Don't forget the wire services. If you don't know the address of your local bureau, then write to the national headquarters as follows: Associated Press (AP), 50 Rockefeller Plaza, New York, NY 10020; (212) 262-4000. United Press International (UPI), 1400 "I" Street N.W., Washington, DC 20005; (202) 898-8000. Reuters, 1700 Broadway, New York, NY 10019; (212) 582-4030. For the addresses of other syndicates, see *Book Marketing Opportunities: A Directory*.

- Also, don't forget your own local newspapers. They are sure to be interested in any local company which is expanding or offering new products. Let them know of your company's new books, big sales, any expansion plans, new personnel, and other items that might interest local readers. Ad-Lib Publications has had a number of such stories in our local press—and we've always gotten orders for our books as a result. In a town of 10,000 people you'd think everyone would already know about us, but that isn't the case. Think of the possibilities if you're located in a city of 100,000 or more.

- Send releases to appropriate college newspapers, in-house publications, association newsletters, alumni newsletters, and other off-the-beaten-track publications.

- Try alternate news hooks. Learning Publications originally publicized their book *Joyful Learning* as a fun way to learn—nothing new there. But when they began publicizing the book as a way to help underachievers, the media jumped on the story—now the book filled a definite need.

- Create a splash with your publication parties. Try something unusual. Hold the press party at a unique place—on a ferryboat, in a penthouse, at a haunted house, in the middle of Yankee Stadium, at an art gallery. When Crown published George Lang's *Cafe des Artistes Cookbook*, they invited the press to a black-tie dinner at a major restaurant. Of course, the press came (they rarely turn down a free lunch, much less an extravagant dinner).

- Hold your author signings at unusual locations. Yankee Books featured a special author signing at the Mondavi winery in California when they published *Italian Provincial Cookery* by Bea Lazzaro and Lotte Mendelsohn.

- Write a letter to the editor responding to something having to do with one of your books. I've seen such letters in local and national newspapers, trade magazines, and other consumer magazines.

- Reply to television commentaries/editorials. When you hear the announcement that "this station welcomes opposing views from responsible spokespersons," why not respond—especially if the subject is related to your book and you can contribute a new insight or way of looking at the situation.

- Write to Mary Ellen with a helpful hint. Write to Sylvia Porter about some money matter. Write to Ann Landers with a comment or question. Write to any major columnist if you can somehow tie your question or comment in with your book.

- Be on the lookout for any freelance writers who are working on books or articles dealing with subjects covered by any of your books. Send them review copies of appropriate books. For example, in the March 14, 1986 issue of *Publishers Weekly*, Marilyn Stasia requested review copies of mystery paperbacks for a feature article she was doing for the *New York Times*.

- Have your say in the pages of *Publishers Weekly*. More than one author (and publisher) have written columns for the "My Say" section—a perfect way to gain exposure before the most important people in the book trade, all of whom read *Publishers Weekly* every week.

- Send an interesting anecdote regarding one of your books or authors to Leonore Fleischer, PW columnist for the "Talk of the Trade." Also send subsidiary rights sales information to Paul Nathan at PW.

- When writing or editing a book, look for ways to mention the name of the major trade journal or consumer magazine covering the subject of the book. Mention the periodical either as a resource or in some other complimentary way. Notice how many times I've mentioned *Publishers Weekly* in this book. It was not all by accident. I doubt, though, that PW would review this book just because I've mentioned them fifty times in this book, but when they do review the book they might look more favorably on it. Who knows? Look what happened to the group who recorded the song, "On the Cover of Rolling Stone." They made it, didn't they?

- Call the Larry King Show during the "Open Phone America" segment. Just call in and say your piece. Phone (703) 6852000.

- Give something away free. When promoting our *Directory of Short-Run Book Printers*, we offered a free report on how to save money in the production of your books. Many periodicals published this free offer where they might not have published the news release about the Directory itself.

- Send your free offers to *FREEBIES* magazine. Send them a sample of your free offer along with descriptive information. Write to Freebies, P. O. Box 20283, Santa Barbara, CA 93120.

- Give a copy of your book to a major news figure. Jeffrey Lant sent a copy of his *Unabashed Self-Promoter's Guide* to Rosalyn Carter when her first book came off the press. As a result, he received mention in several news articles. Proctor Jones, who self-published his own collection of photographs as *Classic Russian Idylls*, sent a copy to President Reagan. A few weeks later he received a phone call from Reagan thanking him for the book. Of course, he let the news media know about the President's reaction to his book.

- Run for president or some other high office. That always makes news. Back in the late 60's Pat Paulsen ran an off-thewall campaign for the presidency. Meanwhile, he received lots of press coverage which helped boost his career as a comedian. Later he wrote a book about the campaign. Of course, if you win the election, all the better. By this time I think almost every major political figure has published at least one book—and many of their books are novels (which sold not so much for their literary value but because of the people who wrote them).

- Make a prediction. Forecast a trend. Predict anything related to your book that is likely to happen. Predictions can make news, especially if an expert makes the prediction (and authors of books are considered experts).

- Write a song. Carol Bayer Sager wrote a song to celebrate the publication of her first novel *Extravagant Gestures*. Johnny Cash also plans to write a song to accompany his new book *Man in White*, the story of the apostle Paul's conversion.

- Give an award. South-Western Publishing Company gives a Gold Book Award to any of their authors who have sold more than one million copies of a book. Thus far, they've given out 64 such awards. Each time, of course, they've received press coverage for both the company and for the book and author receiving the award.

- Hold a contest (more on this possibility in a later chapter).

9:17 Publicity Generates More Publicity

When you are pursuing publicity, remember four essential points:

1. 75 to 80% of all news is planted. That means, that most of the news you read in newspapers and magazines has grown out of news releases sent to the media by businesses, associations, government offices, and other organizations or individuals with something interesting to say.

2. If you can provide real news for the media, they'll be glad to feature your authors and books. Hence, you should keep refining your news hooks until you find one that really meets a need. Don't send out a press release announcing any of your books until you can show that the book provides at least one benefit for potential readers—whether that benefit be entertainment, information, instruction, or enlightenment.

3. Publicity begets more publicity. Once you get the ball rolling, it will often go on by itself. Local news features are often picked up the wire services and spread across the country. Local radio and TV shows can lead to bookings on network shows. One or two features in the major review media, and soon every newspaper in the country is calling to ask for a review copy (or simply reprinting the review from one of the major sources).

4. If at first you don't succeed, try, try again. Persistence, above all, is the key to success in generating favorable publicity for your books and authors. Believe in your books and authors, keep on plugging away, and the reviews will come.

CHAPTER 10

Tips on Advertising Your Books

The most effective way of promoting your books is to combine advertising with publicity efforts. Although publicity and word-of-mouth may be sufficient by themselves to put some books on the best-seller lists, most books will also benefit from some well-planned and well-placed advertising.

When advertising to consumers, you have five basic options: direct mail, telemarketing, magazine advertising, newspaper advertising, and radio/TV commercials. Of course, you can apply these five basic options in a variety of ways. Moreover, there are many other less well-known advertising approaches which have been used successfully by book publishers.

When planning your advertising campaign for each book (or your entire line of books), you must decide which approach or method will produce the best results for that particular book (or series of books). In making your decision, you must consider the subject of the book, its audience, its price, its format, your advertising budget for the book, its method of distribution, and its competition. In addition, you must consider how the advertising will fit into the promotions for your other books and with the company image you want to project.

10:01 Some General Guidelines

No matter what approach you decide to take with your advertising, there are certain basic principles that apply to almost any kind of advertising. Here's a short list of such principles:

- Test, test, test. Whenever you place any ad or do any direct mailing, be sure to test before committing your entire budget to that specific approach. Test everything that is important. Test the advertising copy. Test the lists or media.

Test the price. Test the offer. (Don't, however, waste your time testing little details such as the color of the envelope, or minute changes in copy.)

- Select your audience carefully. Choose magazines with a reader profile similar to your book buyer profile. Select lists made up of recent book buyers rather than a compiled list.

- Track the results of your advertising so you know which media are producing the best return on your investment. Use these results to guide you in placing further advertising, not only for the book currently being promoted but also for future related titles. The basic principle here is to continue using the advertising media and approaches which are producing results before trying other media or approaches.

- A corollary to the above: Focus your advertising efforts on a few select approaches. Don't scatter your attention by trying to advertise everywhere in every way. It won't work. Only when your prime approaches no longer produce a good return should you test other approaches.

- Make sure you have distribution. For example, if you are going to advertise on national television, make sure you have mass distribution—that your book is available in all the local bookstores. Of course, if you are going for a direct sale on television, then you don't need mass distribution. In that case, however, you will need to make it easy for people to order by offering a toll-free number, charge card or COD privileges, and a clear and firm guarantee of satisfaction.

- Have enough books in stock to handle the anticipated demand created by your advertising. Don't roll out a big advertising campaign if you don't have enough stock on hand and a smoothly functioning fulfillment department.

- A toll-free 800 line and acceptance of credit cards will generally increase response to any advertising regardless of the media or approach.

- Focus your advertising on a prime objective: more sales for a particular book, more sales for your entire line of books, creating an image for your company, creating a brand name, or whatever. The clearer you are in your own mind about what your objective is, the more effective you will be in creating and carrying out an advertising campaign.

10:02 The Advantages of Direct Mail

I must admit that of all advertising methods I prefer direct mail. Here are just a few of the advantages of direct mail:

- It is quick. You can prepare and mail a small promotion within days rather than weeks or months. Hence, it is perfect for testing prices, titles, and potential audiences. Of course, more elaborate and carefully targeted promotions do take longer to prepare, but even then they usually require a shorter lead time than most magazines.

- Not only is a direct mailing quicker to prepare, but response time to direct mail is usually quicker as well. Thus you can project the final results of a mailing more quickly and accurately than you can with a magazine.

- It can be cheaper, especially for smaller tests. Using a computer to generate the sales letters, Ad-Lib has done personalized mailings to lists as large as 500 for only the cost of paper, envelopes, and postage (about fifteen cents per piece).

- It does not require as much design time. A standardized direct mail format (letter, response card, folder or brochure, and return envelope) is much easier to design and produce than a magazine advertisement or a television commercial.

- It can be highly targeted. If you choose your lists carefully, you can target your mailings much more selectively than you can with magazines or radio/TV. You can reach almost any market segment, buyer profile, or area of the country you feel is most appropriate for each particular book.

- Direct mail allows you to reach audiences you might not be able to reach through any other method. Rodale Press has sold over a million copies of their book *Stocking Up* since its 1977 publication. Only 10% of those sales were made through bookstores.

- It is more flexible. After testing a promotion, you can change almost anything right away without waiting. You have complete control over the media, the audience, and your offer.

- Mailing packages can offer more details than can any other form of advertising. You can pack a lot of information into one envelope, far more than you can on a full-page magazine or newspaper ad, or in two minutes on radio or TV.

- Your advertising message does not have to compete with other advertising messages or editorial matter. At least, it doesn't have to compete once the envelope is opened.

- Direct mail can be more personal than any other advertising media. Not only can letters be personalized via mail-merging techniques, but you can use more informal language in writing your letter and can direct your letter to the specific interests of the reader.

- The inclusion of an order card and return envelope makes it easier for the consumer to respond to direct mail as compared to magazine advertisements (unless, of course, you include a bindin card opposite the ad or advertise a toll-free order number).

- A direct mail piece is more likely to be retained for future reference than a magazine ad since many readers will either find it inconvenient to tear an advertisement out of a magazine or will be reluctant to do so. Other forms of advertising (radio, TV, and telemarketing) offer nothing to retain.

- You can build an advertising campaign with more confidence by testing small lists, then building to larger lists, and then rolling out to a full list or lists. Strawberry Hill Press turned to direct mail after selling only 3000 copies of Stephen Chang's *The Book of Internal Exercises*. They started small with a four-page direct mail letter to a list of 10,000 proven health-book buyers. When that mailing pulled a 9% response for a net profit over $9000, they tested a variety of other lists which, in turn, produced a net profit of $40,000. When they finally rolled out to larger lists, they sold almost 100,000 copies of the book within a year (for a net profit of $150,000).

- Direct mail allows you to build and maintain an in-house list of prime prospects for your future books (and backlist books). Furthermore, you can make money renting the list. Strawberry Hill Press, in the example above, also had over $20,000 worth of list rental income in that same year.

10:03 15 Ways to Use Direct Mail

Direct mail advertising can be used for other reasons besides making a direct sale. Here are just a few other ways you can use direct mail to increase the sales of all your books:

- Obtain inquiries—You can use an inexpensive direct mail package to obtain inquiries about your books which you then follow up with a more expensive and elaborate informational package.

- Obtain leads—Use direct mail to obtain leads for direct sales representatives or telemarketing staff. This method would be useful for high priced series or collections (encyclopedias, continuity series, or multi-volume reference works). It is also useful for sales to independent retail stores.

- Offer free trials—One of the most effective ways to sell expensive books is to offer a fifteen (or thirty) day free trial period. When a customer sends in his or her request, you send the book with an invoice. Upon receipt of the book, the customer then has fifteen days to either return the book if not satisfied or to pay the accompanying invoice.

- Supplement retail sales—Harlequin uses direct mail to make sales they would not reach through retail stores. According to their president, Harlequin's direct sales do not cut into retail sales. This additive effect of direct mail sales has also been noticed in many other industries (such as the toy and gift industries).

- Boost retail sales—Reader's Digest Books have found that many of the people they mail to actually buy the book at a retail bookstore rather than order direct by mail. Inevitably when they make a mailing on a backlist title, there is a clear jump in bookstore sales.

• Increase sales to libraries—By increasing consumer demand via the mails, you also increase the number of people who go to libraries to request the book. Whenever there is a demand for a book, libraries will inevitably order the book. (You can also stimulate college library sales by mailing to college instructors rather than direct to librarians.)

• Make special sales—To reach potential volume buyers (for premium or catalog sales), direct mail followed up by telephone calls is the most cost-effective media.

• Sell subsidiary rights—Again, one of the most cost-effective ways to reach subsidiary rights buyers is via direct mail followed up by telephone calls.

• Publicize your books—Most publicity is generated via direct mail, again followed up by telephone calls.

• Maintain contact with key customers—Direct mail can be used to send newsletters, updates, and other customer communications to help you maintain contact with your key customers. Such continuing contact can lead to better customer relations and, hence, to more sales.

• Build your customer list—One of the great advantages of direct marketing is that you can build up a list of buyers who are interested in the areas related to your publishing specialty. Many direct marketers will even lose money on their first mailings just so they can build up their list—not only for their own future use but also to rent to others.

• Conduct research—You can use direct mail to do market research and surveys. Many published surveys, opinion polls, and other research is already conducted via this method.

• Prepare new editorial material—You can use direct mail to help you prepare your editorial content. For example, direct mail is the most cost-effective way to update directory listings.

• Sell advertising—If you publish directories or other reference books where advertising is accepted, you can sell advertising space by mail.

10:04 The 3 Fundamentals of Direct Mail

More than any other elements, the following three are vital to the success of any direct mail promotions. If any of these are missing or inadequate, the chances of success are slim. Here they are:

1. **The offer**—Your books must be worth the cost. Make an irresistible offer, and your chances of success are much greater than if either the book is inadequate or the price is too high (or low).

2. **The advertising copy**—The format of your direct mail is not nearly as important as its message. The copy must speak to the interests of the reader. The letter must stimulate the reader to act.

3. **The list**—You can have the best offer and the most irresistible copy in the world but if you mail to the wrong list, none of that will have any effect. Hence, of the three fundamentals, many direct marketing professionals would insist that the list is the most important.

10:05 How to Improve Your Offer

The most important element of your offer is the book. If the book answers a definite need, your offer may need little else to be effective. Nonetheless, here are a few other suggestions on how you can improve your offer to make it more enticing to the mail order buyer.

• Offer a premium for buying the book. As a publisher, an ideal premium would be another printed product (brochure, booklet, or book) related to the main book offer. When Ad-Lib first offered my *Directory of Short-Run Book Printers* for sale by mail, we offered a choice of four reports for ordering early: 1) "20 Ways to Save on the Printing of Your Books," 2) "16 Points to Consider When Selecting a Book Printer," 3) "70 Full-Color Catalog/Brochure/Direct Mail/Card Printers," or 4) "68 Books about Publishing and Self-Publishing—a Bibliographic Review." We found the response to these free premiums to be so great that we included the first two reports in the new Third Edition of the *Directory*. The fourth report has now been expanded into the 80-page perfectbound bibliography, *The Independent Publisher's Bookshelf*. Whatever premium you do offer, be sure it has a high perceived value regardless of its actual cost.

• Set a time limit. If you limit the availability of the book or some special offer (such as the premium offer described above), you can increase the response. At the very least, most people will respond more quickly (which can be very important if you require a faster inflow of cash).

• Offer a discount if they order within a certain time limit or if they order more than one book. For years now, Ad-Lib has offered a 10% discount to anyone ordering three or more books at the same time. And because of this offer, we seldom get orders for two books; when customers order more than one book, they invariably order three or more. Indeed, we have gotten many comments from customers saying that they couldn't resist the discount.

• Offer payment options. Allow payment by credit card, or check, or billing, or whatever. The billing option is almost an absolute necessity if you are selling to companies.

- Make it easy for them to order. Allow them to order by phone, or to call collect, or to call via a toll-free number. Provide a BRE (business reply envelope) to make it easier for them to send in the order.

- Offer a free trial period, or a 30-day money-back guarantee, or a life-time replacement warranty. The free trial period works particularly well for advertising in card decks where your advertising message is so limited by the available space that you almost have to offer people a chance to see the book itself if you expect them to buy it.

- Offer several versions of the product, one higher priced and more exclusive, the other standard. For example, offer a limited edition of a book or an autographed copy or a hardcover/softcover option. In our latest mailing for the Third Edition of the *Directory of Short-Run Book Printers*, we offered both the standard book (for $13.00 postpaid) and a Deluxe MailMerge Edition (for $30.00 postpaid). About 15% of the resulting orders were for the higher priced edition.

- Make a special offer. For example, do as Mark Nolan of *Information Marketing Newsletter* recommends: Send discount coupons to all your customers in celebration of your company's anniversary saying, "'It's our birthday, but you get the present!" The coupon could, for instance, offer $3 off for any order regardless of size.

10:06 How to Design Effective Direct Mail

Although the format of your direct mail package is not nearly as important as the advertising copy itself, variations in format can have measurable effects on the response. Hence, in this section I will be describing not only how to write more effective advertising copy but also how to design your direct mail programs to produce greater response.

- Above all, write copy that sells the benefits that can be derived from reading the book. Don't leave any doubt about what the benefits are. And don't expect the readers to guess what the benefits are from a listing of the book's contents. Tell them. Spell it out in clear language that any bozo could understand.

- Use "you" copy. Write in a personal, comfortable style. Don't use overly long sentences or paragraphs. Underline words to make a point. Vary the length of paragraphs. Ignore your high school English teacher. And even begin sentences with "and" or "or" or "but" or whatever. In short, write in a conversational tone as if you were writing to a friend rather than being graded by the queen's grammarian.

- End each page of a letter with an incomplete sentence so the reader will turn the page. End the page by offering a special benefit or asking a question. Answer the question on the next page.

- Besides underlining words, you might also circle certain words or write something in the margin (using legible handwriting). Don't overdo this, but use whatever seems appropriate to emphasize a point or make the letter more personal.

- Direct your offer to the people reading the letter. If you switch lists and the customer profile is different, you should rewrite your letter if necessary to appeal to the new audience.

- Print your name and address in many places (at least once on each enclosure in the mailing package). First, this prevents the loss of an order when the customer misplaces the order form. Second, it adds a greater measure of credibility to your offer. If you were not proud of your product, you would try to hide your name.

- Some key words: You, your, free, new, bonus, satisfaction guaranteed, order now, success, . . .

- Offer a benefit right away. The first paragraph, indeed the first line should perk the interest of the reader, should inspire the reader to read on. You must capture the reader's interest right away, or the entire letter will fail simply because the reader stops too soon.

- Remember the classic formula for writing direct mail copy that sells: AIDA—Attention, Interest, Desire, Action. First, get the reader's attention. Second, once you have their attention, keep them interested by asking questions, answering questions, giving examples, and stating benefits. Third, stir their desire by demonstrating to them all the advantages of owning the book you are offering. And, finally, inspire them to act. Ask for the order. Make it easy to order. And don't let them delay.

- Note once more: Ask for the order. Make your offer clear to them in simple, direct English. Repeat the offer again on your response card or order form.

- Don't be afraid to be redundant. Repeat if necessary. Say the same thing several times just to be sure that the reader has gotten the point. You don't have to repeat everything in the same paragraph, but you should repeat your main offer and the major benefits of the book several times in your mailing package—at least three times. Repetition helps to make your point clear and avoids any possible misunderstandings. (You can even repeat the exact same sentence again later on in your letter. If it's a good sentence, it can bear repeating.)

- You might try including a second order form in your mailing package. This second order form could be printed in your brochure. Not only does a second order form reduce the chance of a person losing the ordering information (price, address, etc.), but it also encourages pass-along orders.

- Print some teaser copy on your envelope. One of the first barriers any direct mail letter faces is at the mailbox. Many letters are thrown away without being opened because the outside envelope did not inspire the recipient to open the letter. One way to avoid this is to print some teaser copy on the envelope that suggests a benefit that would interest the recipient. Another way to avoid this is to make the envelope look important (either by making it look like a telegram, like a bill, like a check enclosure, like an important business letter, or like a personal letter).

- Use testimonials in your letter. Again, when we mailed out our latest letter offering my *Directory of Short-Run Book Printers*, we included the following testimonial both on the front of the envelope (as teaser copy) and as the lead to our letter: "*Without* Kremer's **Directory** I paid $12,500 for the first printing of one book—and got plenty of production hassles. *With* the **Directory** I paid $4,500 for the identical job—and no problems!" That testimonial not only allowed us to sum up the two main benefits of the *Directory*, but it did it in an objective, yet very dramatic way.

- Include a reply envelope in your mailing, with or without return postage guaranteed. A pre-addressed reply envelope makes it easier for the person to respond. It's also more secure than a reply card by itself. Anytime you ask for a check or credit card payment, you are better off including a reply envelope (note that American Express, as a security measure, requires any orders charged to one of its cards to be inserted in an envelope).

- Use actual stamps (either precanceled bulk mail rate stamps or first class) rather than a printed bulk mail indicia. Or, if you're making a large mailing, use metered bulk mail rather than a printed indicia (bulk metered mail is not easily distinguished from first class metered mail; hence, it actually looks very businesslike). Or, finally, you could have a bulk mail indicia printed in red ink that appears exactly like metered mail (check with your post office to make sure you do this exactly according to specifications).

- Break any of the above rules if it makes sense to do so. However, if you do break a rule, make sure you thoroughly test your mailing promotion before you roll out to a large audience.

10:07 How to Get the Best Lists

As mentioned above, of the three fundamentals of direct marketing, perhaps the most important is the list. Put simply, if you mail to the wrong list, neither your offer nor your message will have any impact whatsoever. Here, then, are a few tips on how to generate, maintain, and select mailing lists that will produce the greatest results for your direct mail program.

- Since 20 to 30% of all addresses change every year, make sure to clean your own house list at least every six months, preferably every three months. To clean a list, simply print "Address Correction Requested" on the envelopes of your own mailings to your list. You'll be charged by the post office for each address correction they return to you.

- Not only do individuals and families move with such regularity, but so do businesses and individual officers. Job titles change, people get promoted or switch jobs (or companies), businesses expand, businesses move, businesses go out of business—these are all responsible for the deterioration of business mailing lists.

- Your own house list will usually offer the best return on any mailing, even when some of the buyers may have originally bought books unrelated to the book you are currently offering. Of course, buyers of previous titles in the same subject area are your best prospects of all.

- The next best list is buyers of similar books from another publisher. If your book is not directly competitive with the other publisher's books, you should be able to rent the list.

- Or, perhaps better yet, you might be able to arrange an exchange of lists with such a publisher. If you do exchange lists, make sure that the lists are as nearly equivalent as possible (in terms of average unit of sale, recency of list, number of buyers in relation to inquirers, number of names on the list, etc.). Ad-Lib has exchanged lists with Para Publishing, publishers of *The Self-Publishing Manual* and *Business Letters for Publishers*, and with McHugh Publishing Reports.

- When you have exhausted all lists of buyers of related titles, then test lists of buyers of items which are related to the title you are now offering. For example, if you have an organic gardening book, you might rent a list of buyers of organic pesticides.

- In almost every case, a list of mail order buyers will outperform a list of inquirers or a compiled list.

- Nevertheless, if no other buyers lists are available, your next best choice is a targeted compiled list. Ad-Lib, for example, regularly rents the R. R. Bowker list of U.S. book publishers, and this list has always performed well for us even though it is a compiled list.

- Membership lists of related organizations can also be superb sources of book buyers. Again, Ad-Lib has used the membership list of COSMEP, the association of independent publishers, which next to our own house list has been our best performer. Indeed, our own list now probably includes 30 to 40% of the COSMEP membership.

- When selecting lists, get recommendations from three or four different list brokers. In such cases, you will undoubtedly receive duplicate recommendations from these brokers. These duplicate recommendations are likely to be the best lists to test first.

- When you are considering another list, try to get samples of direct mail promotions which have worked with the list. Ask the list owner to provide you with samples or to give you the names of some previous renters. The best samples to review are those from repeat renters of the list (no sane direct marketer would ever rent a list twice if it had not performed well the first time). When you do get samples, look for any similarities in appeals, or copy, or format which apparently worked in the past. These should give you some insight into how to best approach the list with your own offer.

- As part of your long range list research, try to get your own name on the lists which you might potentially use. Code your name so you will know when that list is used. You can, for example, code your name by using different initials for each list (J. L. Kremer for one list, J. A. Kremer for another, John F. Kremer for still another, etc.). How, then, do you get on other lists? Buy something, or make an inquiry, or ask for their catalog, or simply ask to be put on their mailing lists for the latest offers. Two of the main advantages of being on a list you might rent is that you will get a good idea of 1) how often the list is rented, and 2) what sort of mailers rent the list. For example, I've been on some lists that are rented out four or five times a week—that's way too often to be effective for many promotions, especially ones for higher-priced items. I've also been on lists which, it turns out, were rented primarily to chain letter opportunists—again, not a list you'd ever want to use.

- To expand your own in-house list, offer a low-priced book that appeals to the same audience as the rest of your books. For example, to add names to our own list, Ad-Lib has offered several inexpensive reports and books including *70 Full-Color Catalog/Brochure/Direct Mail/Card Printers* for $3.00 and *The Self-Publishing Book Review* (now expanded to the 80 page book, *The Independent Publisher's Bookshelf*) also for $3.00. We offered these through press releases, small classified ads, and even as giveaways. Although in most cases we did not make money on these offers, we did add a good number of regular customers to our in-house list. These low-priced books, then, function the same as loss leaders: They bring in the customers, and once these customers discover all the other books we have to offer, they order more—enough, in the final analysis, to make the entire proposition pay off.

- Similarly, you could offer freebies to attract potential customers. Just be sure to offer a freebie that is related to your main line of books. Such free offers can bring in as many as 20,000 inquiries when offered in a magazine with national circulation (such as *Family Circle* or *Parade*).

- Add a section to your catalog order forms which give your current customers an opportunity to "Do a friend a favor." Ask them to give you the names of any friends who they think would like to receive your catalog. This has worked well for a good number of mail order companies.

- One final tip: When testing lists, ask for a random selection based on the last digit or two digits of the zip code (for example, the 56 of 52556, 77856, 10056, etc.). Then if the test is successful, you can skip those zip codes when you roll out to the entire list. On the other hand, if you ordered every nth selection for your test (as is commonly done), when you finally roll out to the entire list you could duplicate many names. Why? Because most lists are constantly changing, and as they change so do the nth selections.

10:08 How to Make Best Use of Card Decks

Card decks, those ubiquitous collections of loose postcards advertising from 30 to 150 offers, are one of the fastest growing areas of direct marketing. You can now choose from over 620 card packs, at least one for almost any audience you want to target (from engineers to doctors, from sales managers to craft store owners). Before you decide to use one, though, you should be aware of the disadvantages as well as the advantages of advertising in such response decks.

Disadvantages

- Since they are cooperative advertising vehicles, it is quite possible to have several of your competitors also advertising in the same deck. (Actually, this could be an advantage or a disadvantage depending on how your book measures up to the other book in price and offer.)
- Because of their small size it is often difficult to sell books which require detailed explanation or extensive copy.
- Again because of the size limitation it is often impossible to offer multiple order or payment options.
- You can't offer a business reply envelope.
- Book returns and bad debts tend to be higher among card deck buyers as compared to magazine advertising or regular direct mail.
- Since many decks are mailed only two or three times a year, they may not allow the best timing for your book promotions.
- Since card deck advertising is more visible than your own direct mail package, such advertising can tip off your competitors to your new offers.
- Response rates are low, anywhere from .2% to 1% are common.

Advantages

- Card decks offer one of the lowest costs for direct mail advertising ($17.00 to $20.00 per thousand as compared to $300.00 to $500.00 per thousand for your own packages).
- They are easy to use.
- Per inquiry or per order insertions are quite easy to arrange in many of the packs (especially with the recent oversaturation of the market).

- Card decks are superb lead generators.
- Card decks offer fast response. You can expect to receive half the response from your deck ad within twelve days of receiving the first response.

Questions to Ask Before Using Decks

1. What is the source of the list? (Make sure it's a reputable source.)
2. Is the list made up of buyers? (Mail responsive lists are better than compiled lists.)
3. How often is the list cleaned? (The more often it is cleaned, the better the list.)
4. How much did the buyer spend on the product? (The price must be at least as high as the price of your book offer.)
5. How often is the deck mailed? (The better decks are mailed four to six times a list, thus allowing you more opportunities to follow up on the success of a card placement.)
6. Is it mailed to the same people each time, or to different lists? (Different lists are often better since they allow your offer to reach new prospects each mailing.)
7. Does the deck offer an A/B split for testing? (A/B splits allow you to mail one offer to half the list and another offer or format to the other half. Such splits enable you to test which offers/formats produce the best results.)

Tips on Using Decks

- Use decks that are sent to mail responsive names rather than to compiled lists. However, avoid hotline names which often represent current respondents only rather than paid buyers.
- Position is important. Some studies have shown that cards in the first half of the deck produce twice the results of cards in the second half of the deck. Hence, if you have to pay a premium for position, it may well be worth the extra payment.
- Free trial offers work better than direct credit card sales. McGraw-Hill has consistently found that 10-day free trial offers work the best for their books.
- If you do use such free trial offers, expect some debt collection problems and some returns (up to 13% or more). Factor these considerations into your calculations when figuring whether participation in the deck will pay off for your book.
- Note that offers for higher priced books are more likely to pay off for you as compared to lower priced books. Again, card decks are best for generating inquiries or leads that can be followed up with sales letters, telemarketing or direct sales visits.

- One option that has worked well for Caddylak Systems is to offer three or four books on the same card. Although each book in itself may be low priced ($9.95 to $14.95), multiple-copy orders usually make participation in the deck pay off. Note also that Caddylak publishes a line of some forty related books. Hence, any orders generated through the card deck usually result in many additional sales from Caddylak's catalog which is sent as a bounceback with the original order.

- Always state the price of your book in the ad.

- Ask for a business card rather than having buyers fill out an order blank. Buyers with business cards are more qualified buyers. Also you can learn more about a buyer from a business card than you can from any information they fill out in an order blank. (Many card deck participants now print a light line saying, "Tape Business Card Here," over the coupon area.)

- Use graphics or a photo of your book in the ad. Multiple colors also work better than a single color. (Note that many card deck publishers will throw in a second color free to encourage you to test their deck.)

- Lay out your offer in a horizontal format. Customers read the deck this way.

- Remember the one second rule: Most cards receive no more than a one second glance from deck recipients as they flip through the stack. That one second is all you have to gain the attention of the recipient and earn a second chance to make a sale. Design your card with this one second rule in mind.

- Many card decks accept per inquiry or per order advertising. Indeed, in many decks up to 30% of the cards are p.i. or p.o. ads. (With per inquiry or per order ads, you only pay the card deck publisher for actual inquiries or orders you receive. For example, if you received 100 orders for a $19.95 book, you would have to pay the card deck publisher about $1000.00, or about 50% of your total income from orders you received. Similarly, you might have to pay $2.00 to $5.00 for each inquiry you received.) When requesting a p.i. deal, make it clear to the deck publisher that if the results are good, you will be placing more ads.

- To save money on your card deck insertions, you might try the DECKMATCH service offered by Bill Norcutt, author of *Secrets of Successful Response Deck Advertising*. Bill has organized a consortium of card deck advertisers whose combined buying power allows him to negotiate ad space at much lower rates (as little as $10.00 per thousand). For more information, write to DECKMATCH, Thinkbank Publishers, P. O. Box 1166, Arlington, TX 76004.

- Some deck publishers will sell on a space available basis which could save you up to 50% of the deck cost. If you choose this option, you run the risk that the deck will fill up and your ad won't run.

- Other decks offer a 15% agency discount (for advertising agencies and card brokers). Many also offer such a discount for direct placement. Main Deck, for example, allows such a discount on the first placement.
- Note that many deck publishers will also typeset, design, and even write the copy for your card. Many offer this service free to first time users (in the hopes, of course, that you will become a regular participant).

10:09 Other Direct Mail Options

Besides the usual letter & brochure format and the card deck, there are any number of other direct mail promotions which have proven successful for other companies. If any seem appropriate for your company, you should certainly test that format. Then, if it proves successful for your books, you might switch all or a large portion of your mailings to that format.

- **Card decks**—Rather than just mail one or two cards in another company's card deck, you could offer your entire line of books in card deck format, with one or two books offered per card. McGraw-Hill and John Wiley offer several different card decks. Academic Press offers a separate deck aimed only at buyers of microbiology books.

St. Anthony Messenger Press has replaced its usual Christmas gift catalog with the card deck format to offer its line of religious books to over half a million customers. Results were "beyond anything else we've ever done."

Garden Way produces an ads-only periodical of direct response cards, called *Gardener's Marketplace*, to sell its line of cookbooks and gardening books. The *Marketplace* is mailed twice a year, in the spring and in the fall, to almost one million gardeners. This format has been very effective for them, with one card alone bringing in over $40,000 in orders.

- **Catalogs**—Almost every book publisher uses this format once they've developed a list of books long enough to justify the cost. Many publishers, however, only send the catalogs to bookstores, wholesalers, and libraries. A growing list of book publishers are beginning to use catalogs to reach book buyers directly. Catalogs can produce excellent results if your own in-house list is large enough or your book list is specialized enough to allow you to target your catalog mailings to specific lists.

- **The Dover format**—Besides mailing special interest catalogs, Dover Publications also mails up to eight 11" × 17" flyers folded to fit inside a normal business envelope. Each flyer features a separate line of about forty books (for example, paper dolls, crafts, graphic arts, or science). Although most books sell for under $5.00, Dover does well with these mailings because the average order is much higher, with most customers ordering three or more books.

- **Tabloid catalogs**—New Society Publishers prints their seasonal catalogs on tabloid-size newspaper stock which allows them plenty of room for describing and illustrating their new and backlist titles while being inexpensive to print in higher quantities.

- **Catalog in magazine format**—John Wiley has issued a catalog in magazine format, even giving it a fancy title, *Excel*, and volume and issue numbers. Their first issue was in the summer of 1985. I haven't seen any further issues, so the format may not have produced the results they had hoped it would. One advantage of the format, though, is that such a mailing format is more likely to be saved during the first sorting of mail—and it also has a better chance of being read. And a mailing that can produce those effects has a much better chance of making the sale than a mailing that gets tossed out without being opened at all.

- **Self-mailers**—Self-mailers are mailing formats which do not require an envelope. They come in many different sizes and formats—from simple folded leaflets to large folded brochures printed on card stock. Self-mailers offer several advantages: 1) They are generally easy and quick to produce, 2) Since they require no outside envelope, they are cheaper to produce, and 3) Again, because they are in one piece with no outside envelope, they require no collating and stuffing; hence, labor costs for preparing them for mailing are much lower.

- **Postcards**—Some publishers have used simple postcards to announce single titles. Postcards have a sense of urgency and informality which might be appropriate for some titles.

- **Broadsides or Posters**—These formats can be very effective for single titles with appealing graphics. Any use of broadsides or posters, whether for single titles or multiple titles, requires careful planning and graphic design.

- **Book jackets as brochures**—Book jackets, printed on the inside with further details about the book, make excellent promotional brochures. They are especially useful for sending with press releases, with your mailings to booksellers (who can then get a better picture of how the book will look on their shelves), and with your prepublication announcements.

- **Statement stuffers**—You can print small 8½ " × 3½ " flyers announcing new titles or older backlist titles to send out with your invoices and statements. These statement stuffers can be cheap to produce and very effective in selling related titles.

- **Stamps**—Little, Brown & Company uses a sheet of full-color stamps each bearing a cover illustration for one of their medical books. Recipients need only select the stamps for the books they'd like to receive, stick them on the order form, and send it in. Such offers work well if your covers are designed to sell your books and if you offer billing privileges.

- **Electronic bulletin boards**—Some publishers have begun offering books on computer bulletin boards. Several publishers, including McGraw-Hill, Bantam, Rodale, and Mercury House, are now merchants in CompuServe's Electronic Mall. This videotext shipping service allows users to scan the offerings of many companies (not only book publishers) and to place orders with their credit card. The Mall now serves over a quarter million Compu-Serve subscribers (an upscale audience especially suitable for books on computers, technology, and business). To learn more about this service and how your company can be listed in the Mall, write to CompuServe, Attn: The Electronic Mall, 3411 Office Park Drive #200, Dayton, OH 45439. Note that there is a charge for such listings.

10:10 Marketing via Your Telephone

Within the next couple of years, most major companies (and many smaller ones) will be offering toll-free phone service for orders and customer service. The cost is now so low and the potential results so great (with proper promotion) that few companies can afford not to offer the service. For more details on the advantages of offering such toll-free service, see section 5:02 in this book.

While the installation of a toll-free number can have a great impact on your sales, you should not limit your telemarketing to passive order taking. As long as you have the customer on the phone, you should take the opportunity to make additional sales or to ask questions of the book buyers (to discover how they found out about your books and why they decided to order your book or books). If you prepare a standard script for your order takers, they can easily increase the sales of your books without any additional costs to you.

After you've organize an effective system for handling incoming orders, you should consider establishing an out-going telemarketing effort as well. While some consumers resent the invasion of telephone sales calls into their homes (and rightly so), outbound telemarketing can still be an effective sales tool for your company. Here's a few ways to use outbound telemarketing to your advantage:

- Test a list fast. You can test a list of a thousand names within a few days by using your telephone. If the results are good, then you have reason to expect a followup mailing to a larger portion of the same list to produce similar results. Such a test is clearly not as reliable as a test mailing, but it can provide you with quick feedback on which of two or more possible lists is likely to produce the best results. According to one telemarketing expert, calls to 100 people will give a response equivalent to a direct mailing to 1000 people.

- Test an offer fast. You can use telephone sales calls to test two or more offers (for example, to test which of two premium offers will produce the most sales).

- Research your market. For example, you might make phone calls to a sampling of doctors to see if they'd be interested in a book on gall bladder operations. Or, perhaps better yet, you could use the same phone calls to ask open ended questions that encourage the doctors to tell you what kind of information they do need. Then you can produce books that would fill that need.

- Follow up inquiries and leads. For example, you could call instructors who have been sent examination copies of textbooks to check whether they will be using the textbook in their classes and, if not, why not.

- Increase sales. Telemarketing can increase the response to an offer by as much as five times. For example, if a list would normally yield a 5% response to direct mail, telemarketing might increase the response to 20 or 25%. Such increases may be attributed to the more personal nature of phone calls, to the greater opportunity for give and take in a phone conversation, and/or to the greater immediacy of phone calls.

- Use the phone to collect delinquent accounts. Probably more publishers use outbound phone calls for this reason than any other.

- To sell new editions. Buyers of previous editions of reference books and manuals are the best prospects for new editions. You can make calls to your own in-house list of buyers offering a prepublication special.

- To sell new titles to your in-house list. Your in-house list is your best prospect for any new titles, especially ones related to the books previously bought by your customers. With a proper computer order entry and tracking system, you should be able to sort out those previous customers who are most likely to buy certain titles. You could then use telemarketing to produce enough prepublication orders to pay perhaps for the cost of producing the new title.

- Open new accounts, especially among booksellers and other key contacts. This application offers the greatest potential for producing profitable orders via telemarketing. You can use the phone not only to open new accounts but also to alert previous customers of new titles or offers.

- Telemarketing can be an inexpensive substitute for direct sales visits. Indeed, with bookstores which are located out in the boondocks, phone calls may be the only practical way to keep in touch with them.

- For smaller publishers who are not able to set up sales representatives (for whatever reason), telemarketing offers a viable alternative, especially if it is used to supplement direct mail offers.

- Outbound phone calls, of course, are also an essential element in any aggressive publicity campaign. Phone calls are often the only practical way to follow up previous contacts. Also, since phone calls allow a certain give and take, negotiations for author interviews and appearances are much easier to conduct over the phone rather than through the mails.

10:11 Tips for More Effective Telemarketing

Telemarketing, to be effective, must be highly organized. You cannot play it by ear. You must plan every step of the process if you hope to make efficient use of what is one of the most expensive and effective media for making sales. Here are a few tips to help you organize your outbound phone campaigns:

• Use highly targeted lists. Don't waste your phone time on general lists or random canvassing of phone books. Your own inhouse list of buyers and inquirers or outside lists of buyers are your best prospects.

• Make a clear, specific offer—one that can be easily stated in a few sentences. Make it easy for the listener to either say yes or no.

• Have a definite script which your callers must follow. The best callers are those who can be casual in their tone and presentation while sticking to the script. Be sure to spend time training your callers to handle any customer questions or other responses. You should anticipate most questions in your script and have clear answers already prepared for the most prevalent ones.

• Hire only phone callers who can handle rejection, who can terminate a phone call politely and proceed right away with the next call.

• Accept purchase orders, C.O.D., or credit card sales. Don't expect people to send checks in response to telephone sales calls.

• Prepare a simple but complete order form that allows the caller to record the order easily while continuing the conversation with the customer.

• Each phone conversation, whether resulting in an order or some other response, should be recorded in writing and filed with your customer files. With outside lists, you may want your operators to check off a simple form recording the number of responses for each general category (orders, requests for more information, simple rejection, vehement rejection, hangups, no answers) rather than writing a complete memorandum.

• Outbound sales calls can be more effective as followups to previous mailings than as cold calls. Such a one-two punch can be far more effective than phone calls or mailings made independent of the each other.

10:12 Advertising in Newspapers

While newspaper advertising outside of the book review sections is not used by many publishers, it has produced some fantastic results for publishers who have the money to commit to an extensive national campaign. Here are a few ways publishers have used newspapers to advertise their books:

• Some publishers have used national newspaper advertising to encourage bookstore sales. Robert Ringer, for example, has used newspaper advertising to market several best sellers, including *Winning Through Intimidation*,

Looking Out for #1, and *Crisis Investing*. His technique was quite simple: He wrote superb mail order copy, took out large ads in major newspapers, and then directed the orders to bookstores rather than to his own publishing company. His aggressive advertising campaign combined with the cooperation of the major book chains pushed his books into the best-seller lists and enabled him to sell mass market rights for close to a million dollars.

Such techniques, obviously won't work for everyone (if they did, you'd see many more publishers trying the same thing). His technique worked because his books were general enough to appeal to a wide audience and because he was a good promoter, making good use of publicity to enhance the effect of his ads.

• Other self-publishers, such as Benjamin Suarez, Ted Nicholas, and Joe Karbo, are all famous for their mail order promotion of books via national advertising in newspapers and magazines. In these cases, they usually went for the direct sale, with all orders coming to them.

• Most publishers, though, use newspaper advertising to supplement book reviews and their other promotional activities. Hence, they tend to focus most of their advertising in the book review sections of major national newspapers.

• Other publishers advertise in sections targeted at a specific audience (for example, advertising a cookbook in the food section of a newspaper).

• Others advertise in the classified sections of newspapers. Such advertising is only effective in newspapers where books are regularly advertised (such as the *Wall Street Journal* and the *San Francisco Chronicle* with its special book mart section). Some classified ads are made up only of words; others are small display ads in the classified section. Hacker Art Books has advertised their sale catalog in the *Wall Street Journal* every year since 1952. Obviously they would not continue to do so if it didn't pay off.

• When planning a newspaper advertising campaign, don't overlook specialized newspapers such as those for army and navy bases, colleges, specific religions, ethnic languages, and so forth. Ace Books, for example, advertised *The Specialist* by Gayle Rivers in armed forces newspapers.

• A relatively new advertising opportunity for smaller presses is the Writer's Choice book promotion project operated by the Pushcart Foundation in cooperation with the Literature Program of the National Endowment of the Arts. Writer's Choice advertisements appear in *Publishers Weekly, Library Journal, New York Times Book Review,* and other major review media. Each month four different books (in the areas of fiction, literary nonfiction, and poetry) are featured at no cost to the participating publishers. The books are selected by well-known writers from hundreds of titles which are submitted by independent literary presses. To submit your books for consideration, write to The Pushcart Foundation, P. O. Box 747, Wainscott, NY 11975.

If your book is chosen, expect to sell about 500 copies as a result of the advertisements.

* One of the most common ways publishers advertise in newspapers is through co-op ads with local booksellers. In such cases the publisher pays all or part of the costs of the ad if the bookseller buys a certain number of books. (See Chapter 12 for more details on offering co-op ads.)

10:13 Tips on Advertising in Periodicals

Many of the tips given above for direct marketing also apply to any print advertising, but here are a few additional suggestions for improving the response to your ads:

* The most important element of most newspaper and magazine ads is the headline. The headline must offer a strong benefit, one strong enough or dramatic enough to get the attention of the reader.

* Consider using a second color. A number of tests conducted over a period of twenty years in the *Long Beach Press-Telegram* showed that two-color ads (one color plus black) outsold non-color ads by 64%.

* Use illustrations or other graphic elements. According to some studies conducted by McGraw-Hill, illustrations increase readership of ads. And increased readership will usually result in increased sales.

* Testimonials in the ad copy usually increase response. They are more believable than straight ad copy.

* Create a sense of urgency by putting a time limit on the offer.

* With smaller ads, the border becomes more important. It should clearly set the ad off from surrounding editorial matter or other advertisements and yet not distract the reader's attention from the ad's message.

* Advertisements which look like editorial copy have often proven to be most effective in producing sales.

* Put a coupon in the ad. Make it easy for the reader to order your book. Even Robert Ringer put coupons in his national advertising; in his case, though, the coupons directed the readers to the nearest chain bookstore.

* Make sure your address and phone number are printed several times in the ad, once outside the coupon and once in the coupon itself. Thus, if someone has already clipped the order coupon, other readers can still find out where to send the order.

* For that same reason, your basic offer (the name of the book, the cost, and any special conditions) should also be repeated outside the coupon.

* Since Sunday newspapers usually have a higher circulation and a longer life, it's generally best to advertise in the Sunday editions as opposed to any daily editions.

- If you are using classified ads, make every word count. Don't be pennywise and pound foolish. If you need more words to describe your book adequately, then use more words. At the same time, don't waste words. You need to strike a balance between minimum word count (and, hence, minimum cost) and an adequate description of your book (and, hence, maximum sales results).

- If you publish a series of books, such as the Silhouette Romances or Sweet Valley High series, and have distribution in most bookstores and, better yet, in many mass market outlets, you might try offering a cents-off coupon to encourage readers to sample one of the books.

10:14 Advertising in Magazines

Magazines offer something most newspapers cannot offer, that is, targeted readership. There are magazines aimed at almost any audience you'd ever want to reach. Here's a checklist of a few samples:

[ ] news (*Newsweek, Time, U.S. News and World Report*)
[ ] people (*People, Us, National Enquirer*)
[ ] sports (*Golf, Running, Sports Illustrated*)
[ ] business (*Business Week, Forbes, Inc*)
[ ] trade (*Gift & Decorative Accessories, Publishers Weekly*)
[ ] food (*Bon Appetit, Gourmet, Cuisine*)
[ ] homemaking (*Good Housekeeping, Family Circle*)
[ ] crafts (*Crafts, Workbasket, Woodworkers Journal*)
[ ] writing (*Inkling, Writer's Digest, The Writer*)
[ ] juvenile (*Highlights for Children, Humpty Dumpty*)
[ ] ethnic (*Ebony, Jet, Scandinavian Times*)
[ ] farm (*Successful Farming, Ohio Farmer*)
[ ] computers (*Byte, PC, Popular Computing*)
[ ] literary (*New Yorker, Grand Street, Pig Iron*)
[ ] genre (*Fantasy & Science Fiction, Analog*)
[ ] home (*Better Homes & Gardens, House Beautiful*)
[ ] health (*Prevention, Bestways, American Health*)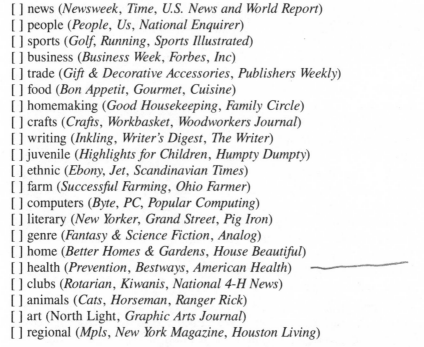
[ ] clubs (*Rotarian, Kiwanis, National 4-H News*)
[ ] animals (*Cats, Horseman, Ranger Rick*)
[ ] art (North Light, *Graphic Arts Journal*)
[ ] regional (*Mpls, New York Magazine, Houston Living*)

And many more, including alumni magazines, religious magazines, company publications, inflight magazines, scholarly journals, entertainment guides, Sunday magazine sections of local newspapers, gossip tabloids, and professional journals. For a complete list of such magazines, see the *Standard Periodical Directory, Ulrich's International Periodicals Directory,* or *SRDS Business Publication Rates and Data.* The first two are available in most libraries; the last can be ordered from Standard Rate and Data Service, 3004 Glenview Road, Wilmette, IL 60091; (800) 323-4588 (SRDS also offers many other directories for community magazines, consumer magazines, mailing lists, spot radio ads, and more).

The same basic rules apply to magazine advertising as apply to newspaper advertising. The one exception is that since you can target your audience more selectively with magazines, you should write more specific ad copy appealing to the special interests of the readers of each magazine.

Here are a few other tips on getting the most for your money through magazine advertising:

• Advertise in regional editions of national magazines. You can buy space in regional editions for much less than the cost of the entire national edition. One company ran a single ad in a regional edition of *Time* magazine and then used reprints of that ad for its window displays and direct mailings for the next five years. Hence, by advertising in the regional edition of such a well-known and respected magazine, the company was able to gain a level of credibility with its customers it could not have gained in any other way.

• Many magazines will accept a per inquiry or per order arrangement for books which they feel will interest their readers. Similarly, some magazines will run an ad for free if you will dropship the orders for them. In this case, orders are sent direct to the magazine; then the magazine processes the order, takes its cut, and sends the order on to you (with their check) for dropshipping. In such cases you will be expected to give a discount of anywhere from 40 to 60% to the magazine.

• Offer free excerpts from your books to magazines in exchange for a tagline at the end of the article telling readers how they can order the book (your company name and address, the price of the book, and other ordering information). When an in-flight magazine contacted one business publisher for permission to serialize a book on business management, rather than charge a fee for the serial rights, the magazine offered to let them run the excerpts for free as long as ordering information was listed at the end of each article excerpt. As a result, the publisher received over 1000 orders from readers of the series.

• Buy remnant space. Ask the magazine to let you know when they have unsold space, which you can then buy at a fraction of the usual cost. Of course, when you rely only on remnant space, you have no way of controlling when and if your ads will appear. Hence, remnant ads are best used for titles which are not time sensitive.

• Rather than working with each magazine to buy remnant space, you might want to buy remnant space through Media Networks. This company offers remnant space in regional editions of almost any national magazine (from *Time* to *Business Week* to *Better Homes and Gardens*). For example, they could get you remnant space in a regional edition of *Time* for as little as a $1000 (as compared to over $50,000 for the entire national press run). For more information, write to Media Networks, 600 Third Avenue, New York, NY 10016; (212) 661-4800.

• Magazines will often prepare and typeset your ad for you—in the hopes, of course, that the ad will pay off for you so you will continue to advertise in the magazine.

• If your advertising budget is currently too small to attract an advertising agency, you might want to set up your own in-house agency so you can get the standard 15% agency discount offered by most magazines. It's not worth your time to do this, though, if you do not spend at least several thousand dollars in advertising each year. Ad-Lib Publications has its own advertising agency, Ad-Lib Consultants, and thus saves 15% not only on the placement of many of its magazines ads but also 15% on the cost of many card deck placements and mailing list rentals. Our agency, however, is not an in-house agency, since we have offered consulting services in the design, development, and promotion of toys and gifts for several years before we established our publishing division.

• You may test some magazines by using classified ads. Not only are classified ads an inexpensive way to advertise, but they can often pull better than normal display ads. Classified ads are a superb way to compare the pulling power of different magazines. The main disadvantage of classified ads is that it is tough to sell books costing more than $5.00 through the classifieds. Why? There are two basic reasons: 1) the space limitation of classifieds may not allow a complete description of your book, and 2) classifieds do not always attract as affluent an audience as normal display ads.

There are, however, apparent exceptions to the rule. Jay Levinson has used classified ads for many years to sell his self-published book *Secrets of Successful Free-Lancing* for $10.00. Why does his ad work where others don't? Because he avoids the two main limitations of classified ads by 1) writing a long ad that describes the benefits of his book in a clear and appealing way, and 2) placing his ads in upscale periodicals such as the *Wall Street Journal* and several professional artist's and writer's magazines.

10:15 How to Advertise on Radio

Radio is not a common promotional vehicle for books. About the only books I've heard advertised on daily radio are mass market paperbacks. For example, Dell conducted a national radio campaign of 60-second spots on late night and drive time network shows and major market radio stations for *Shattered Moon* by Kate Green.

Nonetheless, you might consider using radio even if you don't have mass distribution. For instance, you might advertise a regional title such as the *Boston Ice Cream Lover's Guide* on local stations such as WBZ, WEEI, WHDH, or WRKO. Or you might advertise a rock biography during a syndicated top 40 show or on several local rock stations. Or how about a religious title on a religious station or show? Or, perhaps best of all, market a Spanish-language book to an Hispanic audience via a local ethnic radio station or a national network (according to one source, 90% of all U.S. Hispanics listen to Spanish-language radio stations as compared to only 75% viewing Spanish-language television and only a little over 50% reading Spanish newspapers).

In each of these instances, you could advertise a specific title to a highly targeted audience. In such cases you would not need to have mass distribution as long as you had local distribution or offered to accept credit card orders via a toll-free number.

So you do not need to limit your advertising to national radio network or syndicated shows. You can also advertise on local AM or FM radio stations which have different audience profiles, from rock to country, from all news to easy listening, from sports oriented to religious oriented. Just select the audience profile that fits your books.

Here, then, are a few guidelines to follow if you do decide to test market your books on radio:

• Rule one, then, is to match your books with the audience profile of any radio stations you intend to use for advertising.

• Radio requires frequent repetition for maximum effect. Hence, you're better off concentrating your ads during a short period of time rather than stretching them out over a longer period.

• 30-second spots can work as well as 60-second spots and are less expensive. Indeed, some studies indicate that people listen more attentively when an announcer speaks more quickly. Thus, you may find it more effective as well as cheaper to squeeze your message into 30-second spots.

• The best time for running ads on radio are during its prime time hours, the morning and afternoon drive times. Afternoon drive time has one plus over the morning drive time: As a rule, people are more relaxed and happier as they head home for the evening. Hence, they may be in a better mood for buying.

• With radio, you have about three seconds to attract the listener's attention. Hence, you should take time to make your lead-in effective.

• As repetition of the commerical makes radio spots more effective, so does repetition within the commercial. Repeat your main message at least three times (in different ways). And repeat the title of your book and name of your company at least twice.

- If you are asking for a direct order, you will also need to repeat the ordering information at least twice. Don't try for a direct order unless you use a 60-second or two-minute spot. You simply would not have time to repeat your basic message and the essential ordering information in less than 60 seconds.
- Both radio and TV rate cards are negotiable. Remember, if they don't sell the time, it is gone forever. Hence, if they have open time, they will be willing to negotiate a lower rate than the one stated on their rate cards.
- After producing a radio spot, listen to the tape on your car audio system. The closer you can get to stimulating how it will actually sound on ordinary car radio speakers, the more accurately you will be able to judge its effectiveness.
- Use professional announcers and studio equipment to make your commercials. Don't skimp on production.
- Since radio is an audio medium, consider using appropriate music to heighten the impact of your commercial. Or use other audio effects to enliven the presentation.

10:16 19 Ways to Advertise on TV

Television has a great advantage over radio: Not only can it be heard, it can be seen. Studies have shown that people's memories improve as much as 68% when they have a visual element to help them remember something. Hence, if your book lends itself to a visual presentation, you may find that television commercials will produce greater sales than radio commericals or print advertisements.

On the down side, of course, television costs more. Thus, your TV commercials must be effective. Publishers have developed a number of ways to increase the effect of their TV promotions. Here's nineteen of them:

- Time-Life Books has used direct response commercials to sell series of books (on topics such as World War II, cooking, and home repair). The advantage of selling such continuity series is that the overall sale (if the buyer continues with the entire series) is high enough to cover the cost of expensive TV time.
- Hal Lindsey's book *Countdown to Armageddon* was advertised via two-minute commercials asking viewers to order through a toll-free 800 number. Within 90 days, they sold over 370,000 copies of the book.
- Mikhail Gorbachev's new book *A Time for Peace* has also been sold via two-minute commercials in smaller cities where the book would not otherwise be generally available. In this case, the TV commercials were used to supplement bookstore sales in major cities.

- Dolphin has been able to get free 30-second spots on the syndicated show "Lifestyles of the Rich and Famous" to promote their book named after the show. The show, which is syndicated to some 200 stations across the country, will continue to run the commercial each week for three months. If you have a book which is somehow tied into a TV series, you might try to arrange a similar promotion.

- Berkeley will advertise the book *Return to Treasure Island* after each episode of the miniseries of the same name. The miniseries will run for ten weeks on the Disney Cable Channel. Berkeley, in this case, is paying for the advertising.

- Morrow found that every time Jeff Smith's cable show "The Frugal Gourmet" moved into another market, sales for his book of the same name picked up dramatically. Morrow supported bookstore sales in these new cities by offering co-op advertising to local booksellers. Most booksellers, however, were reluctant to promote the book until the show came to the city. Eventually, though, as the show moved into more and more markets, the book became a national best seller.

- Another TV tie-in, Knapp Press's *New York's Master Chefs*, sold over 110,000 copies through telephone sales generated by the show of the same name. Another 40,000 copies were sold through bookstores.

- New American Library promoted the *Weight Watcher's Quick Start Program Cookbook* through 30-second commercials in major cities. Ads were featured for two-week periods in each city. Both major bookstore chains found that sales of the book increased by over 40% during those two weeks, and that sales remained high for at least another week after the commercial stopped airing.

- Collins has promoted their *Day in the Life* Series by televising documentaries based on the books as well as by organizing travelling exhibits of the photos included in the books. Carl Sagan's *Cosmos* and Kenneth Clarke's *Civilizations* both gained wide publicity and best-selling status as a result of the associated television documentaries.

- Don't overlook local cable TV shows when planning your TV promotions. Local cable TV is still quite inexpensive as compared to local network TV. If your book can be linked in any way with a popular cable feature, you have a good chance of making the commercial pay for itself.

- The Beckley Group markets its *Millionaire Maker Course* through one-hour shows in major and minor markets all over the country. They, in short, purchase the entire hour time period during which time they present an informational seminar on how to get rich in real estate. Interspersed throughout the hour are commercials which present the hard sell for the course. The advantage of this format is that the hour long shows, which are packed with information of interest to the potential buyers of the course, presents the soft sell while the commercials close the sale. Their courses sell for $295.00, and orders are taken via credit card, C.O.D., or check either by phone or through the mail. Using this method, they have sold as many as 20,000 courses in one week (with a C.O.D. refusal rate that can sometimes hit 25%, their net sales in such a week may be 15,000 courses).

- Advertise on videotapes. If your book is tied in to a movie or other popular videotape title, you might arrange to advertise your book at the end of the videotape. Since many readers, after seeing a miniseries such as *Shogun* or a movie such as *Out of Africa*, buy the book to read, you may find a similar immediate response to popular videotape titles.

- Advertise in *TV Guide*. Although *TV Guide* is a print medium, it is so closely connected with TV viewing that you can reach much the same audience for a fraction of what it might cost to advertise on TV itself. Of course, the impact of a print ad is not as great as the impact of a TV ad.

- Advertise in the cable TV guides. Book-of-the-Month Club, Grolier, and Franklin Mint have all advertised in the *The Cable Guide* network of magazines serving 600 local cable systems (with a total circulation of over 5.5 million). Similarly, Doubleday, Grolier, and Encyclopedia Brittanica have all inserted direct response ads in *On Cable*, another network of magazines with a circulation of almost 1.5 million.

- A new video marketing tool is now being offered by PromoView. The company duplicates videos containing your advertising message, gift wraps them, and then ships them to targeted audiences. The advantages of such direct mail is that 1) it is perceived as something of value, so it is not likely to be tossed out without a second glance, and 2) because recipients are involved with sight, sound, and action (and not sight alone) when viewing the tape, they are more likely to get involved with your message as well.

- Remember that television is a mass medium. Don't use it, therefore, if you don't have mass distribution (either through bookstores and mass market outlets or through a toll-free telephone order-taking system).

- Per inquiry or per order advertising opportunities are not as available as they once were in television. With so many more advertisers using TV for direct response advertising, the demand has exceeded the available time. PI opportunities are currently more available on cable TV stations than on broadcast stations.

- The basic rule for how long your commercial should be is as follows: If you are asking for a direct order, use two-minute spots so you have enough time to adequately describe the book and to provide viewers with ordering information. If you are using the commercial to stimulate bookstore sales, then a 30 second time spot is plenty of time to make your point.

• If you are planning major TV exposure for direct sales via your own toll-free number, make sure you have enough operators to handle the response. According to one TV advertiser, you will need at least five lines to handle most local campaigns, even more lines to handle a larger regional or national campaign. If you are not prepared to hire and train operators and lease adequate phone lines to handle any response, then you should hire a professional telemarketing agency to organize and handle your phone orders.

10:17 Tips on Producing Your TV Spots

While major TV commercials currently cost as much as $70,000 per 30 seconds to produce, it is possible to create an effective TV commercial for much less. While you balance your budgetary contraints against your need for a quality production, don't try to do it all yourself. Use your in-house staff where your expertise is strong (for example, in the area of copywriting), but hire professionals where your expertise is weak (for example, in video production). As a guideline, remember that your audience is accustomed to high quality production values and will notice any commercials which are not carefully produced and edited (and will most likely not respond to such ads).

To help you in designing and producing your own television commercials, here's a few guidelines:

• The key to TV success, according to a number of regular TV advertisers, is your media buying skills. If you do not have knowledgeable media buyers, don't try to do the buying yourself. Use a professional agency. As noted above, radio and TV rate cards are essentially works of fiction—they are highly negotiable. Hence, make sure your buyers are highly skilled negotiators; the money you save could make the difference between profit and loss. The Beckley Group has as many as twenty buyers negotiating for media time whenever they roll out one of their national TV campaigns.

• If you are working with a local TV station, let them provide all the technical production assistance (equipment, camera operators, lighting technicians, directors). Often they will provide such assistance for a minimum cost as long as you are buying time on their station. (In most cases, however, don't let them write your commercial unless you want it to sound exactly like every other local commercial on the station.)

• While many ad agencies use storyboards to lay out the story line of a commercial, you may find you don't need one especially if your commercial is well-written, with all the action clearly described in the script. Storyboards can add anywhere from $200 to $500 to the cost of a commercial.

• Perhaps the best way to save money is to do most of your work at the preproduction stage rather than during the actual taping (when costs can skyrocket if you have to stop taping to work out a problem). Hold preproduction meetings to make sure everyone understands the script and knows what to do. Check the scripting details, the lighting, the timing. Hold a dress rehearsal. Never go before a camera crew and other production assistants until you are sure that the production will go smoothly.

- Tape more than one commercial at a time. Since in most cases you will have to pay for a minimum amount of production time regardless of how much time you actually use (as well as travel and set up time), make the best use of the production time by taping two or more commercials or variations at the same time.

- When you plan the taping of your commercial, try to arrange the segments so that editing costs are kept to a minimum. Editing can cost anywhere from $250.00 per hour on up.

- Remember that TV is a visual medium. So be sure to create a strong visual message in your commercial. If the commercial can make its point even with the sound turned off, then you have a sure winner. Use music, sound effects, and words to enhance the visual impact not to replace it.

- If possible, show your book in use. If it is a cookbook, show someone using it to create a scrumptious meal. If it's a mystery, tease the viewers with a look at the unsolved crime.

- As with radio, commercials on TV must gain the attention of the viewer within the first few seconds. Make sure your commercials have a captivating lead-in.

- And, again, as in radio, don't be afraid to repeat.

CHAPTER 11

Offbeat Advertising and Other Promotions

While most books are advertised through direct mail, newspapers, magazines, radio, and TV, a good number of other creative methods have been used both by publishers and other companies to advertise and promote their products. This chapter presents a random collection of some of those methods.

When you consider using some of these offbeat advertising methods, don't just think of them as gimmicks. Rather, think of them as sales tools which should be integrated into your other advertising and promotional activities. Few of these methods will work alone; they must be part of a well-planned and well-executed advertising strategy.

11:01 Inserts in Shopping Bags

Some paper bag companies are now offering to insert advertising messages inside shopping bags at a relatively low cost per thousand. If you have a line of cookbooks, beauty and diet books, or romance novels, you might test this new method.

11:02 Printed Bags, Cartons, and Matchbooks

You might also test having your advertising message printed on the outside of grocery bags and other shopping bags where other people besides the recipient will see your ad. Some producers of milk cartons are also offering to print appropriate advertising messages on the outside of their cartons. And, of course, there are always matchbooks, a long-time advertising vehicle for correspondence courses which might also work well for do-it-yourself books or opportunity books.

11:03 Movie Theater Commercials

Theaters have begun interspersing commercials with movie previews before the main shows. Thus far I've seen ads for Wrangler jeans, GE radios, and O'Dell's butter (besides, of course, the popcorn and candy commercials produced by Coke, Pepsi, or Seven-Up). If you are publishing a book that ties in to a movie, why not test advertising in movie theaters during the run of the movie? Indeed, you will probably find it just as effective to promote the book for several weeks before and after the movie as well as during the run of the movie.

11:04 Ad Specialties and Premiums

When you advertise your books, you might offer a premium with the book—for example, a slide chart with baseball schedule for a book on baseball; or a calorie counter slide chart for a diet book; or a coupon clipper for a book of money-saving ideas.

You could also send these advertising specialties with your publicity releases and review copies to draw attention to your book. Or send them to your key bookselling contacts to help remind them to push your book. How about an imprinted coffee cup with a cookbook? Or matches with a fire safety book?

Try to match the premium or advertising specialty to the contents or style of your book. Please don't send any more pens. But how about stickers, decals, buttons, balloons, paper clips, memo cubes, note pads, rubberstamps, golf balls, calculators, rulers, playing cards, key tags, ice scrapers, wine glasses, yo-yos, pot holders, thermometers, magnetic message holders, or any number of other items?

11:05 T-Shirts and Other Apparel

T-shirts are walking billboards. If you can get people wearing your T-shirts (especially bookstore personnel), then you'll have a much better chance of getting your books noticed. Dell is offering T-shirts imprinted with "It's Heaven . . . and Heller" to promote Joseph Heller's new book *God Knows*. NAL offered T-shirts to promote Stephen King's *Skeleton Crew*.

How about baseball caps for a book on baseball, or sun visors for a book on golf, muscle T-shirts for an exercise book, bikinis for a diet book?

To distribute such imprinted apparel, offer a free T-shirt with every order of ten or more books. Or give them away to a sampling of people at a public event (for example, imprinted baseball caps at a baseball game). Or give them to people who will wear them on crowded streets at lunch time (when many office workers do their shopping for reading material).

Remember that the main value of any imprinted item is to draw attention to your books and to act as reminder advertising. To accomplish these goals, the imprinted items must be seen. Hence, if you are going to use imprinted apparel, be sure that they get into the hands of people who will wear them (or who will, in turn, give them to someone who will wear them).

11:06 Calendars

Calendars are a superb way to advertise your books (of course, they are also a superb way to advertise your calendars). Send copies to all your main bookstore accounts and other key contacts.

Whatever you do, don't send generic calendars imprinted with your company name. Use photos or illustrations from one or more of your books to enliven the calendar. One approach you might use is to print an illustration from a different book for each month—ideally from a book whose publication date is printed in large red numerals on that month's calendar (to do this, of course, you will have to schedule at least one new book for each month of the coming year and will have to commission artwork for that book ahead of time).

A calendar that would have great appeal for booksellers would be one with different promotional ideas outlined for each day or week or month of the year—a calendar similar to the promotional calendars now printed every four months in *American Bookseller*.

11:07 Party Kits

Bantam Books offers a Sweet Dreams pajama party kit free to anyone who requests one. The kit includes one of the latest novels in the Sweet Dreams romance series for young adults, menu ideas for the party, game ideas, and other items to enliven a pajama party.

How about a similar kit for a wine and cheese party to promote a cookbook or book on wines? Or a trivia party kit to accompany a book of lists, records, or ratings? Or a dance party kit to accompany the bio of a rock star?

11:08 Fan Clubs

Many authors already have a fan club. If so, work with that fan club to promote new books or reissues from that author. And, if there are no fan clubs, why not organize some by putting query coupons in new editions of your authors's books, especially those authors who have three or more books published by you? Fan clubs can be a very effective way of starting the word-of-mouth band-wagon for a new book.

11:09 Local Flyer Distribution

If you have a local title (as, for example, the *Boston Ice Cream Lover's Guide*), why not print up some flyers and have them distributed in the local area by neighborhood kids or by a professional distribution service? Or how about distributing the flyers under the windshield wipers of cars in shopping centers or downtown parking lots?

11:10 Public Posters

Why not poster the town? Whenever I visit New York, I always see thousands of posters decorating construction sites announcing new plays or movies. Why couldn't a book be publicized in the same way? Especially in New York. I think such postering could be especially effective for celebrity bios and entertainment titles (rock music, movies, artists).

11:11 Samples

Another ubiquitous phenomenon I've noticed on New York streets are the people giving away samples (cigarettes, candy, whatever). Again, why not give away samples of a new book? Holt, Rinehart and Winston printed sample chapter brochures of Marek Halter's new novel *The Book of Abraham*. I don't know how these were distributed, but certainly some could have been distributed quite effectively on the streets of New York. What a marvelous way to get word-of-mouth going.

You could also distribute samples through participating bookstores, exhibits, conferences, book fairs, meetings, and other group events or public areas. Distribute samples, then, anywhere there are plenty of people who might be interested in the book being sampled. When you distribute samples, make sure your book is widely available in local bookstores so people can buy the book once their interest is sparked.

Daytimers, through 1500 trained counselors, has distributed over 750,000 samples of their products in one year. They have found sampling to be the best method to introduce their time schedulers to new audiences.

11:12 Computer Bulletin Boards

Besides publishing your books or other information on electronic bulletin boards for a royalty, you could also just publish a sample chapter or two of the book to stimulate interest. That's what Leisure Books has done with Jaron Summers's detective novel *Safety Catch*. They posted the first chapter of this mystery featuring a computer detective on CompuServe and the Source. When they posted the first chapter, they also posted a notice offering $5.00 to anyone who would post the first chapter (and the $5.00 offer) on another bulletin board with at least 1000 regular users.

This procedure provides a quick and easy way to offer many readers a sampling of your book. Other individuals have already offered similar samplings of science fiction works-in-progress, trivia books, and computer guides.

If your authors compose their manuscripts on computers, why not try a similar approach? A few months before you publish the book, post the first chapter (or another sample chapter) on one or more bulletin boards. It's a superb way to get word-of-mouth going.

11:13 Stadium Advertising

Berkeley used multi-media advertising in Yankee Stadium to promote Mickey Mantle's autobiography *The Mick*. Certainly, you could do the same with any book that would appeal to a sports audience or other public audience. You don't have to limit such advertising to baseball stadiums; you could also use football stadiums, basketball fieldhouses, boxing gyms, dance halls, or convention centers—wherever, again, an audience interested in the topic of your book might gather.

11:14 Blimps, Balloons, and Skywriting

Goodyear is probably better known for its blimp than any for any other advertising it does. Currently a number of other companies are now flying blimps as well as hot air balloons, all used to publicize the company name at public events. Although such extravagant advertising may not be appropriate for a single book, it might be appropriate for your company as a whole or for a series of books (for example, a series of adventure novels).

Skywriting or banners flown from an airplane, on the other hand, could work very well for a single title. For example, an airplane could fly over the beaches of Florida carrying a banner saying, "Palm Beach, the Novel" to advertise Pat Booth's new novel. Or how about a banner flying over the beaches of Cape Cod announcing the *Boston Ice Cream Lover's Guide*?

Airplane advertising would be expensive so such methods would probably be cost-effective only for books with mass distribution, not only in bookstores, but also in food and drug stores.

11:15 Next Exit: Billboards

Billboards can be very effective as reminder advertising to reinforce other forms of advertising or promotion. Dell, for example, has used billboards combined with a national advertising and author tour to promote Joseph Heller's new novel *God Knows*. Dell also used a billboard on Sunset Boulevard to advertise Kate Green's first novel *Shattered Moon* (the setting for the novel was Hollywood and environs).

Billboards work best for book publishers in areas where there is a high density of book buyers. You might try billboards in Silicon Valley, for example, to promote a series of books about computers. Or, if you publish a travel guide or atlas that is well distributed in gas stations, restaurants, or tourist spots, you might try billboards announcing that your guide is available at the next exit.

A few pointers: Use no more than six words in the ad. Motorists usually have the billboard in view for only a few seconds, so the message has to be simple and clear (hence, the book's message probably also has to be simple and clear). Try placing billboards where there is high foot traffic as well (as, for example, on Sunset Boulevard). Again, billboards are most effective when used as reminder advertising.

11:16 Display Billboards in Malls

Many shopping malls and airport terminals now offer space on their walls for billboard advertising. Why not test advertise one of your major books (a general book that would appeal to an affluent audience) in a mall billboard, especially one near a chain bookstore?

Day-Timers has found that its advertising on billboards in airport terminals has yielded thousands of inquiries and orders every week.

11:17 Transit Advertising

Books have been advertised in transit ads on buses, subways, and taxis. For example, a few years back one author, who was able to buy transit ads quite cheaply because of a family connection, filled the buses of New York with ads for his new novel. As a result, he received publicity in *Publishers Weekly*, the *New York Times*, and other major newspapers in the city. He also sold a lot of books to people who saw the ads in the buses. If I recall, he even got on a local bestseller list.

New American Library also used transit advertising to promote the paperback edition of *Smart Women, Foolish Choices* by Connell Cowen and Melvyn Kinder.

If you do advertise any of your titles via transit ads, try to include a "Take One" order pad attached to the ad so that interested commuters can easily remember the title of the book and where to buy it.

Note that transit ads can appear on the outside as well as the inside. You might use outside ads on buses and taxies in the same way you might use a billboard ad. One advantage of transit ads over billboards is that the transit ad travels all over the city (that may also be a disadvantage if you are trying to target a specific district of the city).

A relatively new variation on the standard transit ad is known as moped advertising. In this case, a company pays a person on a moped to drive around (at a beach, in certain areas of the city, or at some public event) carrying a small billboard advertisement. Moped advertising has the advantage of allowing you to specifically target the areas and audiences you want to reach. You can also test advertise more cheaply than with other transit ads which usually require a minimum number of ads (whose cost, while cheap per advertisement, can add up quickly to become quite expensive).

11:18 Other Billboard Ads

A few other billboard-type ads which have been used include bench ads (at bus stops or park benches), sandwich boards carried around in heavy pedestrian traffic, picket advertising, parking meter ads, shopping carts, ski lifts, bumper stickers, and Johnny Ads (yup, you guessed it, these are ads in public toilet facilities).

One way you might use such billboard advertising is to hire pickets to carry signs advertising one of your books in front of a major bookstore in a high traffic area. Before you do this, be sure you obtain the permission of the bookstore owner. Also, this type of advertising would probably be more effective if the advertising message were humorous or warmly appealing in some other way.

11:19 Business Cards

The use of business cards has already been discussed in Section 4:01. The only reason I mention them here is that you should think of your business cards as wallet-sized billboards and use them accordingly. Business cards can be one of your most effective promotional tools. Hence, be sure to remind your authors, editors, and marketing representatives to carry a few of their cards with them at all times. Business cards are great facilitators of networking opportunities.

11:20 The Yellow Pages

People rarely look at the Yellow Pages unless they are actively interested in buying something. Hence, advertising in the Yellow Pages may be a great opportunity for you to sell your books, especially if you publish a regional title that would be of interest to people who use the Yellow Pages to do their walking for them. For example, if you published a local restaurant guide, why not advertise the guide under the Restaurants section of the Yellow Pages?

Indeed, you need not limit your advertising to the local directory. It is possible to buy space through a national network of Yellow Pages if you have a book that would interest a specific national audience.

For instance, we at Ad-Lib have been considering using the Yellow Pages in major cities to advertise our *Directory of Short-Run Book Printers*. It would be a natural marketplace for our Directory since most Yellow Pages do not carry a separate listing for book printers. Hence, if someone is searching for a book printer, they have to wade through all the quick printer listings under the Printing heading to find anyone who can print their books. Even then it is difficult to locate a quality book printer because they camouflage themselves as directory and manual printers. The only printers who advertise themselves as book printers are usually vanity presses. Our Directory would save the self-publisher much time in locating a reliable book printer.

11:21 Other Directory Listings

Don't forget to get your books and company listed in any appropriate directories. Also, consider advertising in directory issues that are most applicable to your line of books. For example, if you publish craft books, you should certainly be listed in the periodic directory issues of *Creative Product News*—and you should also consider advertising in such issues. Dover Publications, Chilton Book Company, and Horizon Publishers all advertise in this trade magazine.

11:22 In-Store Broadcast Ads

Some grocery stores and shopping malls now provide their own in-store background music programming. Often they also sell advertising on these broadcasts. Campbell Soups has used such in-store ads to build consumer interest in their LeMenu frozen dinners. Why couldn't a publisher of a series of romance novels use similar in-store ads to build consumer interest in their books?

Two major advantages of such advertising are that it reaches buyers *when* they are in a buying mood and *where* the product is readily available for purchase.

11:23 In-Flight Audio Magazines

W. H. Freeman has a segment from Linus Pauling's new book *How to Live Longer and Feel Better* featured on Eastern Airlines's Audio Magazine Program. I'm not sure if this segment is an excerpt from the book or a paid advertisement.

Nonetheless, if you publish a book that would interest an affluent business audience, you should look into getting your book on similar programs (perhaps combined with an advertisement in the airline's in-flight print magazine).

11:24 Ads in Mail Order Catalogs

Some major mail order catalogs have begun accepting outside advertising in their catalogs. For example, *The Sharper Image* now carries four ads in each monthly issue of its catalog. Bloomingdale's carries as many as twelve ads in their catalog.

While advertising in these high-ticket catalogs is expensive, it might be appropriate for promoting an expensive limited edition title. You should also be on the lookout for other catalogs who might offer more affordable advertising rates and better demographics for your particular titles.

11:25 Game Show Giveaways

If you publish books that might interest the viewing audience of TV game shows, you should look into getting your books placed as giveaways on "The Price Is Right" or "Hollywood Squares" or 'Family Feud" or "The Wheel of Fortune." One company that specializes in arranging such placements is Game-Show Placements, 7011 Willoughby Avenue, Hollywood, CA 90038; (213) 874-7818.

For example, you might give away a set of encyclopedias, or a set of do-it-yourself manuals, or a collection of romance novels or travel guides (to take with them their Mediterranean cruise), or an exercise or diet book (with home exercise equipment), or a microwave cookbook to accompany a microwave oven, or a dress for success book to accompany a new wardrobe, or a racy novel to accompany a fancy waterbed.

If you use your imagination, I'm sure you can think of a prize to tie in with almost any book you publish. That way, although your book itself may not be that expensive, it would make a nice addition to a larger prize (just as they currently give away a year's supply of macaroni and cheese dinners with a new stove).

11:26 Multi-Level Marketing

Though multi-level marketing is both a method of advertising and a means of distribution, we can consider it here. Many books and reports (especially opportunity and home business titles) are already marketed through some form of multi-level marketing. Personally, though, I would be hesitant to use this method because the multi-level marketing industry still has a rather weak reputation.

Too many fly-by-night operators are attracted to multi-level marketing programs. Besides, many of the programs themselves are too close to being pyramid schemes.

Multi-level marketing still hasn't developed its full potential. Perhaps someday someone will come up with a way to draw upon the strengths of multi-level marketing without incorporating its weaknesses. Until then, I cannot advocate it.

11:27 Special Offers

Addison-Wesley has arranged for special offers to be included with several of their new books. In cooperation with the National Gardening Association, they are offering a free subscription to the *National Gardening* magazine with any purchase of *Gardening: The Complete Guide to Growing America's Favorite Fruits and Vegetables*. Similarly, for their updated edition of *The New Joy of Photography*, they tucked in coupons worth $10.00 in film processing charges from Kodak.

Certainly any cookbook publisher should be able to arrange similar promotions for ingredients, cooking tools, aprons, or other kitchen utensils. How about offering free gambling tickets with a mystery novel set in Las Vegas? Or, how about convincing tourist attractions to offer two-for-one specials to accompany a travel guide? Or, to accompany an investment guide, why not work with a reputable stock brokerage house to offer 10% discount coupons for brokerage services?

11:28 Refunds and Rebates

If you publish a series of books, you might experiment with offering a rebate with proof of purchase of a minimum number of books. Or, to encourage readers to try the series, offer a rebate for the purchase of even one title. One advantage of rebates is that you can offer a discount on your books without hurting the bookseller's profit margin or causing other unnecessary administrative hassles (which would result if you offered direct cents-off coupons).

Rebates have also been used by other manufacturers to move surplus inventories; perhaps publishers could use rebates to sell stagnant backlist titles or to remainder titles direct to consumers (such rebates could replace the current attempts to remainder books in place).

- For a new series of gardening books, Houghton Mifflin offered a rebate to any reader who bought a second book in the series. All the consumer had to do was send in the coupon direct to Houghton Mifflin for a rebate.

11:29 Sweepstakes

In a recent poll conducted by *Premium/Incentive Business*, over 96% of the companies which ran sweepstakes accomplished their goals. For these companies, sweepstakes helped to increase sales, public awareness, brand recognition, and/or store traffic.

Here's a few of the ways different publishers have used sweepstakes to promote their lead titles:

- For the new novel by Pat Booth, *Palm Beach*, Crown offered a free one-week vacation at the Breakers, a luxury resort in Palm Beach. An entry form, printed on the inside flap of the hardcover book, could either be clipped out or copied and then sent in to the sweepstakes office. To encourage bookstore promotion of this sweepstakes, Crown also offered to give the same vacation to the owner of the bookstore where the winner had obtained the sweepstakes information.

- Abingdon Press ran a "Win a Trip to the Holy Land" consumer contest to help promote William Gentz's *The Dictionary of Bible and Religion*.

- To promote the tie-in novel for the movie *Jewel of the Nile*, Avon ran a consumer sweepstakes with a grand prize of a trip to Morocco where they movie was filmed. To draw attention to the sweepstakes, Avon provided bookstores and travel agencies with floor displays, brochures, and movie posters.

- Villard offered a $10,000 scholarship and ten personal computers in a "Dollars for Scholars" sweepstakes to promote *The Princeton Review: Cracking the System: the SAT*. Coupons for the sweepstakes were available at any stores which displayed the "Dollars for Scholars" poster and shelf talker.

- Harlequin offered consumers a chance to have their "dreams come true" by winning a Rolls-Royce or a trip to Paris in their fall 1985 First Class Sweepstakes. The sweepstakes was announced on the covers and in four-color inserts of all fall releases in Harlequin's romance novel series. Harlequin also provided stores with posters and shelf talkers to draw attention to the sweepstakes. Entry forms were available in each book as well as on point-of-purchase coupon entry pads.

- Bantam sponsored a sweepstakes to promote its series of books featuring Disney characters. The prize? A free trip to Disneyland for a family of four.

Sweepstakes are an excellent way to spur interest in one of your books, especially one which you are backing with a major advertising budget (because sweepstakes work best with highly visible titles). Sweepstakes can also boost response to direct mail promotions by as much as 50%.

If you decide to offer a sweepstakes, you should hire a company which specializes in managing sweepstakes and other contests. The legal requirements for sweepstakes is so exacting that you shouldn't even try to offer one without advice from an experienced consultant. Besides helping you to meet the legal requirements, such companies can provide creative development, prize selection and acquisition, judges, and fulfillment. They are well worth any additional cost.

For more information write or call one of these companies (which all have excellent reputations): Don Jagoda Associates, One Underhill Boulevard, Syossett, NY 11791; (516) 496-7300 or (212) 529-1500. Ventura Associates, 200 Madison Avenue, New York, NY 10016; (212) 889-0707. D. L. Blair, 185 Great Neck Road, Great Neck, NY 11021; (516) 487-9200 or (212) 688-1500.

11:30 Other Contests

Another way to generate interest in your books is to sponsor contests which are in some way connected with the contents of your book or series of books. Unlike sweepstakes, these contests could be tests of skill, or knowledge, or some other capability.

- For instance, Bantam sponsored a cover-girl contest to help promote its Sweet Dreams series of novels. Bantam also sponsored a Choose Your Own Adventure writing contest to help promote its series by that name; the winning manuscript, in this case, would be published by Bantam as part of the series.

- John Magel, author/illustrator of *Dr. Moggle's Alphabet Challenge* published by Rand McNally, offered a set of alphabet blocks enclosed in a handmade cherry case as a prize to the reader who correctly identified two hidden words which he had designed into the book's illustrations. Besides identifying the two words, the winning reader also had to explain in 40 words or less the significance of those two words.

- Morrow, publisher of *Who Killed the Robins Family?* by Thomas Chastain and Bill Adler, offered a $10,000 prize to the reader who submitted the best answer to the title question.

- Houghton Mifflin and five Twin Cities bookstores ran a Curious George Word-Search Contest for children through a full-page ad in *Minnesota Monthly*, the member magazine for donors to Minnesota Public Radio. Houghton Mifflin provided 75% of the $1200 ad cost through co-op monies due the five bookstores; the bookstores each paid $60.00 as well. All the participating bookstores reported increased sales of Curious George titles plus a large mail order response to the contest. The prizes for the contest were children's dictionaries.

11:31 Brandstanding

Brandstanding is the linking of special events with specific brands or products. For instance, Budweiser's and Pepsi's sponsorship of various races,

Miller's sponsorship of golf games, or Virginia Slims sponsorship of tennis tournaments. Why couldn't a publisher of an exercise book help to sponsor a run-for-fun event?

• When Bantam launched its Sweet Dreams line, it tied into the nationwide fashion shows sponsored by *Seventeen* magazine.

• How about sponsoring an attempt to break a world record? If the record was broken, the chances are that your company name or book title would be mentioned in *Guinness*, which currently sells over one million copies every year. That's a lot of free advertising.

11:32 Book Fairs

Participating in local book fairs is an excellent way to introduce your books to new readers. Most of the people who come to such book fairs are avid readers who, if they like one of your books, will very likely order others as well. Make sure everyone who passes your booth gets a brochure or catalog.

Some of the best-known book fairs include the New York Is Book Country fair (October), the Great Midwestern Book Show in Minneapolis (October), Books-by-the-Bay in Miami, and others in San Antonio, San Francisco, Boston, and Seattle.

• The Marin Self-Publishers Association sponsors a fair every year to exhibit books published by its members. The fair, usually held in September, draws a good number of book buyers as well as some media attention.

• The Philadelphia Publishers Group donated $3000 worth of books to a city-sponsored literary celebration called Philadelphia Ink. The celebration included a book fair, seminars, and book readings, plus drawings for seven free collections of books.

• At the Great Midwestern Book Show last year, Ad-Lib sold over $600 in books. A number of other smaller presses did even better—so good, in fact, that they had to close early because they had run out of stock on most of their titles.

11:33 Other Festivals and Fairs

Besides participating in book fairs, seek out other fairs or festivals which might offer a market for your books. For example, if you publish books on crafts, why not exhibit at some local craft shows? Or, how about exhibiting your books on automobiles at a car show? Or books on sailing or fishing at a boat show?

• When Signe Carlson exhibited her book *North of Skarv Island* at Scan-Fair in Portland, Oregon, she sold 52 copies of the book in one day.

- Redbird Productions, as noted earlier, sold over 27,000 copies of their self-published book *Cream and Bread* by exhibiting at any festival attended by people of Scandinavian heritage.

CHAPTER 12

Getting Distribution

The key to bookstore sales is two-pronged: 1) you have to get your books into the stores, and 2) you have to get them out of the stores. You won't make any bookstore sales if you do not have your books in the stores when your major advertising and publicity hits the public; hence, you need to get distribution. But once you get distribution, you must be sure to promote your books so that they move off the booksellers's shelves into the hands of readers rather than back into your warehouse as returns.

No sane bookseller will carry your books for very long if you do not provide advertising and other promotional support that will help him or her sell your books. The average turn at retail for bookstores is somewhere between three and four times a year—that means that booksellers, in effect, replace their entire inventory of books about every three or four months. No bookseller can really afford to stock books on his or her shelves which do not have sufficient demand to turn at retail within six months at the very latest. For the sake of completeness, they might carry a few titles just to fill out a special section but, even then, they will not tolerate slow moving books for very long.

What all this means is that if you intend to sell to bookstores, you must produce high quality books—both in content and design. It also means that you must be prepared to handle the problem of returns.

At present about one out of every four hardcover books sold by publishers is returned. The return rate can be even higher for new books. You can cut down this return rate by not overselling your books. Don't push more copies of your book on booksellers than you actually expect them to sell.

Now that I've cautioned you, I'd like to describe some of the different ways you can go about getting your books distributed to the trade. In one recent survey of independent bookstores, it was found that 51% of the booksellers used publishers as their primary source of supply, while 12% bought primarily from one wholesaler, 23% bought from more than one wholesaler, and 14% gave no response. Of course, many of the booksellers who used publishers as their primary source also bought from wholesalers as their secondary source.

Before describing how to go about distributing books on your own (which is a very difficult way for new publishers to get national distribution for their books), I'd like to review the other possible avenues for distribution: distributors, wholesalers, other publishers, chain stores, and sales reps.

12:01 Why Bookstores Buy from Wholesalers

Bookstores have a number of good reasons for buying from wholesalers or distributors rather than direct from a publisher. Here's just a few of them:

1. By combining a number of smaller orders, they can usually get a higher discount from distributors.

2. By consolidating orders with one distributor, they save a lot of time by eliminating the paperwork necessary to deal with many small orders. Not only do they save time in ordering, but they also save time when it comes time to pay bills. It's far easier for them to keep track of one bill than many bills.

3. If a book doesn't sell, they can use their credit on returns to buy other books from the distributor. In the case of a one or two-book publisher, they could be stuck with no options for using the credit.

4. Distributors tend to be more reliable. They usually ship books faster than a publisher. Even major publishers are two to three times slower than wholesalers in shipping books.

12:02 Distributors and Wholesalers

Because there is such a wide variety of wholesalers and distributors in the book trade, the distinction between the two is not always clear. In this book, however, and in our *Book Marketing Opportunities: A Directory*, we do make a general distinction between the two functions.

A distributor stocks books, reps the books to its accounts, handles all fulfillment, and pays for the books on consignment (i.e., only when they are actually sold). A wholesaler, on the other hand, functions essentially as an order taker for its accounts. Wholesalers generally do little promotion outside of a catalog, order books as the need arises or in small stock quantities, and pays for the books under normal terms (usually net 30 or net 90).

12:03 Distributing through Distributors

Why, then, use a distributor to represent your books when you could simply sign up a number of wholesalers to carry your books? The main reason is simply this: Distributors have sales reps and/or other active means of promoting your books. Also, because they tend to represent fewer books and often specialize in certain kinds of books, they are more likely to promote the titles they carry.

The main disadvantages of using distributors is that they stock books on consignment (usually paying 90 days after they've sold the books), and they usually ask for a hefty discount (effectively, as much as 65%).

Distributors vary widely in their ability to cover the book trade or any other outlets. Hence, you should avoid signing an exclusive deal with any distributor unless they can demonstrate to you that they do offer full coverage of the book trade. At the very minimum, they must have sales representation in all major areas of the country, must make regular visits to the key chains and wholesalers, and should offer other means of promotion (such as catalogs and other mailings).

Here are the names of a few leading distributors. For a more complete list (with names, addresses, phone numbers, territories served, subject interests, and other details), see the companion directory to this book, *Book Marketing Opportunities: A Directory*):

- General distributors: Associated Booksellers, Caroline House, Independent Publishers Group, Kampmann & Company, Pacific Pipeline, Publishers Group West, Publishers Marketing Group, and Talman Company.

- Literary and small press distributors: Bookslinger, the distributors, Inland Book Company, Small Press Distribution, and Subterranean Company.

- Religious and new age distributors: Genesis Marketing Group, The Great Tradition, and Spring Arbor Distributors.

- Specialty distributors: Ardic Book Distributors (travel), Bradt Enterprises (travel), Carrier Pigeon (alternative, gay), Cogan Books (cookbooks), E-Z Cookin' Book Company (cookbooks), Horizon Publishers and Distributors (crafts), New Leaf Distributing (health, new age), Nutri Books (health, new age), and Unipub (business).

12:04 Selecting a Distributor

When selecting a distributor for your books, be sure to ask each of them for the following information which will allow you to make a reasonable choice:

1. The discount they require from you—Be sure to verify how they figure the discount. Get a firm idea what the resulting average discount will be (since many require a discount on net sales, the actual figure you pay them can vary depending on the net sale price).

2. Their terms—How often will they pay? How often will they report sales? How soon after sales are made will they pay?

3. Their territory—Are they asking for exclusivity? If so, what territory do they cover? What markets do they serve? Is the exclusivity only for a certain territory or market, or for the entire book trade?

4. Insurance—Do they insure your books while on consignment in their warehouse? If so, for how much?

5. Their sales expectations—Ask them how many of each title they expect to sell. Are they enthusiastic about your titles or only lukewarm?

6. Other contract provisions—Ask to see a sample contract. Check to see what the duration of the contract will be. If need be, how can the contract be terminated? What are your responsibilities? What are the responsibilities of the distributor?

7. References—Ask for the names, addresses, and phone numbers of other publishers they distribute. Phone these references, and check to see how well the distributor has served them. How many books did the distributor sell? Did they pay on time? Any problems? Any dramatic successes?

8. Customer references—As long as you are checking references, you might also ask for the names of some of their accounts. How well do they service their accounts? What kind of reputation do they have? Obviously you would not want a distributor who has a dishonest, sloppy, disorganized, or otherwise unhealthy reputation.

9. Financial statements—If you have any questions about the viability of a distributor, ask to see their financial statements to verify that they are sufficiently well-financed. You don't want to tie up your stock with a distributor who is teetering on the edge of bankruptcy.

When you do choose a distributor, remember one thing: The distributor cannot sell your books without your help. You must be prepared to back up their sales efforts with your own advertising and publicity campaign. Don't expect them to perform miracles without your help.

Furthermore, once you have signed up with a distributor, keep in touch with them. Let them know about your upcoming titles. Send them review copies as soon as they are off the press. Get their feedback on the cover designs, titles, and contents of your books before you go to press. Also, get their feedback on your promotional plans. Let them help you help them. The more you communicate with them, the more sales they can make for you.

12:05 Distributing through Wholesalers

Instead of distributing your books exclusively through distributors, you might want to set up your own accounts with major wholesalers. In this case you would make your own sales presentations to the wholesalers (either by mail, over the phone or through direct visits), take their orders, and handle all fulfillment and collection on your own.

Wholesalers can often provide you with as much distribution to the book trade as can a distributor. More bookstores order through Ingram and Baker & Taylor, the two largest bookstore wholesalers, than through any other distributors or wholesalers.

The advantages of using wholesalers rather than distributors are:

1. Wholesalers usually require a smaller discount (typically 46% to 50%).

2. They pay by invoice (usually within 60 to 90 days), rather than stock books on consignment.

3. They do not require exclusive contracts. Instead, they will stock any books for which there is customer demand.

The disadvantages of using wholesalers rather than distributors are:

1. Wholesalers tend to be passive order takers. Although they usually publish a catalog of titles they carry and will often also do some telephone marketing, few of them have sales representatives who regularly call on bookstores to promote new titles.

2. Since they carry so many more titles, they cannot promote your individual titles as aggressively as can a distributor who has fewer titles to offer.

3. Wholesalers do not offer complete fulfillment services for publishers.

Since wholesalers do not require exclusivity, you should try to set up accounts with as many as possible. Ingram and Baker & Taylor, of course, are essential for any general books, but if you publish highly specialized titles, you should also seek out those wholesalers who specialize in your subject area.

When approaching wholesalers, you will need to show them your catalog of books, your upcoming list (and promotional plans), your terms and discount schedule, and your returns policy. If you can demonstrate to them that you are producing quality books with general appeal, offer standard terms, and are well enough capitalized or committed (so that you will still be in business when— and if—it becomes necessary to return titles to you), you should have no trouble selling your books to them.

12:06 Working with Ingram Book Company

Ingram is probably the largest wholesaler to independent bookstores. Because Ingram offers a large selection of books, toll-free ordering, fast shipping, and easy returns, many booksellers would prefer to order through them rather than go direct to the publisher. As a result, if you want to reach the independent bookstore market, you need to get your books into their system.

If you are a small publisher or new to Ingram's system and want to get your books stocked by them, send your catalog, terms and discount schedule, and a short letter outlining your publishing plans and promotions to Cathy Clarke (if your company name begins with a letter from A to L) or Jim Batte (if your company name begins with a letter from M to Z), Ingram Book Company, 347 Reedwood Drive, Nashville, TN 37217; (615) 361-5000.

Ingram takes an active role in promoting the books they carry. Here are just a few of the services they offer to bookstores:

- Monthly magazines—In their monthly magazines *Advance* and *Paperback Advance*, which are mailed to about 9000 bookstores, Ingram lists the major new titles they have begun to offer. As a publisher, you may buy advertising in these magazines to help promote your books. Indeed, Ingram often requires that a publisher buy some advertising in one of its magazines or catalogs to help support the promotion of that title to booksellers.

- Telephone promotions—Ingrams offers telephone promotions of titles with wide general appeal. When bookstore customers call in, they are asked if they would like to hear about some interesting new titles. If yes, then the telephone operators describe the three or four new titles being promoted that week. Some publishers have report sales increasing by 600% during the week they paid Ingram to promote one of their titles.

- Best-sellers lists—Ingram publishes its own best-sellers lists, both for general hardcover and softcover books and for specific areas like computer books, inspirational titles, cookbooks, how-to books, and so on. Booksellers use these lists as guides for ordering new and continuing titles.

- Laser-Search—Ingram has developed database of over 1,275,000 titles on a CD-ROM laser disc. This database allows booksellers and libraries to identify and acquire almost any book still in print.

- Bookseller's Assistant—A fairly new offering still being tested, the Bookseller's Assistant allows bookstore customers to browse through computer records looking for books of interest and will then print out a listing of any recommended titles. When not being used by a customer, the Bookseller's Assistance runs commercials. Crown, Dell, Doubleday, McGraw-Hill, Morrow, Simon & Schuster, and Viking Penguin have all advertised on this system.

- Bookshelf—Ingram issues a monthly full-color consumer buying guide which they provide to bookstores at their cost ($5.00 per 100). The guide lists the best-selling books as well as new potential best sellers.

- Special catalogs—Last fall Ingram published a Children's Books catalog aimed at consumers. The 16-page catalog featured over 150 new and backlist titles. Booksellers could get 100 free catalogs with each order of 100 or more featured titles. Ingrams also produces other special interest catalogs, some aimed at consumers (such as their Gift Book and Computer Book catalogs), some aimed at booksellers for title selection (such as their guide to business and economics books). In every case, you may buy advertising space in the catalog to promote your titles in that category.

- A.I.D.—Ingram provides an Automatic Inventory Distribution program which allows booksellers to automatically receive a certain number of copies of any new title selections made by Ingram's own buying staff.

- ROSI—Ingram also provides a Recommended Opening Store Inventory selection service for new or expanding bookstores. ROSI is a computerized printout of best-selling titles by subject categories based on the popularity of those titles in a particular region. The bookseller can then edit the printout to their own needs and return it as an order.

- Microfiche—ReadyStock is a weekly microfiche service listing all title currently in stock in Ingram's warehouses. By using this service, booksellers can special order any title in stock for their customers and expect shipment within days (rather than weeks or months if they ordered direct from the publisher).

- Statement stuffers—Ingram will insert your advertising flyer into their microfiche and statement mailings. The cost? About $1000.00.

- Other services—Ingram also offer inventory control systems, co-op advertising summaries, audio/video and software stock, and many other services that aid booksellers in their business.

Because Ingram offers so many services to booksellers and because many of these services rely on their in-house selection of book titles, you should make a special effort to get your books stocked by them.

12:07 Working with Baker & Taylor

Baker & Taylor is the other major wholesaler to booksellers (and an even larger wholesaler to libraries). To get your books listed with Baker & Taylor, write to Vita Balsoni, Publishers Contact Section, Baker & Taylor, 6 Kirby Avenue, Somerville, NJ 08876; (201) 526-8000. Or fill out their Vendor Profile Questionnaire (you may copy the one included on page 128 of my *Book Marketing Made Easier*) and return it to them.

Then, whenever you complete your Advance Book Information forms for listings in Bowker's *Books In Print* database, send a copy to Baker & Taylor as well. Also send any other information about the book (brochures, copy of the cover, etc.) that will aid them in their title selection.

When your books come off the press, send a review copy to Baker & Taylor right away. These review copies will be evaluated by their staff of librarians for selection in their Final Approval Program. If your books are selected, the opening order would be for about 100 copies. Three factors affect their selection of a book: 1) sustained demand for your books, 2) the viability of your company (how long has it been in business, etc.), and 3) whether you offer normal terms of doing business.

Baker & Taylor is especially strong with libraries. If you are a new or small publisher, you can expect that as many as 75% of your library orders will be placed through Baker & Taylor. Here are just a few of the services that Baker & Taylor offers its customers:

- Final Approval Program—Some libraries order every title that is selected by Baker & Taylor for inclusion in this program.

- Cataloging—Baker & Taylor will catalog all new titles they stock. The cataloging of these titles encourages library and school orders because it makes the books more accessible and easier to process.

- Special orders—Baker & Taylor offers one-stop buying to its customers. Hence, even if your books are not stocked by any of its four centers (in New Jersey, George, Illinois, and California), they will still order books from you when a customer requests your books. Such orders trickle in (one or two copies at a time) until such time that the demand warrants a larger order.

- Journals—Baker & Taylor publishes two bibliographic journals which they send to libraries to encourage orders. *Forecast* goes to 17,000 public libraries in the United States and Canada. *Directions* goes to about 7000 academic and special libraries. Your books will be listed in the appropriate journal or journals if selected for the Final Approval Program. Plus, you can also advertise in either journal.

- Book Alert—Baker & Taylor also publishes a catalog of new titles which it sends to over 4500 booksellers and 4000 libraries. Advertising is also accepted in this catalog.

- Exhibits—Baker & Taylor exhibits selected titles at overseas book fairs, including the Moscow and Frankfurt book fairs. They also distribute certain books overseas.

- Other services—As with Ingram, Baker & Taylor offers telephone solicitation of selected titles, statement stuffers, approval programs, and other special services.

As with Ingram, all these services mean that Baker & Taylor has developed a loyal following of booksellers and librarians who will not order a book which is not available through their programs. Hence, it would be well worth your while to spend some time to get your books selected for Baker & Taylor's Final Approval Program.

12:08 Working with Other Wholesalers

While courting the big three (Brodart is another major wholesaler, though they primarily focus on library sales), you should not overlook the good number of other regional and special wholesalers who offer great service to booksellers and librarians. For instance, Bookpeople is well-known as a wholesaler of books from independent publishers, especially on the West Coast. Gordon's Books, which covers the Rocky Mountain region, is another strong regional wholesaler.

To attract these regional and special wholesalers, you must woo them the same way you woo Ingram and Baker & Taylor: Produce great books. Offer standard terms. Let them know about forthcoming books early enough so they can have them in stock before publication date. And support your books with sufficient advertising and promotion.

Here's the names of a few of the best known wholesalers (again, for more detail, please see *Book Marketing Opportunities: A Directory*):

* General wholesalers—Bookazine, Bookpeople, Dillon Book, Dimondstein, Golden-Lee Book Distributors, Gordon's Books, Koen Book Distributors, Pacific Trade Group, Riverside Book and Bible House, and Yankee Book Peddler.

* General library wholesalers—The Book House, Brodart, Eastern Book Company, Emery-Pratt, and those listed above.

* Academic and special libraries wholesalers—Academic Book Center, Ambassador Book Service, Ballen Booksellers, Blackwell North America, EBS Book Service, Key Book Service, Midwest Library Service, Scholarly Book Center, Scholium International, Siler's Library Distributors, Taylor-Carlisle, and University Book Service.

12:09 ID's—Independent Distributors

Independent distributors (otherwise known as ID's or paperback jobbers) are responsible for the distribution of most mass-market paperbacks and magazines. These distributors are local agencies which distribute to booksellers, schools, drug stores, food stores, newsstands, and other paperback outlets. Most of them get their stock from such national distributors as Kable News Company, Select Distributors, and Simon & Schuster Mass Merchandise Company rather than direct from the publishers.

Although most of their business involves magazines and mass-market paperbacks, some of these local jobbers also carry hardcovers and trade paperbacks. Some will also represent textbooks to schools and colleges. Hence, if you publish regional titles which might interest these jobbers, you should check to see if your local jobber handles anything other than magazines and mass-market paperbacks. You might find a willing accomplice for your local distribution.

Tom and Marilyn Ross met with the truck drivers of their local jobber, San Diego Periodical Distributors, to promote their book on *Creative Loafing*. This meeting helped them to get greater local distribution for the book than they could have accomplished on their own time.

And, as mentioned previously, Jacqueline Susann was famous for her breakfasts with such truck drivers, working to convince them to give her books the best positions in the paperback racks.

12:10 Distributing through Other Publishers

Many major book publishers also distribute other publishers's lines. If you've developed a line of books and are looking for distribution to the trade, you could contact another publisher whose publishing philosophy you admire. You might find them amenable to taking on distribution of your line.

Most publishers who do distribute other publishers's books require a hefty discount to do so, as much as 25% of the list price of the book. In turn, they take care of all sales visits, distribution, fulfillment, and collection. Meanwhile, you would still be responsible for editing and producing the book, plus all advertising and promotion. Hence, in order for such an arrangement to be profitable for you, you would have to sell quite a few books.

Here's a list of a few major publishers who distribute other publishers's books:

* Harper & Row distributes Wesleyan University Press, Beacon Press, Basil Blackwell, Ungar, Garden Way Publishing, Harvard Business School Press, Microsoft Press, Newmarket Press, Kodansha International, Feminist Press, Oxmoor House, and Faber & Fabor, among others.

* Random House distributes Shambhala Publications, Reader's Digest Books, Shelter Publications, Sierra Club Books, and TSR Hobbies.

* W. W. Norton distributes Sandpiper Books, Pushcart Press, Saybrook Publishing Company, Ecco Press, New Directions, John Muir Publications, Dembner Books, The Taunton Press, and Thames and Hudson.

* Farrar Straus Giroux distributes North Point Press, AARP Books, PAJ Publications, and the hardcover and trade paperback editions of Mysterious Press.

* Besides distributing all its own imprints, Simon & Schuster also distributes for Baen Books, Zebra Books, Harlequin, Seven Seas Press, Meadowbrook Press, Kodak Guides, and Golf Digest.

12:11 Selling to Chain Stores

Rather than go with a distributor, you could handle your own distribution through wholesalers, chain stores, and direct sales to independent booksellers. In that case, you would have to make your own sales to the major chain stores. In 1985, the four major chain stores (B. Dalton, Waldenbooks, Crown, and Barnes & Noble) accounted for almost 30% of all retail bookstore sales. Hence, you can hardly afford to ignore them if your books are of general interest.

Here are a few guidelines and suggestions on how to sell your books to chain stores:

• The major chains stores will rarely take on a one-book publisher unless the book has great promise and the publisher guarantees cash refunds on returns. Usually, in the case of one or two-book publishers, the chains would rather order the books through a distributor or wholesaler.

• In most cases, the chains are looking for publishers who can offer a steady flow of new books of broad general interest each season.

• They are more likely to take on a book from a small publisher if the book fills a need.

• The books from smaller publishers that are finally chosen for the major chains's backlist often start off as good sellers in some of their local stores.

• Most chains have central buying offices that do most of the buying for all the stores in the chain. In some cases, individual stores may also buy regional titles or other books of special interest to their local customers.

• The best way to begin contact with the major chains is to call and find out which of their buyers would be the most appropriate one to send your materials to. Then, on a regular basis, send that person information about your forthcoming books.

• Once you have books in hand, send them a copy of the bound book before you call to ask for an order. Especially with new or unknown publishers, they would prefer seeing a finished copy of the book so they can see for themselves that the book is of high quality in both production and contents.

• Keep your key contacts informed. Let them know about any major rights sales, publicity, new promotions, and author appearances. Especially keep them informed of any strong local promotions you'll be doing so they can order books for their local outlets. For example, as part of their promotion of the new edition of *The TM Book*, Fairfield Press worked with Walden-books to do a special co-op advertising test in a number of major cities.

• A recent study indicated that 38% of the chain store buyers found out about new titles by reading direct mail promotions sent by the publishers themselves. In another study of smaller chain stores conducted by the *Huenefeld Report*, over 90% of the respondents reported that catalogs and flyers were the most effective way (other than personal visits) for publishers to keep them informed. Hence, don't be hesitant to mail information about your new books to these buyers.

• Work with the editors of those chains with newsletters such as Kroch and Brentano's *Book Chat* and Walden's *Xignals* (sent bimonthly to 250,000 science fiction book buyers), *Crime Times* (for mystery fans), *WaldenCooks* (for cookbooks), *Fiction Finds* (first novels and midlist titles), and *Walden*

Journal (for business titles). For example, when books are promoted in *WaldenCooks*, sales can increase by as much as ten times. And Knopf claims that the B. Dalton newsletter (with its enthusiastic rave reviews) was almost single-handedly responsible for putting their cookbook *The Vegetarian Epicure* on the best-seller lists.

• Be cautious about selling too many books to the chains and overextending your supply of books. Note, for one thing, that returns from chain stores average about 25% as compared to about 10% returns from independent stores.

• Finally, don't put all your eggs in the same basket. While the major chain stores may have a significant impact on retail sales, don't overlook the smaller regional chains and the great number of independent and specialty stores. For the names and addresses of almost 200 large and small bookstore chains, see *Book Marketing Opportunities: A Directory*.

12:12 Sign Up with BOS

BOS (Booksellers Order Service) is a new service provided by the American Booksellers Association for its member bookstores. Thus far about 30 publishers and about 100 bookstores are participating in this electronic ordering service that permits booksellers to order in smaller quantities (by combining their orders from all participating publishers) and yet earn higher quantity discounts.

BOS also offers an electronic bulletin board where participating publishers can announce their new titles, changing terms, and any other information that might interest participating booksellers.

In order to participate in this innovate ordering system, you must have a computer and telecommunications capability in house. For more information, write to Sandra K. Paul, BOS, 160 Fifth Avenue, New York, NY 10010; (800) 523-6789.

12:13 Distributing through Independent Sales Reps

As part of your overall strategy to handle your own distribution, you could assign certain regions of the country or certain markets to sales rep groups. Or you could have representatives handle all your sales calls, from visits to the major chains and wholesalers to regular trips to see independent booksellers.

To set up your own network of sales reps groups, consult the list in *Book Marketing Opportunities: A Directory* and write or call those which look like they could fill your needs. To cover the entire country, you will probably have to contact six to ten groups since few of them cover more than ten states. When you do write to them, send them the same information you would send to a prospective wholesaler or chain store.

Most sales rep groups ask for a commission of 10% on all retail sales and 5% on all wholesale sales in their area, irrespective of whether they made the sale or not. The main advantage of having sales reps is that many booksellers still respond better to sales visits than to direct mail. The main disadvantage of having sales reps is that they only sell; they do not handle warehousing, fulfillment, and collection as do distributors.

One caution on setting up independent sales reps: Check their references as thoroughly as you would for distributors. When I was consulting in the gift industry, one of the companies I was working with hired a new rep without checking his references very carefully. At first, everything seemed fine. He sold many new accounts and, hence, seemed to be doing a good job. Unfortunately, he sold most of those accounts by telling them that they didn't have to pay for 90 to 120 days and if they hadn't sold the product by that time, they could return it for full credit (in effect, without our knowledge, he sold them the product on consignment rather than at our normal net 30 terms). Meanwhile, he collected his commissions. Only when we began having problems collecting these accounts did we discover what he had done. Since he would take no responsibility for the situation, the company ended up losing close to $10,000 in bad debts.

12:14 Hire Your Own Sales Reps

Many major publishers hire their own network of sales reps to cover the entire country. Having your own reps is, perhaps, the best of all distribution alternatives. The only difficulty with hiring your own reps is that you need to have at least $350,000 in net annual sales to the book trade before you can justify the cost of hiring even one rep. With salary, travel expenses, and other costs, each sales rep will cost you anywhere from $30,000 to $60,000 per year.

If you do decide that you can afford to hire a rep or two, start small by hiring one or two to cover your own region first. In that way you can keep their travel expenses down while you test the effectiveness of having reps for your line of books.

12:15 Handle Your Own Distribution

As an alternative, you can test the effectiveness of hiring reps by first asking some of your regular personnel (sales manager, editors, or yourself) to handle the local sales calls. In this way you can get experience on what works best for your company before you commit your time and money to organizing a separate department for sales representatives.

Another advantage of handling your local sales in this way is that you give your sales manager and editors experience in the field. Prentice-Hall requires that all new employees begin by going on the road for three years before they are allowed to edit or market books. A number of other companies also encourage this policy. Only by going out into the stores can you see what kind of books are actually selling, what kind of merchandising actually works, and what sort of people buy what kind of books. Moreover, being out in the field is one of the best ways to get ideas for new books.

If you do decide to use your other employees part time as sales reps, train them well before you send them out. Make sure they know your list of new titles, not only the names of the books but also why the bookstore should carry them— why, for instance, these new titles will interest the bookstore's customers. Also, be sure they are familiar with your backlist—which titles are selling best, what other titles might interest a particular group of people, any titles you are offering at a special discount, and so on. Finally, have them memorize your company payment terms, discounts, returns policy, co-op advertising terms, and any other promotional programs you offer.

Don't send out anyone who you do not feel will represent your company in a professional manner and in keeping with the image you want to project for your company. And don't force anyone to go out who really does not want to go.

The next chapter on Working with Bookstores goes into more detail on how to handle your own distribution through bookstores.

12:16 Why Exhibit Your Books

One of the best ways to get your books known to booksellers is to exhibit your books at their conventions. Not only can you show your books to as many as 15,000 booksellers, but you can also attract new distributors, corporate buyers, and subsidiary rights buyers.

The major book show in the United States is the American Booksellers Association (ABA) Convention which is held over Memorial Day weekend. In 1986, it will be held at New Orleans, in 1987 at Washington DC, and in 1988 at Los Angeles (Anaheim).

Other major shows include the Frankfurt Book Fair (held in October at Frankfurt, West Germany), the Bologna Children's Book Fair (held in the spring in Bologna, Italy), the Christian Booksellers Association convention (July), the American Library Association convention (July), the Canadian Booksellers Association convention (July), and the National Association of College Stores. Major international shows are also held in London, Barcelona, Cairo, Jerusalem, and Moscow. Regional booksellers associations also hold book fairs at various times of the year.

When planning your book exhibits, don't forget other trade shows besides the major book shows. For example, if you publish children's books, you might want to exhibit at some of the regional toy shows. Or, if you publish craft books, how about exhibiting at some of the annual craft shows (Dover Publications exhibited at Quilt Market '85). Or, if you publish books of interest to various academic disciplines, you should consider exhibiting at conventions such as the American Institute of Biological Sciences, or the American Sociological Association convention, or the American Political Science Association convention.

Besides selling books, here are a few other reasons why you should attend at least one of these shows every year:

• Your number one reason, of course, should be to sell books. That means you should be prepared to take orders right at the show, to offer special discounts for orders placed at the show, to staff your booth with sales oriented people, and to have catalogs and brochures ready to give out to all who attend the show.

• You will be able to display your new books to the trade and to any media in attendance at the show. Book shows are superb times to give away samples of your books to the major opinion makers in the industry.

• Rather than place an emphasis on book sales, you may choose to use shows to establish your company name and image more firmly in the minds of booksellers and the media. Book shows are one of the best ways to gain such exposure.

• You will be able to make valuable marketing contacts. In many cases you'll have an opportunity to meet with buyers for major chain stores, wholesalers, distributors, and corporations. At no other event would you find such a concentration of buyers.

• Such conventions provide a superb learning opportunity—to see how others display and merchandise their books, to network with other publishers to discover new ways to market your own books, and to meet booksellers face to face to learn what more you can do to fill their needs.

• Many major rights deals are made at conventions. Not only can you sell rights to your books, but you can also pick up the rights to other people's books. Even smaller publishers can get into the act. I know of a good number of smaller publishers who have obtained English language rights to books by attending the Frankfurt show and other shows.

• Conventions are a most concentrated form of market research. In just two to three days, you can get a detailed overview of the publishing industry, discover what sorts of books other publishers are promoting, and learn what new lines your competitors are bringing out. You may even uncover an emergent trend that you can exploit before others follow suit.

• Conventions are also an excellent place to meet new and established authors and to come up with ideas for new books. This book grew out of my experience at the 1985 ABA convention in San Francisco. Almost every small publisher I talked to at that convention had one questions to ask me: "How do I get my books into the hands of the people who can use them most?" This book, I hope, provides a few answers to that question.

12:17 How to Exhibit Your Books

To mount a successful exhibit, you must plan ahead. You must not only design your booth, but you must also decide which of your books you will display (and which will get the limelight), what promotions you will run, who will staff the booth, and how the booth will be shipped, set up, maintained, dismantled, and shipped home.

To help you plan your exhibit, read Dan Poynter's excellent book *Book Fairs* and use the Exhibit Planning Checklist in my book *Book Marketing Made Easier*. The checklist will ensure that you cover all the necessary steps in preparing and packing for a book exhibit.

Here, then, are a few other pointers on how to go about exhibiting your books:

- If there are certain people you want to be sure to meet during the convention, contact them in advance to arrange an appointment to see them during the show. Don't expect that you will be able to just drop by their booth and meet them. Chances are that they will be out on the floor just like you. So be sure to make appointments ahead of time with any major buyers or other key contacts that you want to meet. Then confirm those appointments the first day of the convention by dropping your card off at their booth with a short message confirming the time and place of your meeting.

- In his *Book Marketing Handbook*, Nat Bodian summed up the best way to work a show: "(1) Make the booth accessible; (2) make your books accessible; (3) make yourself accessible."

- Arrange your booth so people can get in and out easily. Have your books, catalogs, and other sales literature readily available so that people can reach them without stooping or running an obstacle course.

- Have a professional design your booth (or, at least, it should look like it was designed by a professional). It should be attractive, open, inviting. It should project an image compatible with one you want for your company.

- Arrange your books so that they are easy to find—either by subject, title, or author. Display new titles up front where they will get the most attention.

- Give away samples of your books—either advance review copies or at least sample chapters. This is one of the best ways to get people talking about your major titles months before their publication dates.

- Staff your booth with friendly, knowledgeable salespeople. The people in your booth must know your line of books well enough to talk intelligently about any title. They must also know your company's terms and discounts, upcoming promotions, and other policies.

- Make sure you have enough people to staff the booth. Staffing a trade show booth can be very tiring, especially after three days, so be sure each person in your booth has enough time off to rest between work periods. Also, make sure each has some time to scout the convention as well.

- Train the people who will staff your booth so they are comfortable staffing the booth. They should be ready to answer any questions that might come up (and they should be aware that if they cannot answer a questions, they should write it down and be sure to get an answer or followup with a letter after the convention). They should be alert and willing to help any passerbys. They should not sit or smoke in the booth.

- Have them make notes of any books which attract the most attention from browsers and buyers. These notes might come in handy in planning future exhibits or sales promotions following the convention.

- Have them also make notes of any questions, comments, inquiries, or other conversations which might come in handy for future promotions or contacts.

- To attract people to your booth, give something away. At the 1983 ALA convention, Festival Publications gave away over 12,000 signs with humorous messages such as, "Ever meet a librarian who wasn't all booked up?" Each sign, of course, also carried a short sales message and ordering information for Festival's publications. Mindy Bingham of Advocacy Press gave away roses to all the women booksellers who came by her booth at the 1985 ABA convention. The roses were very much in keeping with the floral cover design of her book *Choices*, which is aimed at helping young girls make choices.

- If the convention has set aside a place where you can offer free literature, use it. At the 1985 ABA convention in San Francisco, several tables were placed outside the convention hall where publishers could place free literature and announcements of any special promotions. I saw many booksellers sifting through the material to select items of interest to them. Such free material, especially if it has your booth number on it, will help to draw more people to your booth.

- To attract more people, some publishers have placed napkins imprinted with their sales message and booth number on the counters of the convention hall coffee areas. One enterprising small publisher placed fortune cookies near the press room coffee pot. Each fortune inside the cookies asked a question and listed the publisher's booth number as the place to go to get the answer. Cable News Network and several other reporters followed up the story.

- To make sure you get the names and addresses of convention goers (so you can send them more promotional material after the convention), place a basket at the front of your booth so people can leave their business cards. To encourage more people to leave their cards, hold a drawing each day for a free prize.

- Hold a special promotion. At the 1985 Canadian Booksellers Association convention, McClelland & Stewart offered a free Macintosh computer to the bookseller who came closest to guessing what the total sales would be for the major M&S titles through December 1985. As part of the contest, they also asked the booksellers to estimate how many of each title they expected to sell in their own stores. This contest not only helped to draw booksellers's attention to M&S's major titles, but it also gave M&S a breakdown of the booksellers's sales expectations.

- If you cannot afford to rent a booth on your own, then join in a cooperative exhibit. Several of the publishers associations, such as COSMEP and the Publishers Marketing Association, offer cost-effective group exhibits at the major shows. Publishers' Book Exhibit, Conference Book Service, and New Pages Exhibits all offer group exhibits at many conferences, association meetings, and smaller book fairs (such as the American Psychological Association meeting and regional library exhibits) which you might not otherwise be able to attend.

- When considering your costs for exhibiting at a show, remember that the booth rental represents perhaps as little as 25% of your total cost. Other costs include travel expenses, housing and food, staff salaries, booth design and construction, promotional materials, shipping, and miscellaneous booth charges.

Again, remember that the most important function of any exhibit is to sell your books. Keep that purpose in focus, and all the minor details will fall into place, making your job easier and more enjoyable.

12:18 Get Listed in Trade References

To aid booksellers in finding you and your books, make sure you are listed in all the major trade reference books. The references used most often by booksellers include *Publishers' Trade List Annual*, *Books in Print*, *Publisher's Weekly* spring and fall announcement issues, the *ABA Book Buyer's Handbook*, and the *NACS Book Buyer's Manual* (National Association of College Stores).

- *Publishers' Trade List Annual* is a multi-volume collection of the catalogs of most major publishers. You must pay to get a listing in this publication, but the cost is quite reasonable for the circulation it provides for your catalog. In a recent survey, 84% of the bookstores and over 90% of the libraries indicated that they used *PTLA* for ordering books.

- In a 1982 membership survey, 97% of the respondents said that the most valuable service provide by the American Booksellers Association was the *ABA Book Buyer's Handbook*. Hence, it is reasonable to conclude that the handbook is a vital source for them when they are ordering books.

• Besides advertising in *PTLA* and *Publishers Weekly*, you might also consider advertising in *Forthcoming Books*, the bimonthly update of the Books in Print series. Over 15,000 booksellers, librarians, and wholesalers use *Forthcoming Books* to help them in ordering new titles.

Listings in these major reference books will not only help you to get additional sales from booksellers and librarians, but should also help you in gaining distribution and representation. If you hope to gain maximum distribution of your books in bookstores, you must do at least some advertising in trade publications as well as in consumer publications.

CHAPTER 13

Working with Bookstores

Once you have a method of getting your books into the bookstores, you must still work to see that your books move out of the bookstores. Besides promoting your books to the general public via advertising and publicity, you can also work with the bookstores to see that your books are properly displayed and merchandised. This chapter, then, will describe different ways to work with bookstores to increase the exposure and sale of your books.

13:01 Setting Priorities

To get the most out of your sales calls to bookstores, you must make your priorities clear. Not only must you decide exactly what you want to accomplish with each visit, but you must also decide which of your accounts you should visit first. Here are some guidelines to help you in setting your own priorities:

- Remember the old 80/20 rule. 80% of your business will come from 20% of your accounts, so be sure to place your greatest emphasis on keeping in touch with these major accounts. At Bantam, they have a core group of experienced salesmen who handle only four or five accounts each. Since 25 major accounts make up almost 60% of their business, they give them extra special service and support.

- You or your reps should visit each major account at least twice a year, preferably more often. At the very minimum, you should call on your key accounts to show them your spring and fall lists. (Your key accounts would probably include several major wholesalers, the biggest chains, and perhaps a few independent stores.)

- If you are a smaller company without your own sales force or distributor, then you should certainly contact these key accounts by mail or by phone at least twice a year, or whenever you are bringing out a major new book.

- If many of your titles are regional in content, you should place more emphasis on stores in your own area. In such a case you could even visit the stores once a month or once every two months, thus providing them with far better service than they will ever get even from major publishers. New England Press does this with bookstores within the New England region.

- As long as you are already in an area visiting a major account, you might also visit some of the independent stores in the area at the same time. For example, if you were in Minneapolis to visit the B. Dalton buyers, you could also call on The Bookcase, Gringolet Books, Hungry Mind Bookstore, Savrans, and Odegard Books, among others.

- Phone or mail your promotional material to those stores and other accounts which you or your reps cannot visit directly.

13:02 Getting the Most from Your Sales Calls

In making sales calls to independent bookstores, smaller publishers have several advantages over major publishers. First, they can offer titles to the independent bookseller that most of the big chain and discount stores do not carry. Second, they can give more personal service to each store they visit. Here are just a few suggestions for making your sales calls to the independents more effective.

- When you visit booksellers, approach them as friends and co-workers. You can work with them to offer the best books to the reading public. Let them know you are there to help them.

- Prepare effective sales literature that you can leave with the stores when you visit them. Give them your catalog, flyers or brochures describing your new titles, a price list with your terms and policies, and any other literature that will aid them in making a decision on which books to buy. For all your new titles, have extra cover samples printed up so you can show the booksellers what the books will look like on their shelves. Better yet, carry the actual books with you.

- If possible, travel with a carload of books so you can stock the store immediately. Since they often have to wait three to six weeks to get books from major publishers, booksellers will appreciate the immediate response. Plus it will save them shipping costs and will save you the time you would otherwise have to spend in packing and shipping them later.

- Give actual samples of your major new titles to your regular accounts. Not only will they appreciate this special service, but they are far more likely to order more copies of the books if they have read them.

- Work with them to prepare an adequate order for your titles. Don't push them to stock too many, but do let them know which titles you will be promoting most heavily so they can stock up on those titles.
- When you come back for a return visit, check their remaining stock of your titles and prepare a proposed reorder that takes into account which of your titles sold best in *their* store.

13:03 Make an Offer They Can't Refuse

Whenever you approach bookstores (whether in person, via the telephone, or by mail), offer them special deals which will encourage them to place an order or to increase their order for your titles. Here are a few offers that have work successfully for other publishers:

- Grant them a 5% discount for cash payment with the order. You can afford to give a 5% or 10% discount to prepaid orders since you will save billing and collection costs on such accounts. Plus, of course, you will get the money several months earlier.
- Grant them larger discounts for books they order on a nonreturnable basis. Because such discounts will allow bookstores to make more profit on the sale of each book and because they cannot return the books, they are more likely to promote your books in their store. Hence, not only will the bookstores tend to sell more copies of such titles, but you will also save time and money by not having to process returns. Thus, the larger discounts will often pay for themselves. Ad-Lib offers a 50% discount on the orders of ten or more books on a non-returnable basis.
- Offer to pay postage on all orders of ten or more books (or some other limit you set).
- Let bookstores know that you participate in the Single Title Order Plan (STOP). This may result in a trickle of single title orders in the beginning, but once a store has become accustomed to ordering from you (and have found your service to be fast and reliable), they will be more likely to place larger orders from you when you do approach them with titles that suit their customer profile.
- Offer white sales. Run special sales on some of your slower moving titles to encourage bookstores to stock up on those titles. Houghton Mifflin runs semi-annual white sales offering discounts of up to 85% on selected titles (all in mint condition). They require a minimum order of 25 assorted books on a non-returnable basis.
- Offer delayed billing on prepublication orders for major titles. To encourage larger stocking orders on its new edition of *The New Doubleday Cookbook*,

Doubleday offered delayed billing on any order of ten or more copies.

- Extend your payment terms. Rather than the standard net 30 terms, offer new customers an opportunity to buy books at net 60 or net 90 terms. In this case you would bill them immediately, but the payment would not be due until 90 days after they receive shipment of the books.

- Set up an agency plan with new accounts. If you have a backlist of ten or more books and publish three to four new titles each season, you might want to develop an agency plan that ensures that each participating store carries a minimum quantity of each of your current titles. With such plans, a store usually is required to order a minimum of five or ten copies of each title, guarantee that they will maintain a stock of at least two to three copies of each title (and reorder when the stock runs low), and put in a standing order for five or more copies of each new title you release. In exchange for such guarantees, you would, in turn, offer them a 5% or greater bonus discount over your normal discount schedule.

- Set up an In-Store Merchandising Program (IMP) similar to the one set up by Houghton Mifflin. IMP offers booksellers incentives for stocking and displaying specific categories of Houghton Mifflin titles. The incentive package includes delayed billing, co-op money, rebates, plus a merchandising kit with materials for preparing special displays. As part of this promotion, Houghton Mifflin also offered prizes to the booksellers who set up the most effective displays. Over 400 independent stores plus a number of smaller chains took part in the first year of IMP programs.

- Organize a remainder-in-place program. Again, Houghton Mifflin organized a Houghton Mifflin Markdown Program (HMP) whereby the publisher and bookseller shared the cost of reducing prices on certain titles. Each book that was sold at a reduced price had to be clipped. The clippings then had to be submitted on a worksheet to Houghton Mifflin so the bookseller could get credit for the greatly reduced price. Waldenbooks, which participated in this program, noticed that sales went up dramatically for some of the discounted titles and several sold out completely.

- If all else fails to entice a prospective account to order your titles, offer to let them have the books on consignment—that means, they pay for the books only after they've sold them. For a sample consignment agreement (which you should have the bookseller sign), see page 140 of *Book Marketing Made Easier*.

When Renny Darling of Royal House Publishing published her first cookbook *The Joy of Eating*, the book sold very few copies until she went down personally to the Beverly Hills B. Dalton store and left five books on consignment for 90 days. Two days later the store ordered fifteen more copies; two days after that, another 30; a few days after that, several cases of the book. Her husband, seeing those results, took to the road and began peddling copies of the book in all the bookstores up and down the state of California. The book has now sold a half a million copies in the past ten years, and Royal House has gone on to publish seven more books. It all started, though, with that first small consignment.

13:04 The Importance of Service

Once you have gained an account, the best way to keep that account ordering your titles is to provide them with fast and friendly service. Make it easy for them to work with you, and they will remain loyal to you. Make it tough, and they will find someone else who can provide similar titles (even if those titles are not as good as yours).

- Fill orders promptly. If possible, ship the books the same day you receive the order. Ad-Lib has had a same-day shipping policy from the beginning, and we continually get rave reviews (and more orders) from our customers because of our prompt response to orders and inquiries.

- When billing, send legible invoices. More than one bookseller has complained because of the sloppy business habits of some smaller publishers. A bookseller will always choose to work with a company which is well-organized and efficient over one that is not. And, as one bookseller noted, the ones who are organized will be the first to be paid.

- Send thank you notes to new accounts and to old accounts who have placed especially large reorders.

- Support your books by advertising and publicizing your books. No bookseller would want to carry a book which does not have the support and commitment of its publisher.

- Follow all the other suggestions contained in chapter five on how to serve your customers best.

13:05 Keep in Touch with Your Accounts

As part of your overall service to your accounts, you should have some means of maintaining contact with them between actual sales calls. You can use the phone, direct mail, catalogs, or newsletters to help you keep in touch with them. The following points provide a few suggestions on how to use each of these means to help you keep in touch with your bookstore customers.

13:06 Reach Out and Touch Someone

One of the best ways to keep in touch with your bookstore customers is to phone them regularly. While this may not be practical if you have a large customer list, you may still use phone calls to keep in touch with your major accounts and other key contacts.

• Again, as I've mentioned before, installing an 800 number will encourage your customers to call you with new orders, questions, inquiries, suggestions, and other matters of importance to your relationship with them.

• Use outgoing calls not only to speed collection of past due accounts, but also to clarify any questions about orders you have received or any problems you might have encountered in fulfilling the order.

• Outbound sales calls preceded by a mailing of your catalog or other sales literature can increase your orders by as much as 60% (in the experience of at least one publisher).

• You can also use outbound phone calls to encourage orders from bookstores which have not previously ordered from you.

For more pointers on using telephones in marketing your books, see sections 10:10 and 10:11 of the chapter on advertising earlier in this book.

13:07 Sell by Direct Mail to Bookstores

Direct mail can be an effective way to reach the person responsible for buying new titles at bookstores. As mentioned in the last chapter, two different surveys showed that chain store buyers relied on brochures and flyers as a major means for finding out about new titles. Review the first part of Chapter 10 for general pointers on using direct mail. Here, though, are a few specific tips for using direct mail in your trade promotions.

• Mail to the book buyer. Unless specifically requested to do so, do not send your catalogs or other sales literature to more than one person at each store.

• For mailing lists, use your own list of bookstore buyers, the R. R. Bowker list, or rentals from ABA (American Booksellers Association), CBA (Christian Booksellers Association), NACS (National Association of College Stores), or the Children's Bookseller Association. You could also develop a list from the *American Book Trade Directory*, which lists over 24,000 retail booksellers in the U.S. and Canada. Or, finally, you could use the list of specialty bookstores and chain stores in *Book Marketing Opportunities: A Database*.

• Mail regularly. Establish a certain schedule, either once a month or once every two or three months, so that booksellers begin to anticipate your mailings.

• Establish a recognizable format so that booksellers can easily recognize your promotions. This, again, will help to establish your company in the minds of the booksellers.

- When you send out invoices and statements, always include some announcement regarding one or more of your titles. Use these statement stuffers to offer special sales or promotions.

13:08 Sell Via Catalogs

Your catalog is probably your best sales tool, other than your books themselves. Hence, you should design your catalog so that it effectively sells your books. Plan to design and publish a new catalog with each new list (usually in the spring and fall). To help you in designing your catalog, here's a few suggestions that might work for your books:

- Mail your catalog only to your own house accounts and other major prospects. Mail flyers or brochures to other marginal prospects offering them the complete catalog upon request.

- Don't be stuck on one format for your catalog. Since most buyers for bookstore rarely refer back to publishers's catalogs after their first perusal, you need not design the catalog for easy filing. Instead, design it so it stands out in the crowd. Stoller Publications's catalog for its line of calendars is another calendar with sample full-color pages from each of its major calendar titles. Not only is the catalog appropriate for its contents, but it also stands out from the crowd. Many booksellers will undoubtedly put the beautiful calendar on the wall above their order desk, where it will be readily available for ordering.

- Organize your catalog so every title is easy to find. Provide a table of contents and a cross-referenced index by author, title, and subject (if appropriate).

- Be sure to include all appropriate bibliographic information so anyone who wants the information will have it easily accessible. Include the title, subtitle, author, price, ISBN number, LCCN number, number of pages, trim size of book, type of binding(s), and the type and number of illustrations, indexes, appendices, and other information. Also describe the audience for the book, something about the contents and benefits of the book, and any other promotional information that will encourage booksellers to stock the book.

- Make it easy to find the order form, easy to detach from the catalog and mail, and easy to use to place an order. Include one or two extra order forms so that the catalog doesn't become obsolete after the first order is placed.

- Include a clear and concise statement of your terms and discounts, returns policy, and any other information a bookseller might want to know before placing an order with your company. If you offer any co-op advertising or other merchandising programs, promote these programs in your catalog so the booksellers know that you back your books with advertising support.

* List the addresses of any distributors or major wholesalers who handle your book. Not only will this list make it easier for bookstores to consolidate their order for your books with other orders, but it will also encourage the wholesalers to stock more copies of your books (be sure they get a copy of the catalog so they are aware that orders may be coming their way).

* Promote the use of your order phone number (whether a standard line or an 800 number) so bookstores can easily find the information if they need to order quickly.

* Provide a return envelope to make it easier for them to order.

* Describe the shipping information—how you ship the books, what the charges will be, and what your usual turnaround time is (of course, if your turnaround time is unimpressive, don't mention it until you have taken steps to improve it).

13:09 Promote Via Newsletters

One of the best formats you can use to communicate regularly with your major accounts is a newsletter format. Newsletters can be more personal, newsy, and informal than catalogs. Plus, since newsletters do not require extensive graphics or design, the cost of producing a newsletter (both in terms of time and money) will usually be less than the cost of producing a catalog or other direct mail package.

Use your newsletter to let your key accounts know about new titles, new promotions, updates on previous promotions, recent subsidiary rights sales, reprintings or new editions, changing trade terms, and any other information that may be of use to them in selling your books. At the same time, however, be sure to keep the tone of the newsletter low-key and personal.

To encourage readership of your newsletter, add informative features on how to set up a display, or how to run a book fair, or other how-to items which would make life easier for the bookseller.

Finally, you could also include short camera-ready articles that booksellers could reprint in any newsletters or other mailings that they make to their own customer list. This copy could feature a special theme or subject (travel, cooking, or back to school) and excerpt material from one or more of your books. In this way you would be helping booksellers to find good material for their newsletters while promoting your books at the same time. When you offer such material, make it clear to the booksellers that they have your permission to reprint the material in their promotions.

* Scribners publishes a quarterly newsletter featuring new titles from their line of mystery books. The newsletter also describes any other recent successes with previous titles. This newsletter is mailed to their house list of bookstores,

agents who might buy subsidiary rights, individual readers who have requested to receive the letter, and to Baker & Taylor's 18,000 library and bookstore accounts.

- Pocket Books published a similar newsletter directed at science fiction and fantasy readers. At the world science fiction convention, they offered a free subscription to anyone requesting one. Since the people who attend such conventions are among the most active and influential readers in that genre, Pocket Books was able to create significant word-of-mouth advertising by mailing its newsletter to these people.

13:10 Advertise in Trade Magazines

Another major way of keeping in one-way communication with your accounts (and other prospective customers) is to advertise your books in the major trade journals such as *Publishers Weekly, American Bookseller, Library Journal*, and some of the wholesaler and chain store publications. At the very least, you should promote your new lists in the spring and fall announcements issues of these magazines.

Along those same lines, you should exhibit at the major book trade conventions whenever possible. Such conventions offer a superb opportunity to meet your customers face to face and to discuss with them how you can better serve their needs and desires.

13:11 Support Your Local Bookseller

Do whatever you can to help booksellers sell more books (whether your own titles or books in general). Provide them with display materials, promotional literature, or any other services that will make their job easier and more productive. Here's just a few of the things you can do for them:

- As mentioned above, one of the most valuable services you can provide to bookstores is camera-ready copy for their newsletters. Since their regular customers enjoy the informative sales format of newsletters, many bookstores have found newsletters to be their most effective advertising media. Any help you can give them to make their newsletters better will certainly be appreciated.
- Provide materials for bookstores who want to host open houses or book fairs for librarians and school teachers. Let bookstores know that you are willing to supply them with giveaway items that would interest teachers and librarians—items such as bookmarks, bookplates, stickers, display materials, and other giveaways.

- Prepare audio or video excerpts of some of your books and send them to booksellers who host local radio or TV book programs (such as Penguin Bookshop's "From the Bookshop" weekly show on cable TV). Of course, you could also send such excerpts to other radio or TV book reviewers.

- Provide support for reading programs. Houghton Mifflin, for example, underwrote a special issue of *Instructor* magazine which focused on helping schools to establish educational partnerships with local businesses and community groups. Suggestions included establishing an after-school read-aloud program, donating a library of special titles to a retirement home, and giving free book coupons to students who help to tutor fellow students to read. As part of this support, you could provide stores with cents-off coupons redeemable for some of your books which would appeal to young readers.

- Arrange author appearances at local bookstores. Better yet, arrange for special demonstrations linked to your books. For a cookbook featuring Virginia seafood recipes, GB Publishing arranged for a chef to give cooking demonstrations at local bookstores. As part of the demonstration, they also gave away seafood samples. Similar demonstrations could be arranged for craft books, how-to books, and even travel guides (with tips for travellers about how to pack), among other topics.

- Provide bookstores with flyers and brochures which can be imprinted with their name and address. Such promotional literature will be most effective if it is targeted at a specific audience (such as school teachers, craft people, corporate accounts, or travellers).

- Support other bookstore outreach programs. Besides providing material for school book fairs, check for any other audiences which bookstores might want to tap—such as corporate accounts, senior citizens, fundraising organizations, churches—and offer to provide the stores with material appropriate for that audience.

- Encourage bookstores to sample your books. The more they know about your books, the more likely they are to recommend your books to their customers. M. Evans offered booksellers a chance to see galley copies of their new book *The I-Like-My-Beer Diet*. With the galley copies, they offered a free case of beer to any bookseller willing to try out the diet.

- Sponsor in-store contests. Times Books sponsored a "'Win a Great Meal" contest to publicize John Mariani's new book *Mariani's Coast-to-Coast Dining Guide*. Winners, chosen in a random drawing, were given dinners for two at selected restaurants featured in the book. Several winners were chosen in each of fifty major cities. Free dinners for two were also given to the bookstores where the winners had picked up their entry blanks for the contest (these free dinners were incentives for the bookseller to promote the contest).

- Participate in the ABA/*Time* holiday insert. Over 800 stores and 55 publishers participated in the 1985 insert which promoted buying books for gifts. 90% of those bookstores participating in the insert were satisfied with the results. The 1986 insert, which will cost publishers almost $7000 to participate (with a photo and short description of one book), will run not only in *Time* but also in the *New York Times* and *New Yorker* magazine.

13:12 Co-op Advertising

Perhaps the best promotional support program you can offer a bookseller is co-op advertising. Under such arrangements, you would rebate a portion of the bookseller's total purchase of eligible titles to be used by the bookseller to advertise your titles in local media. A typical rebate percentage would be about seven or eight per cent of the net dollar amount of the bookseller's order. Here are a few guidelines to follow in setting up a co-op advertising program:

- If you offer co-op advertising to one bookseller, you have to offer the same terms to other booksellers. Not only is this the fair thing to do, it is an FTC regulation. So set your terms, and then stick to them.

- Offer co-op advertising only for your titles which have wide distribution. Be selective. Titles of wide general appeal are best for national co-op advertising programs; titles of regional appeal are best for regional co-op advertising programs.

- Provide booksellers with appropriate copy for the ad, preferably camera-ready ad slicks which can be inserted with the bookstore's logo and address (or prerecorded tapes for radio ads).

- Allow booksellers to use the co-op money for alternative advertising promotions as well as the usual newspaper and radio ads. For instance, if they want to feature your titles in their direct mail literature, newsletters, or catalogs, work with them to arrange a co-op ad that satisfies both of you.

- Both the chains and independent booksellers are open to such co-op advertising. Few booksellers will refuse such help.

- One drawback to co-op ads is that some booksellers may stock up heavily on your co-op titles in order to get a larger co-op advertising allowance and then end up returning most of the books. In such cases, there is no way for you to get any of the co-op money back. To limit your risk, set an upper credit limit for such co-op ads.

- For more details on how to create a co-op advertising policy, see the sample statement of terms on page 141 of my book *Book Marketing Made Easy*. You may adapt this standard policy to suit your own needs.

13:13 Point of Purchase Displays

As many as 50% of bookstore customers have no specific purchase in mind when they first enter the store. Because such a large percentage of readers come to browse and window shop, you should do everything you can to encourage impulse sales of your books. There are any number of point-of-purchase (POP) sales aids which you can provide bookstores to help them help you sell books. Here's just a few of them:

- **Book covers as billboards**—Above all, the covers of your books should be designed to sell books. When designing the covers, think of them as billboards which must attract the attention of the casual browser (and then make the sale).

- **Bookmarks**—Supply bookstores with attractive bookmarks featuring your lead titles. Since many readers collect bookmarks, such giveaways will help to attract buyers into the store while at the same time bringing their attention to your books. To promote Leo Buscaglia's *Bus 9 to Paradise*, Morrow distributed approximately 100 bus-shaped bookmarks to each bookstore receiving Ingram's monthly *Advance* magazine.

- **Shelf-talkers**—Shelf-talkers are promotional cards, tags, or labels which help to draw attention to books on the shelf. For example, Crown uses tent cards to promote a number of its cookbooks as lifestyle books. When the cookbooks are promoted on sight in this way, they sell far faster than they would if shelved along with many other cookbooks. To promote its *The New Doubleday Cookbook*, Doubleday provided a shelf talker with a pad of tear-off recipe cards which had a cookbook comparison chart on the back side. Guess whose cookbook came out on top in the chart?

- **Bag stuffers**—Doubleday provided the same recipe cards in loose sheets as well so booksellers could place the cards into the bags of any book buyer who purchased a related title.

- **Book bags**—You can help bookstores save money by providing them with book bags advertising your books (and, if practical, imprinted with the store name). One advantage of imprinted bags is that they expose your advertising not only to the book buyer but also to the general public. Avon provided special imprinted shopping bags to help promote Gail Godwin's *The Finishing School*. Dell did the same for Richard Adams's *Maia*.

- **Buttons**—Send the bookstores buttons advertising one of your books. Their employees can wear these buttons and/or give them away to customers. NAL used buttons to help promote the mass-market edition of *Smart Women, Foolish Choices*.

- **Window streamers**—NAL also sent stores window streamers to help promote *Smart Women, Foolish Choices* as well as Robin Cook's *Mindbend*. Since most bookstores have only a limited amount of space to devote to window streamers, don't use them for any but your major books which you will be advertising and promoting extensively.

- **T-Shirts**—Provide imprinted T-shirts for each employee of your major bookstore accounts. Encourage them to wear the shirts on (and off) the job. To promote its new book *Boomerang*, Workman handed out T-shirts that read "I Am the Thrower" on the front and "I Am the Catcher" on the back. Whenever you do provide imprinted items to bookstores, be sure that the imprint has some connection to the book you are promoting.

- **Posters**—Provide free posters with any order of ten or more books. Posters can be especially helpful in promoting children's books and science fiction books or, for that matter, any other books which are valued for their cover designs or interior illustrations.

- **Coupon pads**—Along with the free poster for display in the bookstore, you could provide a coupon pad which would allow any consumer to order a free copy of the poster with the purchase of any of your books. Again, such offers would be especially suited to any books which are valued for their cover designs or interior illustrations.

- **Mobile displays**—Tyndale House not only supplied shelf talkers and full-color posters to promote their Campus Life series; they also provided a full-color mobile. Such active displays are more likely to attract attention.

- **Floor displays**—Anytime you can get the bookseller to give you some space all for your own books, the better chance you have of attracting the attention of browsers and impulse buyers. Floor dumps or risers are an effective way to convince booksellers to give you that space. Note, however, that booksellers are not likely to give up such space except for titles expected to be best sellers.

If you can combine copies of previous titles from the same author in the display with his or her newest best seller, then you'll have a good chance of increasing sales of those backlist titles. Random House combined Robert Ludlum's latest best seller *The Bourne Supremacy* with copies of his previous best sellers.

- **Counter displays**—Counter displays have one great advantage over almost any other sort of display: They can be placed right next to the checkout counter to encourage last minute impulse sales. Such counter displays work best for inexpensive humor and novelty books.

Klutz Books was able to get prominent display of its instruction books on how to juggle and how to use hacky sacks by providing stores with ready-to-use counter packs of ten books each.

The best displays are those which get the customer involved. Ingram Audio has prepared a special display of audio tapes which includes a personal tape player so bookstore browsers can listen to samples of the tapes featured in the display. Such a display not only gets the customer involved, but it also allows the customer to sample the product before buying.

• **Window displays**—By encouraging booksellers to display your books more creatively, you will help them increase their sales at the same time you increase the sales of your titles. For your main titles, provide special display materials to any bookseller ordering ten or more copies. Addison-Wesley supplied booksellers with a watering can and other gardening paraphernalia to promote the sale of its new book *Gardening*.

Wilshire Books provided booksellers with copies of the sheet music from Tommy Boyce's most famous songs (*Last Train to Clarksville, Come a Little Bit Closer, I Wanna Be Free,* and *Valerie*) to accompany display copies of his book *How to Write a Hit Song and Sell It*.

To draw attention to his book about two famous San Franciscan dogs, *Bummer and Lazarus*, Malcolm Barker of Londonborn Publications had a designer prepare a special display for his booth at the 1985 ABA convention. These two dogs were said to be so close to one another that their "tails wagged as one"; hence, the display showed two dogs with their tails wagging in unison. After the ABA convention, Malcolm offered the display to a local bookseller who immediately put it into his window. Not only does the display help the bookseller sell ten copies of the book every week, but it also draws people into the store. Hence, the bookseller loves the display and won't give it up.

• **Window display contests**—To encourage booksellers to use the display materials you provide or to develop their own displays for your books, offer a special prize for the bookseller who puts together the best display.

Pantheon Books offered a two week vacation in Paris for the bookseller who came up with the best display for its *Hachette Guide to France*. In this case Whole Earth Provision Company of Austin, Texas won the prize by setting up a temporary outdoor cafe offering French food and music.

To promote *The Mollen Method* exercise book, Rodale Press offered a free four-day Caribbean cruise to the bookseller who put together the best display for the book. Rodale supplied a fitness display kit including a gym bag, T-shirt, ankle weights, sweatband, jump rope, and poster to be used in putting the display together.

• **Boutiques**—As part of its 50th anniversary celebration last year, Penguin offered booksellers a 47% discount on any order of ten or more books if they would establish a permanent Penguin boutique consisting of a wall section or floor fixture given over solely to Penguin titles. Penguin also offered a 50% discount on all orders of ten or more books to any bookseller joining their 2500 Club, which requires that the bookseller commit to stocking all 2500 Penguin titles (and buy at least three copies of each new Penguin title).

• **In-store video ads**—Fleming H. Revell provided bookstores with video tapes of Zig Ziglar in action to help promote his new book *Top Performance*.

CHAPTER 14

Selling through Other Retail Outlets

According to publisher David Godine, only 32% of the population of the United States has ever been in a bookstore, much less bought a book there. Whether his figure is accurate or not, there is certainly a large proportion of people who do not visit bookstores regularly. Hence, if you want to reach these people, you have to get your books into the places where these people will see them.

14:01 The Advantages of Other Retail Outlets

The major advantage of distributing your books in non-bookstore retail outlets is that you can get your books before people who would not otherwise enter a bookstore. That means, if David Godine's estimate is true, that you could triple the number of people you reach by getting your books into other retail outlets. Here's a few other advantages of distributing your books through these outlets:

- You can target your audience much more sharply by distributing through specialized retail outlets. For example, you are far more likely to sell books about fishing in a sports shop than in a bookstore.

- Your books do not have to compete with as many other books. Bookstores carry anywhere from 500 to 25,000 titles in stock; how many of your books could possibly stand out in such a crowd? On the other hand, most other retail outlets usually carry only a few other titles, thus giving your books a better chance of attracting the attention of casual browsers.

- Your books are more likely to be displayed prominently in non-bookstore outlets. In many stores, they will be give space right next to the cash register.

- Many special retail outlets will have greater in-store traffic than many bookstores. This is especially true of tourist spots, stationery stores, and many gift stores.
- Your books can be sold just about anywhere. New England Press, for example, sells its Vermont titles in cider mills, wood-products stores, pottery shops, T-shirt shops, country stores, drug stores, lodges, and even the ferries which cross Lake Champlain.

14:02 Alternative Retail Outlets: Some Examples

Because books provide information, instruction, and entertainment applicable to just about every field of life, they can be sold in almost any type of retail outlet. Here's a few examples of how other publishers have approached getting their books into alternative retail outlets:

- Supermarkets—Before the rise of the major chain bookstores, HP Books sold almost all their books through supermarkets. To make it easy for the supermarkets to offer their books, HP designed spinner floor racks which could display a range of their cookbook, crafts, and gardening titles. HP also pioneered the use of cross-merchandising in selling books to other retail outlets. For example, they'd supply wire racks that would allow their pasta cookbooks to be displayed right next to the boxes of noodles and spaghetti. Finally, they offered supermarkets highly competitive terms including far better discounts than they were accustomed to getting from most other suppliers.
- Home improvement centers—According to the *National Home Center News*, 30% of all how-to books on home repair and interior decorating are sold through home improvement centers. Because the sale of how-to books enables customers to do their own home improvement work, these centers encourage the sale of such books.
- Gourmet shops—Barron's has over 40 reps selling their cookbooks to gourmet shops alone. 101 Productions has set up their own distributorship network to sell their cookbooks (as well as those of other companies) to gourmet and gift shops.
- Food stands—Garden Way sells its *The Apple Cookbook* and *Simply Strawberries* in orchards and at roadside fruit and vegetable stands. A Good Thing Publishing sells *The Florida Citrus Cookbook* at citrus stands across the state. The book makes a perfect tourist item—and extra sale—for these stands.
- Shoe stores—New England Press sells its autobiography of running great Clarence DeMar in Bill Rodgers athletic shoe stores. It's their only title that sells in those stores, but because it ties in so well with the main line of those stores, the book sells well.

• Toy stores—In 1984, over 142 million books were sold through toy stores for a total value of $188 million. If you want to sell in this market, you should produce full-color story or learning/activity books which can retail for less than $8.00 (most titles sell for prices ranging from $1.00 to $5.00). You'll have a better chance of placing your books with toy stores if you offer them sets or series of books.

• Record stores—Wilshire Books sold more copies of *How to Write a Hit Song and Sell It* in record stores than they did in bookstores. Here's another case where matching the book to its potential audience allowed a publisher to open new markets.

14:03 Alternative Retail Outlets: A Checklist

Use the checklist below to aid you in locating other possible outlets for your books. For example, if you publish cookbooks, you could sell to appliance stores, campgrounds, candy shops, Christmas stores, coffee houses, cookware stores, doctor's offices, fish markets, fitness centers, food stands, garden supply stores, gift stores, grocery stores, gourmet shops, health food stores, hospital gift shops, houseware shops, marinas, supermarkets, and tourist shops. Of course, out of this list you would have to select those shops which are most appropriate for your particular cookbook titles. A regional cookbook could be sold in gift shops, campgrounds, and tourist shops while a natural foods cookbook would be most appropriate for health food stores and fitness centers.

Here then is a checklist of alternative retail outlets for your books:

[ ] art supply stores—graphics, art, architecture
[ ] appliance stores—house & home, how-to, cookbooks
[ ] automobile dealerships—automobiles, how-to, travel
[ ] barber shops—sports, recreation, novelty, humor
[ ] beauty shops—beauty care, fashion
[ ] camera shops—photography, art, travel, coffee-table books
[ ] campgrounds—recreation, sports, travel, novelty
[ ] candy shops—cookbooks, diets
[ ] chain stores—general, mass-market, novelty, celebrity bios
[ ] children's stores—juveniles, games, humor, child care
[ ] Christmas stores—Christmas titles, juveniles, crafts
[ ] churches—religious, family life, inspirational
[ ] clothing stores—fashion, beauty care, diet, exercise
[ ] coffee shops—cookbooks, poetry, general
[ ] college stores—textbooks, general, literature, novelty
[ ] cookware stores—cookbooks, diets, health
[ ] computer stores—computers, business

[ ] craft stores—crafts, how-to, hobbies
[ ] discount stores—general, remainers, mass-market
[ ] doctor's offices—health, diet, cookbooks, recreation
[ ] dress shops—fashion, beauty care, sewing
[ ] drug stores—general, mass-market, novelty, beauty care
[ ] fabric shop—sewing, crafts, fashion, beauty care
[ ] fish markets—seafood cookbooks, recreation, sports
[ ] fitness centers—health, diet, recreation, cookbooks
[ ] florists—gardening, how-to, crafts
[ ] food stands—cookbooks, gardening, how-to
[ ] garden supply stores—gardening, crafts, cookbooks
[ ] gas stations—travel, atlases, humor, novelty
[ ] gift stores—coffee-table books, humor, novelty, hobbies
[ ] golf clubs—sports, recreation
[ ] gourmet shops—food, cookbooks, diet, crafts
[ ] grocery stores—food, cookbooks, diet, crafts
[ ] gun shops—sports, recreation
[ ] hardware stores—crafts, how-to, sports, recreation
[ ] health food stores—cookbooks, health, alternative lifestyles
[ ] hobby shops—crafts, hobbies, how-to
[ ] home improvement—house & home, how-to, crafts, design
[ ] hotel gift shops—travel, novelty, coffee-table books
[ ] hospital gift shops—cookbooks, diets, humor, health
[ ] houseware shops—cookbooks, crafts, how-to
[ ] law offices—business, law, politics, social issues
[ ] marinas—seafood cookbooks, recreation, sports
[ ] maternity shops—juveniles, child care, education
[ ] military PX's—general, military, adventure, recreation
[ ] movie theaters—celebrity biographies, movies, entertainment
[ ] museum shops—coffee table books, art, literature, juveniles
[ ] music stores—music, celebrity biographies
[ ] newsstands—local titles, general, novelty
[ ] novelty shops—humor, games, novelty, recreation
[ ] office supply stores—business, humor, novelty, computers
[ ] print shops—graphics, art, novelty, business
[ ] prison commissaries—general, literature
[ ] record shops—music, celebrity biographies, novelty
[ ] religious stores—religion, family life, general
[ ] school supply stores—education, juveniles, crafts, how-to
[ ] shoe stores—fashion, beauty care, running, exercise
[ ] specialty shops—novelty, regional, entertainment
[ ] sports shops—sports, recreation, games, humor, novelty
[ ] stationery stores—novelty, humor, calendars

[ ] supermarkets—cookbooks, mass-market, juveniles
[ ] tourist shops—travel, regional titles, novelty, humor
[ ] toy stores—juveniles, child care, novelty, games, sports
[ ] travel agencies—travel books, regional titles, recreation

14:04 Tips on Marketing to Other Retail Outlets

To work with other retail outlets, you must first learn what their standard operating procedures and expectations are. Few other stores operate in the same way as bookstores. For example, grocery stores operate on a 20% discount for many food items (they make up for the low discount with much higher volume), though they've come to expect and appreciate higher discounts for non-food items. Gift stores, on the other hand, usually buy at a 50% discount (they have a lower volume, higher risk business where fads and heavy promotions play an important role in their success or failure).

These differences in operating procedures and expectations are governed by a number of factors: the type of product the store normally sells, the average price of items sold, the volume of sales, the type of customer, the distribution network for that industry and, of course, tradition.

If you are not aware of these differences, learn them. Ask local retailers how their industry works, who they buy from, what kind of discount they get, what their expectations are, and any other questions that will help you to sell your books to other similar stores.

Here, then, are a few other tips on how to market your books to other retail outlets:

• Many other retail outlets are accustomed to buying direct from manufacturer's sales reps (perhaps even more so than in the book industry where many bookstores have now become accustomed to buying through major wholesalers and direct from publishers). To locate commission sales reps for these other outlets, go to the various trade shows for that industry, read their trade magazines, ask your local retailer who their favorite reps are, and visit showrooms of reps in the nearest major city.

In the gift industry, reps are accustomed to commissions of 12% to 20%. Many reps won't even take on a new item unless they get at least a 15% commission. So your pricing formula must be able to support the larger commissions and larger discounts of the gift industry if you hope to sell to that market.

When you are ready to sign up commission sales reps to represent your line, be sure you get a signed agreement that outlines their responsibilities, territories, and markets. You may use the sample sales representative agreement on pages 133 and 134 of *Book Marketing Made Easier* to help you design an agreement that meets your needs.

- Attend the trade shows for that industry, especially when you are first starting out. Trade shows are the best place to get an overall view of the industry as well as an education in the detailed policies and procedures of that industry. Later, if your sales in those retail outlets are good, you might consider exhibiting at the trade shows. For example, WRC Publishing and Garden Way Publishing both exhibited special cookbooks at the San Francisco Gourmet Products Show. Among their titles, WRC displayed *Chocolate Truffles* and *Knowing Beans About Coffee*, while Garden Way displayed *Simply Strawberries*.

- Read the trade magazines in that field. Again, in the gift industry, these means reading *Gift and Decorative Accessories*, *Giftware Business*, *Giftware News*, and a new magazine *Gift Reporter*. In the toy industry, the two major trade magazines are *Toy and Hobby World* and *Playthings*. These magazines will not only give you a good idea of what is currently happening in the industry, but they will also provide you with many key contacts (such as sales representatives, wholesalers, and retail stores).

- Learn where to go for distribution. You will discover that there are many book distributors who can already provide you with distribution into these other markets. For example, 101 Productions, Cogan Books, and E-Z Cookin' Book Company all provide distribution into cooking stores, gourmet shops, and other cookbook outlets. Riverside Book and Bible and Spring Arbor Distributors both distribute to religious stores and churches. Business Books Marketing Group is now representing business titles in office products stores.

  On the other hand, you will find that in some industries you will be better off working within their distribution system. This is especially true in the drugstore and toy markets, where major wholesalers dominate many local and regional markets (just as the ID's and national distributors control much of the distribution for mass-market titles in the book industry). Again, you can learn who these major wholesalers are by asking your local stores, going to trade shows, and reading the trade magazines. Also, if you've set up a rep network, they will undoubtedly take care of these contacts for you.

- Set your discount schedule and terms to suit the industry. In the gift industry, these means giving 50% discounts for packaged deals (such as a prepack display of ten or more books). In many cases you will not need to offer a returns policy. Let your sales reps and local retailers help you to set a reasonable discount schedule and statement of terms. As a caution, always verify any advice you get from one source by checking with another source.

- Design packaged programs that make it easy for other retailers to order, stock, and display your titles. Since many retailers may not be set up to display books, be sure to offer a display with your books. The easier you make it for them, the more likely they will buy from you.

- When you send out display packages, always include reordering instructions with the display. You might put these instructions in front of or inside of the last copy in the display. If you hope to get reorders, you have to provide some procedure such as this to make it easy for the retailer to place the order.

- When you approach stores, you must convince them that they can make an easy profit, that the title or titles will sell well. Perhaps the best way to accomplish this is to demonstrate how well other stores have done. If you can tell them how often your books turn at retail (how often other stores have to reorder), or can demonstrate the profit potential of your books (how many dollars in sales they can expect to make per square foot per year), then you have a chance to make the sale.

- Better yet, show them how well your titles fit into their product mix. One way is to show how your books can serve as easy reference guides for their customers. For example, Aris Books was able to place *The Grilling Book* in hardware stores and *The California Seafood Book* in fish markets because both books were superb guides to using the products of those markets.

- Show stores how they can cross-merchandise your books with their product line. Barron's offers dumps to supermarkets so their seafood cookbooks can be placed near the fresh fish and their salad cookbooks near the fruits and vegetables. They have also packaged dessert cookbooks with baking trays so the books could be sold in cookware departments of stores. Similarly, 101 Productions has recommended to stores that they package a few tools with their new book about kitchen tools.

- Publish special editions for some markets. For example, pop-up and other special effects books sell better in toy stores than books with no play value.

To make their booklet *Key to North American Waterfowl* more usable by hunters and bird watchers (who could easily drop the book in a lake or swamp), Schroeder Prints printed their booklet *Key to North American Waterfowl* on special waterproof paper which actually floats. Because of its unique design, the book has sold well in sporting goods stores where it is often displayed submerged in a pail of water.

CHAPTER 15

Selling to Schools and Libraries

Schools and libraries form a larger market than retail bookstores. In 1984, U.S. sales of school textbooks amounted to about $2.7 billion, while sales to libraries were almost $1 billion—that's close to 40% of all U.S. book sales. Hence, if you are looking for new markets for your books, look into selling to these two big markets.

15:01 School Textbooks: How to Get Adopted

School textbooks make up the major portion of book sales to schools. The best way to get your books adopted for classroom use is to get samples of your books into the hands of the instructors who make the adoption decisions. And the best way to reach these instructors is through direct mail.

To obtain lists of college faculty sorted by any criteria you care to use, write to College Marketing Group, 50 Cross Street, Winchester, MA 01890; (617) 729-7865, or to Educational Directory, One Park Avenue #1102, New York, NY 10016; (800) 541-0100 or (212) 889-8455. For lists of elementary and high school teachers, write to Market Data Retrieval, Ketchum Place, P. O. Box 510, Westport, CT 06880; (800) 243-5538 or (203) 226-8941.

If the universe of instructors in a particular discipline is very small, you could send them review copies of the books right away. In most cases, however, you will want to pre-qualify recipients to make sure that they are responsible for making the adoption decision. Hence, when you send them your direct mail package describing your new textbook, enclose a reply card that allows them to request a complimentary examination copy (also known as a teacher's desk copy). On the card, ask them to answer the following questions:

1. Instructor's name,
2. Department and school where course is taught,
3. Address of school (where book should be shipped),
4. Title of course,
5. Current and/or previous textbooks used in the course,
6. Age and grade level of students taking the course,
7. Estimated number of students in the course,
8. Date course will begin,
9. Office phone number and office hours, and
10. Author and title of book they'd like to review.

Not only will requesting this information help to weed out casual inquirers, but it will also provide you with some valuable marketing data for future promotions. When you send the review copy, enclose a review slip which asks the instructors to give you feedback on why they did or did not select your title for adoption. This information will also be helpful in producing future textbooks and marketing promotions.

For reproducible copies of an Examination Copy Request Form and a Complimentary Book Acknowledgement form, see pages 123 and 124 of *Book Marketing Made Easier.*

15:02 Factors Affecting Textbook Adoptions

When instructors review books for possible adoption, the most important factor influencing their decision is the quality of the text. The book must provide a reliable and comprehensive treatment of the subject. Here, though, are a few other factors that could influence their decision:

- The timeliness of the information—The book must be current; it must reflect the trends of the time. As a result, you should consider updating a textbook at least every three or four years.

- Author's reputation—The author's reputation is not that important for elementary or secondary texts or even, for that matter, for introductory college-level texts, but it can be crucial for upper-level textbooks. In such cases, the author should be a recognized expert in the field.

- Suited to the teacher's style—The textbook must suit the teaching style of the instructor who will be using the text in the classroom. If the instructor is uncomfortable with the format, style, or content of the text, he or she will not use it unless there is no other comparable text on the market.

- Special features—If the textbook includes quizzes, exercises, review questions, or other material that makes the teacher's job easier, it is more likely to be selected. Also, if you provide an accompanying teacher's handbook, transparencies, tests, and other teacher's aids, your textbook will have a better chance to be selected.

- Binding—Because they tend to take more abuse and last longer, hardcover bindings are preferred over paperback bindings. This can be a crucial factor in school districts which provide textbooks for their students. It is not so important at the college level where the students have to buy their own texts.

- Price—Price is much more important to school districts which must pay for their own texts than it is for colleges where the students must pay the price. At the college level, the quality of the text is given primary consideration.

- Graphic design—The design of a book is rarely a factor in the decision. The only time the design might come into play is when two textbooks are equally matched on all other points but one is more graphically appealing than the other. Hence, the increased use of graphics in introductory textbooks.

15:03 The El-Hi Textbook Adoption Market

The el-hi textbook adoption market is complicated by the varying standards and requirements set by state departments of education. Some states restrict teachers' options to only those books approved by the state; others allow more flexible purchasing.

At present, the following states restrict purchases to a select list of books deposited in or consigned to a state depository: Arkansas, Florida, Georgia, Louisiana, Mississippi, New Mexico, Oklahoma, Oregon, Tennessee, Texas, and Utah.

The following states maintain an official adoption list but do not require publishers to consign copies with them: Alabama, California, DC, Hawaii, Idaho, Indiana, Kentucky, Nevada, North Carolina, South Carolina, Virginia, and West Virginia.

While the following states maintain no adoption list, they do require publishers to register with them and/or meet other requirements (such as price guarantees): Arizona, Illinois, Missouri, Montana, North Dakota, and Ohio.

All other states currently have no requirements or adoption lists. For more information, write to the appropriate state agencies. You can find their addresses in *Book Marketing Opportunities: A Directory* or the third edition of *The Huenefeld Guide to Book Publishing*.

15:04 Other Sales in the El-Hi Market

Breaking into the el-hi textbook market could be difficult against the dominance of the already established publishers, but there are other ways to sell books to schools. Here are a few examples of how other smaller publishers are selling books in the school market:

- Instead of aiming for textbook adoptions, publish workbooks, practice guides, and other supplemental texts which do not have to be approved by the state agencies and which may be purchased from supplemental funds.

- Sell your books through the school supply stores where teachers go to buy teaching aids and other supplies to enrich their lessons. To learn more about this market, read *Educational Dealer*, the trade magazine for these stores. Write to Educational Dealer, Peter Li, Inc., 2451 East River Road, Dayton, OH 45439.

- Organize book fairs. For example, Gryphon House sells preschool centers sample copies of their books which the schools can then display at book fairs. The schools then take orders for additional copies which they, in turn, buy from Gryphon at a 20% discount.

- Use your books as fundraisers. Student clubs, bands, sports teams, and even the PTA might be willing to sell some of your titles in order to raise funds for their programs. For example, sports teams could sell your fishing guides or other sports books to help raise money for special team trips. Look into any student function that might tie into one or more of your titles. Then send information on your fundraising programs to the faculty advisors at those schools which you feel would be most open to such fundraising. Before committing a lot of time or money into such a program, though, test it with some local schools first.

- Form a book club. Again, Gryphon House mails a tabloid listing about 100 of its titles to over 10,000 preschool centers. The teachers at these schools, in turn, consolidate orders received from parents and send them on to Gryphon House for fulfillment. Gryphon processes the combined order and ships the books to the schools where the books are distributed to the students. Under this program, the schools get to choose free books for their libraries, the number of books dependent on the amount of orders which were placed by the parents.

- Sell to adult education programs. Because teachers of adult education programs usually have much more flexibility in choosing which textbooks they use for their courses, you might be able to establish your new textbooks first through these programs. Sales to these programs might be enough to support the development and marketing of your textbooks until you are able to work your way through all the ins and outs of the school adoption processes in various states.

- Finally, of course, you can sell your books to school libraries. While school libraries may buy only one copy of each title, there are so many school libraries (over 100,000 public, private and parochial libraries on the Bowker lists) that even one copy per library could make your books best sellers.

15:05 Other Sales to the College Market

In 1984, college textbooks accounted for over $1 billion in sales. Unfortunately for the smaller publisher, over two-thirds of those sales were made by the twelve largest publishers (with the largest publisher alone accounting for almost 18%). Nonetheless, one-third of $1 billion is still a huge market. Again, the major way to reach this market is to get your books into the hands of the instructors who make the adoption selection. Here, however, are a few other things you can do to sell more of your books in the college market:

- Direct mail to faculty members is still the best way to reach this market. Whether you want to sell textbooks, supplemental readings, or reference books to colleges, instructors are still the people who make the major adoption decisions.

- Nonetheless, when you do send direct mail to faculty for books that might merit library acquisition, enclose a library routing slip that will make it easy for the faculty members to recommend your titles to their libraries. If you want to sell to the 3000 college and university libraries, you need to bring your books to the attention of the librarians. Faculty members can help you to do that if you make it easy for them. (For a sample routing slip that you may use in your promotions, see page 125 of *Book Marketing Made Easier*.)

- Look for ways to adapt your trade titles as supplemental readings for college courses. You may find it easier to compete against the major publishers by going after these supplemental sales.

- College travellers (sale representatives) can help to bring your books to the attention of faculty members. While fewer publishers are currently using such representatives, you might test using reps in certain regions (or try doing your own repping in your local area).

- To bring your books to the attention of specific faculty, exhibit the books at academic conferences and conventions. For example, exhibit your city planning texts at the Urban Affairs Association, the American Society of Public Administration, or the Population Association of America. Conference Book Service offers cooperative exhibit services for several hundred conferences each year. Write them for their schedule: Conference Book Service, 80 South Early Street, Alexandria, VA 22304; (703) 823-6966.

- Work to get reviews in the appropriate scholarly journals, especially those which are most applicable to your specific titles. If the reviews bring good results, then advertise in subsequent issues to capitalize in that interest.

- Advertise in *The College Store Journal* to bring your books to the attention of the college store book buyers. These bookstores carry not only textbooks and supplemental readings, but also other general trade titles that they feel will interest college students. For more information on advertising in the *Journal* and exhibiting at their yearly convention, write to the National

Association of College Stores, 528 East Lorain Street, P. O. Box 58, Oberlin, OH 44074; 216-776-7777.

15:06 The Importance of Sales to Libraries

Since libraries buy $1 billion worth of books every year, they represent a major market you should not ignore. Library sales are especially crucial for the over 2000 children's titles published every year, the majority of which are still bought by schools and libraries.

Libraries offer several other advantages to book publishers:

- You can sell books to libraries at a discount half that you must give to bookstores. Many publishers offer a 10% to 25% courtesy discount to libraries, although some offer no discount at all on single copy orders.

- You don't have to offer a return privilege to libraries. They seldom return a book.

- The greatest advantage of library sales, though, is that they often result in further sales. If your book is the kind that readers would want to refer back to again and again, those readers who first discover your book in a library will often order the book direct from you rather than continue to check the book out of their local library. Personally, I've bought many books in just this way.

In one study of technical book buyers, it was discovered that 2% to 3% of all such buyers bought the book because they had first seen the book in a library.

15:07 The Diversity of the Library Market

The library market is not a homogeneous whole. Instead, it is made up of many smaller markets, each with its own special audiences and interests. Of the $1 billion in annual sales, 23% of those sales are made to public libraries, 33% to el-hi school libraries, 27% to college libraries, and 17% to special libraries.

There are well over 150,000 libraries in the United States, including almost 9000 public libraries, 3000 college libraries, over 100,000 el-hi libraries, 1000 governmental libraries, almost 2000 business libraries, over 2000 medical libraries, 1000 law libraries, and over 1000 formal church libraries (and an estimated 50,000 smaller church libraries). Plus almost every business and organization in the country has its own small collection of books.

Most of these figures are taken from the mailing list catalog of the R. R. Bowker Company, the major supplier of library mailing lists in the country. For more information, write to R. R. Bowker Company, Mailing List Department, 205 East 42nd Street, New York, NY 10017; (212) 916-1699.

Another major source for lists of public libraries is Market Data Retrieval (listed in point 15:01 above). For lists of Canadian libraries, write to Micromedia, 144 Front Street West, Toronto, ON M5J 1G2; (416) 593-5211. For special libraries, write to the Special Libraries Association, 235 Park Avenue South, New York, NY 10003; (212) 477-9250.

15:08 Why Libraries Buy from Library Jobbers

According to several studies, anywhere from 65% to 75% of all library orders are placed through wholesalers. Of these wholesalers, Baker & Taylor is far and away the most significant for library sales. As many as 50% of all your library sales will come through Baker and Taylor. Other major wholesalers include Ingram, Bookazine, Brodart, and Blackwell North America.

There are also strong regional wholesalers such as Pacific Pipeline, Midwest Library Service, Eastern Book Company, Emery-Pratt, and others, as well as a good number of specialized wholesalers such as J. A. Majors (medical books), Riverside Book and Bible (religious books), Maxwell Scientific International (reference books), Bilingual Publications Company (Spanish books), and Small Press Distribution (literary and poetry books).

Why do libraries prefer buying from these wholesalers rather than direct from publishers? Here's just a few reasons:

- Library jobbers provide many more services, such as cataloging cards, book processing, and special bindings.

- Jobbers offer a greater selection than any one publisher can hope to offer. In essence, they offer the library one-stop shopping.

- There is less paperwork and check writing involved in placing a large order from one source as compared to placing many smaller orders from a number of sources.

- There is also less work in processing the books when they are received as one shipment.

- Jobbers usually offer equal or higher discounts than those offered by publishers, especially on larger orders (which the library can place when it consolidates orders for books from many different publishers).

- Jobbers, in general, offer faster and more reliable service than publishers (we as publishers should not be proud of this fact, but a fact it is).

- Jobbers tend to publish more frequent catalogs and other announcements of new titles. Many publish monthly, thus enabling the librarian to keep up to date on all new titles.

- Many jobbers offer continuation, standing order, or on-approval plans for specific subject areas. Because most publishers do not publish enough books in any one subject area, they cannot possibly compete with jobbers in offering a comprehensive standing order plan for specific subjects.

15:09 How to Appeal to Libraries

To make it easy for librarians to order your books, you must provide them with the information they need to make informed decisions. Do not clutter your sales literature with hype. Instead, provide them with the following information in a clear and simple presentation:

- ISBN and LCCN numbers—State the ISBN and Library of Congress Cataloging numbers for every title listed.

- Publication dates—List the publication dates for your new and forthcoming titles so librarians can be sure when the books will be available; then be sure to meet those publication dates. List the month and year of publications for your backlist titles as well; librarians like to know how current the information is in any book they order.

- CIP data—If you participate in the Library of Congress's Cataloging in Publication program, be sure to indicate this. The CIP program provides ready-to-use cataloging information which any library may use. Libraries are more likely to order a book if they know that catalog card information will be readily available even prior to a book's official publication date.

- Prices—Indicate the prices for each and every edition of your books. Librarians must have prices if they are to prepare book orders within their allotted budget. Librarians rarely choose on the basis of price alone, but if your book is less expensive than another equivalent book on the same subject, most librarians would undoubtedly order yours. The key word here is 'equivalent." If one book has gotten better reviews, even if it is more expensive, librarians will almost always order it. Quality of content and format is far more important to them than is price alone.

- Edition statement—Whenever one of your titles has just been published in a new edition (or as part of a continuing series), make that fact clear. Many libraries which have been satisfied with previous editions of a book will order new editions of the book to keep their collections as current as possible.

- Contents—Give the librarians some idea of what your books contain. Either reprint the table of contents, or print a short representative excerpt, or write a short descriptive statement.

- Reviews—Quote from any favorable prereviews from leading library journals or from endorsements provided by people who are well-known in the book's field. These outside testimonials carry far more weight than anything you can write about the book.

- Supplementary material—State the number of pages, number of illustrations (photographs, drawings, tables, forms, graphs, etc.), and what other additional information the book provides—especially whether it provides any appendices, a glossary, bibliography, index, and so on.

- Author credentials—If the author is an expert in the field or has other credentials that make him or her particularly suited to writing the book, be sure to state these facts.

- Physical qualities—Indicate whether your books are available in both hard and softcover versions and, if so, at what prices. Also indicate any editions with special library bindings or acid-free paper which make for a more durable, longer-lasting book.

In short, provide libraries with any information that demonstrates the benefits of your books for readers, makes it easier for the librarian to place an order, and indicates that your books will stand up to heavy library use.

15:10 Some Tips on Selling to Libraries

Libraries are really quite easy to sell to if you publish books that fill a need, whether it be entertainment, information, or instruction. Once you've produced a book of quality, all you have to do is to let the librarians know about the book.

Perhaps I make it sound too simple but, nonetheless, it is easier to get the attention of librarians than it is to reach booksellers or consumers. The main point to remember is that librarians are information specialists. They are continually and actively seeking new titles which can help them better serve their library patrons. Hence, you don't have to overcome as much sales resistance as you would with consumers or booksellers who have many other activities demanding their attention.

Here, then, are a few ways you can attract the attention of librarians to your books:

- First and perhaps foremost, you must work to get reviews of your books in the major library review media such as *Publishers Weekly, Library Journal, Booklist, Kirkus Reviews, Choice* (for books of interest to graduate and undergraduate libraries), *Horn Book* (for children's books), *Small Press Review* (for small press literary titles), and *New Pages Press* (for alternative press publications), as well as in the general review media which librarians rely upon (such as the *New York Times Book Review*). Since they don't have time to read every book that is published, librarians must rely on reviews from respected media to help them make informed buying decisions. A review in *Library Journal*, for instance, can result in orders for over 1000 books.

- Advertise in these journals, especially in *Library Journal* and *Choice*. Librarians like to know they are dealing with reputable and reliable suppliers. Ads in these journals ads help to reinforce your company image and also indicate to librarians that you are seriously pursuing their market.

- Send your catalogs and other seasonal announcements to libraries. Arrange your catalogs by subject area, then by author. Clearly indicate any new or forthcoming titles with the month and year of publication. Use simple, clear layouts with wide margins (for making notes). Provide an easy-to-use order form arranged by subject.

- If you want libraries to order direct from you, provide some incentive for them to do so. Offer sale prices on certain titles, or prepayment discounts, or free postage. Be sure to set a time limit on these sales to encourage the libraries to order right away and to prevent orders from trickling in for years (which could cause all sorts of problems in your fulfillment department). At the same time, though, since many libraries have rather elaborate purchasing procedures, allow ample time for ordering; hence, set a deadline that is at least 60 to 90 days from the date you will be mailing the promotion.

- Offer standing order plans for annuals, series, or subject areas where you publish many books (such as poetry books or children's books).

- Refer readers to their local library. Librarians are especially sensitive to the needs and requests of people who use their library and will often order a book simply because one or two people request the title. Melvin Powers of Wilshire Books often sends readers of his advertisements to their local library to check out his books before they buy them. Not only does this allow readers to preview the books before they buy them, but it also increases the demand at local libraries which, in turn, will order extra copies if the demand persists. He claims to have sold thousands of copies in this way.

- Work with the major library wholesalers. Send them information on your forthcoming titles in plenty of time for them to place orders before they, in turn, receive purchase orders from libraries. Remember that as much as 75% of your library sales will come through these jobbers so make it easy for them to work with you.

- Sign up with Quality Books. While most library wholesalers do not go out of their way to promote your titles (but, instead, passively process the orders they receive from libraries), Quality Books actively distributes non-fiction adult books to libraries throughout the country. They have sold many books for small presses, are easy to work with, and pay on time. For more information and for a copy of their new title submission form, see pages 41 and 126 of *Book Marketing Made Easier*, or write directly to them: Quality Books, 918 Sherwood Drive, Lake Bluff, IL 60044-2204; (312) 498-4000.

- Exhibit your books at the major library association meetings: the American Library Association convention in mid-summer, their mid-winter meeting, and the conventions of the Special Library Association, the Association of College and Research Libraries, and the many regional associations. If you cannot afford to exhibit on your own, join one of the cooperative exhibits

(Conference Book Service, Publishers Book Exhibit, New Pages Exhibiting Service, COSMEP exhibit service, and others).

- Write to the ALA to receive their free newsletter on *Selling to Libraries*: American Library Association, Attn: Selling to Libraries, 50 E. Huron Street, Chicago, IL 60611.

- Join cooperative mailings to libraries such as the ones provided by the Publishers Marketing Association, the Business Books Marketing Group, or Direct Mail Promotions. Many publishers have reported superb results using these inexpensive promotions. For a more complete list of such co-op marketing plans, see *Book Marketing Opportunities: A Directory*.

- Arrange distribution in special subject catalogs such as those issued by North Carolina Biological Supply, Social Studies School Service, Ross Book Service, or Gryphon House. Some of these are cooperative ventures; others are catalogs issued by publishers who also distribute other publishers's books.

- Finally, be sure you are listed in the standard reference works used by librarians in placing orders (such as *Books in Print*, *Small Press Record of Books in Print*, and *Publishers Trade List Annual*). Few librarians will track down a publisher who is not listed in these standard reference works if there is another publisher who is listed and who can supply a similar title. Furthermore, such listings can often lead to many direct sales since librarians use these books not only to locate publishers but also to locate books of special interest. For example, Davis Publications found that most of the library sales for Carolyn Hall's *Soft Sculpture* were directly attributable to the fact that it was the only book listed in the title volume of *Books in Print* under "soft sculpture."

CHAPTER 16

How to Sell Subsidiary Rights

The sale of subsidiary rights is now a major source of income for trade book publishers. Indeed, if it were not for subsidiary rights income, many publishers would lose money on their lead titles as well as on their midlist titles. For this reason, many major publishers have established a separate department of three or more people whose sole responsibility is to arrange sales of subsidiary rights. Given the potential for income, you too should seriously consider establishing your own subsidiary rights department or at least assign someone to spend a portion of each day pursuing sales of subsidiary rights. Nick Lyons Books, a small New York City publisher, has set up such a department which brings in $6000 to $12,000 a year just from the sale of serial rights. If you publish five or more titles of general interest every year, you might well discover that an organized pursuit of subsidiary rights sales will more than pay for itself.

16:01 6 Benefits of Subsidiary Rights Sales

While subsidiary rights sales are a great source of income for any publisher, there are many other reasons why you should pursue the sale of subsidiary rights. Here's six of them:

1. First and foremost, of course, the rights income itself will help to pay for the printing and promotion of your books. Such sales are especially useful in helping to pay for an increased advertising budget which can, in turn, mean increased sales in the retail stores.

2. Prepublication rights sales can increase the visibility of your titles and, hence, can lead to larger bookstore orders and more prominent displays and, thence, to greater sales.

3. Rights sales increase the credibility of any book which can, again, increase the exposure and sales of the book.

4. Rights sales beget other rights sales. For instance, a first serial sale to a major magazine can spark interest in the book from the major mass-market reprinters or from independent movie producers.

5. The exposure given a book by a first serial in a magazine can increase bookstore sales significantly. For instance, the serialization of Erich Segal's *Love Story* in *Ladies Home Journal* caused such a positive reaction from the readers that most went right out and bought the book. The excerpt thus helped put that book on the road to best-seller status.

6. The sale of movie or TV rights can create a second wave of book sales when the movie plays in the theaters or the TV show is aired. This second wave of sales can sometimes be greater than the first wave.

16:02 Tips on Selling Subsidiary Rights

To make subsidiary rights sales, you must be persistent, well-organized, and attentive to details. Here are a few steps you can follow to increase your effectiveness in selling subsidiary rights:

- Before you do anything else, do your homework. Above all, this means developing a contact list for each major subsidiary right you might sell. Hence, you should have a separate list for serial rights sales, another for dramatic rights, another for reprinting, another for book clubs, and so on. In addition, each list should be broken down by category—for instance, those interested in fiction, or biography, or science, or whatever categories you specialize in publishing so you can match your new titles to each potential buyer.

  Such a database should be quite easy to develop with a computer. As a starting point, you could begin with the *Book Marketing Opportunities* database developed by me. Among other listings, this database includes listings for over 1500 major newspapers and magazines, their addresses and phone numbers, the names of their editors, whether or not they buy serial rights (or do book reviews), and the topics they are most likely to buy (or review). The listings can be sorted by name, zip code, category, and a number of other criteria—and can be exported to an ASCII file for importation into any other database you might already have developed.

- Once you've developed a list, keep these key contacts informed of any forthcoming books. Send news releases to them the moment you have signed an author for a new book and have set a proposed publication date. Send them your catalogs, noting especially those titles which would most interest their audience. Finally, once you have a manuscript in hand, send a letter to each of your key contacts offering them a preview galley copy or photocopy of the manuscript.

- Send out review copies as soon as you receive requests. The quicker you sent them out, the less chance the editor or buyer will have to lose interest in your book. In most cases, these review copies must be in the hands of major rights buyers at least six months before publication date so that they have plenty of time to make a decision and schedule their use of the rights they buy.

- When you send out the review copies, be sure to include the following vital information: 1) a letter or memo outlining why the book should interest their audience, 2) a biography of the author, and 3) a fact sheet highlighting the contents of the book and your promotional plans for it. If you have prepared a mockup of the cover of the book, send that also. Finally, be sure to note the publication date.

- Don't be afraid to approach more than one rights buyer at a time; it's standard operation procedure at the major publishing houses. As a courtesy, though, let the buyers know that others are also being approached. The advantages of such multiple submissions are that 1) you can approach more potential buyers in a short period of time, and 2) if more than one buyer expresses an interest in your book, they might well bid against each other thus raising the final price tag for the sub rights.

- Some rights buyers prefer to be telephoned first so they can screen a title. Others prefer to have some promotional literature or a review copy in hand before you call. Here's a general guideline of how to decide whether to call first and mail later or mail first and call later: If you are unsure whether or not a rights buyer would be interested in a particular title, call him or her and ask; on the other hand, if you are sure that the book will interest him or her (because the book is highly targeted to his or her audience), then send the book or promotional literature first and follow up with a call.

- Regardless of whether you call first and mail later or mail first and call later, always be sure to do some sort of followup on every contact you make. Don't assume that just because they have not contacted you that they are not interested. There could very well have been some foulup in shipment or receipt that caused your contacts not to receive their review copy. So always follow up your initial contacts.

- When you do get an offer or expression of interest from one buyer, don't sell that particular subsidiary right until you have heard from other potential rights buyers who've received a review copy. If the others haven't called you, call them and ask if they'd like to make a counter-offer.

- If more than one rights buyer expresses a strong interest in one of your books, you could hold a rights auction. To hold an auction, set a closing date for bids, lay down the basic rules for the auction, and set the minimum opening bid you will accept. You may offer the "floor" to any buyer who will guarantee payment of that minimum opening bid. In exchange, that buyer usually gets the right to sit out the bidding and to top the last bid by 10% or some other agreed upon figure.

You can ask for written bids to be submitted by the closing date, or you can accept telephone bids on the closing date. In either case, once the auction date has arrived you should review all the bids and then call the lower bidders to see if any of them want to top the highest bid. Continue this procedure until every bidder but one has dropped out. Then sell the rights to that highest bidder.

If someone has the floor, call them back at the end to see if they'd like to top the final bid by the agreed upon percentage. If they'd like to, then they gain the rights. If not, the highest regular bidder gains the rights.

• While the best policy is to pursue rights sales in an organized way, there have been a number of cases where rights buyers discovered the book rather than the publisher discovering the rights buyer. Sometimes this has occurred even several years after the original date of publication. So don't give up. If you have published a worthwhile book and it is selling well, the subsidiary rights buyers will come to you sooner or later if you don't find them first.

16:03 The Subsidiary Rights Contract

While many subsidiary rights buyers have their own contract which they require you to sign when they buy rights from you, you may also want to develop your own contract. To ensure that all points are covered in such a contract (whether theirs or yours), you may want to use the sample subsidiary rights license on page 151 of my *Book Marketing Made Easier*. Here are the major points which need to be covered in any subsidiary rights agreement:

• Title and author of book—Be sure that the title, edition, and name of author are spelled out correctly in the agreement.

• Rights being granted—State exactly what rights are being granted. Be as specific and as clear as possible. Make sure that both parties clearly understand which rights are involved.

• Territory covered—State whether the rights are for North America only, or the English language only, or whatever territorial restrictions might apply.

• Duration of rights—State the term of the assignment of rights. For example, most mass-market paperback rights are sold for a term of five to seven years. Other rights might be sold for the life of the copyright. Others, such as serial rights, are only sold for the one use.

• Use of the book material—If there is any question about how the rights may be used, spell them out clearly. Can the rights buyer change or edit the material? Are there any restrictions on how they may advertise or promote their version of the book?

• Amount to be paid—The amount to be paid should be clearly spelled out, including any advances and royalties. Due dates for payments and methods of accounting may also need to be delineated in detail.

• Other limitations—For certain rights you might also want to include some other limitations. For example, in selling mass-market paperback rights, you will undoubtedly want to require a limitation stating that no such edition can be published until at least one year has passed since the publication date of your hardcover edition. That will give your hardcover edition a decent chance to sell out before the mass-market edition is published.

16:04 First Serial Rights

First serial rights are the rights sold to magazines and newspapers to excerpt part (or sometimes all) of a book before its date of publication. While most first serial rights are sold for anywhere from $400 to $5000, sales have gone as high as $200,000 (*Woman's Day* paid that much for the exclusive right to excerpt from Rose Kennedy's autobiography *Times to Remember*). Aside from the income such sales can generate, the other main benefit of first serial rights is the exposure they provide for new titles. This exposure can sometimes make or break a book. For example, Lee Iacocca's autobiography was launched through a pre-publication excerpt and interview in *Newsweek*. This cover story was all the publicity Iacocca did for his book, and yet it was enough to create the word-of-mouth which made his book one of the first mass-market hardcover bestsellers. *Newsweek* has since provided similar sendoffs for Geraldine Ferraro's biography and David Stockman's *The Triumph of Politics*.

Since first serial rights are so important to launching any major title, here are a few guidelines on how to handle such sales:

• To place first serial rights, contact the book editors at magazines which you believe would be interested in the subject of your book. Send them a copy of the manuscript at least six months in advance of publication. For a highly illustrated book (such as a travel guide or photography book), it is better to send a copy of the finished book if at all possible, or quality photographs with the manuscript if no finished book is available. In general, the other basic procedures for handling serial rights sales and contracts are similar to those outlined above for any other serial rights sales.

• First serial rights can be sold on a non-exclusive basis. That means that you can sell excerpts from different parts of the book to as many buyers as are interested. For example, Patricia Breinen, rights director at Holt, Reinhart & Winston, made ten first serial sales for Louise Erdrich's episodic novel *Love Medicine*. She sold chapters from the book to *Ms.*, *Atlantic*, *Mother*

Jones, *Kenyon Review, North American Review, North Dakota Quarterly, New England Review,* and two excerpts to *Chicago.*

Stanton & Lee, a regional publisher out of Madison, Wisconsin, sold 34 separate serial rights to their book *Haunted Heartland*, a collection of 150 "true" stories of the occult by Beth Scott and Michael Norman. Because these purportedly true stories take place in 108 different locations in the Midwest, Stanton & Lee found it quite easy to sell first serial rights to 34 Midwestern newspapers including most of the major ones. Because of the attendant publicity, the first printing of the book sold out the day after publication.

• Note that you can also sell exclusive first serial rights to various categories of publications. For example, Marcia Chellis's agent sold exclusive newspaper syndication rights for her book *Living with the Kennedys* to the New York Times Syndicate for $30,000 and sold exclusive tabloid rights to the *National Enquirer* for $75,000, for a total first serial sale of $105,000.

• First serial sales can be made to newspapers, magazines (both consumer and business), tabloids, and syndicates. Plus, within each category you can make sales to any number of publications. For example, if you have a health book, besides selling first serial rights to *Prevention* or *Today's Health*, you might also be able to sell rights to sports magazines such as *Running*, women's magazines such as *Self* or *New Woman*, alternative magazines such as *Mother Earth News*, and business magazines such as *Inc.*—all dependent on how appropriate the contents of the book are to the different audiences. Don't overlook potential sales just because a magazine has never used such material in the past. Editorial trends are always changing. Keep up with them, or even ahead of them.

• When negotiating book contracts with your authors, try to get a 50/50 split on the income from serial rights sales. While some authors (or their agents) insist on an 90/10 or 80/20 split, you should try to convince them to go for a more equitable split—one which would make it worth your while to pursue such sales. The income generated from such rights sales should at least pay for your costs in obtaining such sales, and that usually requires at least a 50/50 split, especially on second serial rights sales. Let the author know that the more such sales you can afford to make, the better off both of you will be—not only because you will both be getting more income but also because of the attendant publicity (which will mean greater sales for the book itself).

16:05 How to Determine a Fair Price

With first serial rights going for as much as $200,000 and for as low as $400, you need to carefully consider what price to ask for such rights. You don't want to price your book out of the market, but at the same time you do want to get a fair price for the book—the highest possible fair price. Here are a few guidelines to use in determining a fair price:

- What is the circulation of the periodical? The higher the circulation, the more the periodical can generally afford to pay. Hence, while *Playboy* can afford to pay $3500 or more for first serial rights to a story, a magazine such as *Fantasy and Science Fiction* could hardly afford to pay more than its going rate per word which would result in a far smaller payment.

- What does the periodical normally pay for such rights? And what is the maximum amount it has been willing to pay in the past? Here are a few examples of high prices paid by some of the major buyers of first serial rights:

  Redbook—$44,000 for *Breaking Point* the story of John Hinkley written by his parents.

  Good Housekeeping—In the upper five figures each for both Eddie Fisher's autobiography *Eddie: My Life, My Loves* and *The Pritkin Diet.*

  Ladies' Home Journal—$120,000 for Betty Ford's autobiography *The Times of My Life*, $100,000 for Sophia Loren's autobiography *Sophia*, and $87,500 for Gail Sheehy's novel *Pathfinders.*

  Woman's Day—$200,000 for Rose Kennedy's autobiography *Times to Remember.*

  Family Circle—$100,000 for Lauren Bacall's autobiography *By Myself*, $75,000 for Richard Simmon's *Never Say Diet Cookbook*, and $35,000 for Nancy Sinatra's *Frank Sinatra, My Father.*

  National Enquirer—$37,000 for the *I Love Lucy Book* by Bard Andrews and $27,000 for *The Duke: The Life and Times of John Wayne* by Donald Shepard and Robert Slatzer.

- How much of the book do they want to excerpt? The more they want to excerpt, the more they should pay. For example, *Family Circle* paid $125,000 for five installments of Marjorie Craig's exercise book *10 Minutes a Day Shape-up Program*. On the other hand, *Good Housekeeping* paid $90,000 for the exclusive right to use a short 2000 word excerpt from Bill Cosby's new book on *Fatherhood*. That's $45.00 per word, far higher than normal for such rights.

- Does the publication want exclusive rights to the entire book or to just a part of the book? You would, of course, have to charge more for exclusive rights since you are giving up the possibility of any other income.

- If they do want exclusive use of all or a part of the book, how long do they want such exclusivity? The longer they want such exclusivity, the more they should pay.

- How badly do they want the book excerpt? Again, the more they want the excerpt, the more you can charge for it. Probably the only way, though, that you will ever be able to tell how much they want it is if some other competitor also bids for the rights. Of course, the more competition there is for the rights, the higher the price will go.

- First serial rights are worth more than second serial rights because of their "scoop" value. The buyer of first serial rights is paying for the opportunity to give the world its first look at a new book.

- Syndication rights should sell for more than first serial rights to one publication. Remember that most syndicators are going to make back whatever they pay for the rights by reselling the rights to syndicate members. For example, the Los Angeles Times Syndicate paid almost a $100,000 for the syndication rights to Anthony Summer's biography of Marilyn Monroe, *Goddess*. Within 48 hours they had recouped their investment by reselling the abridgement to 17 newspapers.

- Celebrity biographies, as a rule, tend to draw the highest bids for first serial rights. Other books usually have to settle for earning smaller first rights sales.

- When pricing the first serial rights to your books, remember these two points: 1) Most first serial rights go for less than it would cost the magazine to commission an article from a freelance writer. 2) A book excerpt is easier to edit than an original article (which saves the periodical both time and money in editorial costs). So don't be hesitant about asking for a fair price for such rights.

16:06 Second Serial Rights

Second serial rights are those serial rights which are sold after a book's publication date. Since the printing of excerpts from a book after its publication does not have the exclusive "scoop" value of excerpts prior to publication, second serial rights are usually sold for a lot less than first serial rights. Standard payment for second serial rights can range from $50 to $2000, depending primarily on the circulation of the publication and the number of first and second serial rights which have previously been sold. Nonetheless, payments for second serial rights can sometimes rival those made for first serial rights. The *National Enquirer* recently paid almost $20,000 to reprint portions of Robert Lenzner's biography of John Paul Getty, *The Great Getty*.

Why would magazines buy second serial rights? Besides the fact that such rights are cheaper, the magazine gets the benefit of the book's publicity and other promotion. Plus, the editor can work from a finished, completely proofread book, thus making his or her job easier. Finally, before buying such rights, the editor has a chance to gauge readers' response to the book and, hence, can better decide if the book would be appropriate for the magazine's readership.

When you do approach periodicals about buying second serial rights, let them know of any previous first and second serial rights sales. Not only is this common courtesy, but it also demonstrates to the prospective buyers that the book has material that lends itself to being excerpted.

16:07 Freebies, Adaptations, and P.I. Deals

Rather than sell second serial rights, you may decide to give away excerpts of one of your books in order to increase the book's exposure to its major audience. These freebies benefit the periodical by providing it with solid editorial material, and they benefit your book by increasing its visibility at no cost to you. These freebie deals can be arranged in at least four different ways:

- Offer free excerpts of parts of the book to any magazine or newsletter that expresses an interest. Stipulate that they may reprint the excerpt free as long as they provide a statement at the end of the article describing how the book may be ordered. That statement should include the title and author of the book, the name and address of your company, and the price of the book, plus any other appropriate ordering instructions.

  Ad-Lib has offered excerpts of several of its books to the newsletters of some of the smaller publishers associations. These associations rarely have a budget for such articles, yet their members would clearly be interested in the information contained in our books and would be likely to order our books if they had a chance to sample the contents of the books. Hence, we look on these freebies as samplers which we are able to get into the hands of prime prospects at no cost to us.

- Offer such freebies in trade for advertising space. Since the advertising space you get will often have gone unsold anyway, the article doesn't cost the magazine anything; and since you would not have otherwise sold serial rights to the magazine, you are able to get a free ad which will reinforce the article's impact and increase direct sales of your book. Since the ad is yours to do as you please, you can have the orders come direct to you.

  A number of business opportunity and trade magazines regularly participate in such exchanges. So do many limited circulation magazines and newsletters.

- If the magazine will not trade advertising space, you could offer them a per inquiry (P.I.) or per order deal. Under such an arrangement, they not only run an excerpt of your book, but they also run an advertisement or bingo card which allows readers to order the book through them. The magazine then sends the orders to you for fulfillment (after taking their cut, which may be anywhere from 40% to 60% discount).

  For its *Office Purchasing Guide*, Lowen Publishing permitted a chain of twenty regional purchasing management magazines to run a year-long series of articles excerpted from the book in exchange for monthly P.I. ads for the book. This arrangement gives double exposure for the book to its prime market.

* Finally, rather than excerpt part of the book, you could adapt material from the book to create new articles. These articles, in turn, could be sold in the same way as any other freelance article or could be given away under one of the above arrangements.

I adapted part of *The Independent Publisher's Bookshelf* for an article about publishers associations which I then sold to *Small Press* magazine. The payment I received for that one article paid for my expenses in preparing the entire bibliographic review.

The one disadvantage of giving away freebies is that such arrangements make it harder to sell second serial rights for your other books. Magazines, which previously have gotten articles for nothing, are not likely to want to pay for excerpts of new books if they can still make other arrangements. Perhaps the best policy, then, is to offer freebies only to periodicals such as limited circulation magazines or newsletters who cannot afford to buy serial rights in the first place. All others pay cash.

16:08 Mass-Market Paperback Reprint Rights

Here's where the big money is. Paperback rights have gone for as high as $3.2 million (that's what Bantam paid for Judith Krantz's *Princess Daisy*). Even reprint rights for midlist titles will often sell for $25,000 to $100,000 or more. Hence, of all subsidiary rights, these reprint rights are probably the most important. So you would do well to research this market carefully. Find out who the major players are, what categories of books they buy, and how much they are willing to pay for major titles. To give you a beginning, here's a few brief notes about some of the major mass-market publishers:

* **Avon**—Avon has recently gotten a new publisher and is revamping its editorial strategy. A member of the Hearst Group (which includes Morrow and Arbor House), Avon has previously paid $1.9 million for Colleen McCullough's *The Thorn Birds*, $1.5 million for Collins and LaPierre's *The Fifth Horseman*, and $1.5 million for Woodward and Bernstein's *The Final Days*.
* **Ballantine**—Owned by Random House, this house publishes both general fiction and non-fiction. Its Del Ray line publishes some of the best science fiction and fantasy novels. Fawcett is also now owned by Random House. Ballantine has previously paid $1.9 million for Marilyn French's *The Bleeding Heart* and $1 million plus for Erich Segal's *Man, Woman and Child*.
* **Bantam**—Currently a major publisher of hardcover bestselling biographies, Bantam has previously been known primarily for its paperback best sellers,

including its two lines for young adults, Sweet Dreams and Sweet Valley High (which do not currently buy reprint rights). Besides paying $3.2 million for Krantz's *Princess Daisy*, Bantam has paid $1.8 million for E. L. Doctorow's *Ragtime*, $3.0 million for James Herriott's *The Lord God Made Them All* (along with the renewals for three previous titles), and $1.9 million for Cynthia Freeman's *No Time for Tears*.

- **Berkley**—Part of the Putnam group which includes Jove, Ace, and several other lines, Berkley publishes general fiction and non-fiction. Berkley recently paid $825,000 for Gerald Browne's *Stone 588*.

- **Dell**—A division of Doubleday, Dell publishes general non-fiction and contemporary fiction. Dell has paid over a million dollars for Erma Bombeck's *Motherhood: The Second Oldest Profession*.

- **New American Library**—An independent company, NAL recently bought E. P. Dutton in order to be able to compete with other publishers for combined hard/soft rights deals. NAL also has its own hardcover line, as well as the Signet line of paperback classics. NAL has paid $2.6 million for rights to Robin Cook's *Brain* and *Sphinx* and over $3 million for two new Cook novels. NAL has also paid $2.2 million for Mario Puzo's *Fools Die* and $1.5 million for Irma Rombauer's *The Joy of Cooking*.

- **Pocket Books**—Part of Simon & Schuster, Pocket Books publishes in most fields with a separate science fiction line, Tapestry romances, and Washington Square Press high-quality paperbacks. Pocket has paid over $2 million for John Irving's *Hotel New Hampshire* and $1.6 million for Judy Blume's *Smart Women* and a renewal of her *Wifey*.

- **Warner**—A division of Warner Communications, Warner Books publishes contemporary fiction and general non-fiction. Warner has paid $1.2 million for Judith Rossner's *August*. They have also paid $2 million for Richard Nixon's *Memoirs* and $2 million for Woodward and Bernstein's *All the President's Men*.

- Other mass-market paperback lines include DAW, Harlequin, Baen Books, Questar, Tor, Mysterious Press, Penguin, Leisure, Revell, Zondervan, Scholastic, Popular Library, and Zebra.

Once you've located those paperback houses who you think would be most interested in your titles, send them a copy of your book for consideration. Reprint rights can be sold at almost anytime, at the time of signing the hardcover edition (a joint hard/soft deal), prior to hardcover publication, or anytime after publication.

What are your chances of selling reprint rights to your titles? Very good if your book is fiction, since nearly 3/4 of the 4000 mass-market paperbacks produced each year are fiction titles. While many of those 3000 fiction titles are original paperbacks, perhaps as many as a quarter are reprints of the 2000 hardcover/trade paperback fiction titles published each year. That would mean that about ⅓ of all fiction titles are sold for paperback reprinting each year. (This estimate, of course, is very rough since I do not know the actual number of fiction reprints each year.)

For nonfiction titles, however, the prospects for mass-market reprint rights sales are not that good. Each of the 35,000 hardcover and trade paperback non-fiction titles published each year in the U.S. must compete to be one of the 1000 mass-market nonfiction titles produced in the U.S. each year. Since a number of those 1000 titles are originals, the opportunities are even more limited.

Here's the odds for a number of categories (based on entries in the *Weekly Record* and *Paperbound Books in Print* databases for 1981 and 1982): For cookbooks and juveniles, about an 8% to 10% chance. For sports and recreation titles, about a 15% chance. For biographies, about a 4% chance. For all other titles, about a 1% to 2% chance.

If you do make a sale, the basic terms of the contract would be about the same as for any other subsidiary rights. Royalty rates range anywhere from 6% to 10% (and higher for a few "brand name" authors). The term for such rights is usually five to seven years. Most contracts also stipulate that the mass-market edition may not be published within a year of the hardcover edition (this allows the hard-cover a decent life span in which to sell out).

16:09 Trade Paperback Reprint Rights

If you do not publish your own trade paperback editions, you could sell such reprint rights before you sell mass-market rights. In this way, a book can have three full lives—as a hardcover, as a trade paperback, and as a mass-market paperback. *The Joy of Cooking*, for example, was a best seller as a hardcover (over 10 million), a trade paperback (over 1.5 million) and as a mass-market paperback (over 5 million).

Trade paperback reprint rights usually sell for a royalty of between 6% and 10%. Other provisions of the contract are similar to mass-market rights and subsidiary rights in general.

16:10 Selling to Book Clubs

Besides the extra income that book club sales generate, there are a number of other advantages to such book club sales: 1) If the book club joins your print run, you could save 10% or more on the production costs of your own copies. 2) Book club sales rarely eat into normal trade sales or other sales by mail; they are, in effect, add-on sales you probably would not have gotten in any other way. 3) The promotional exposure provided by book club magazines helps to support your own promotional efforts and often leads to more bookstore sales.

Royalties for book club sales are usually around 10% of the club's list price (which itself is often 70% or less of the book's original list price). The royalty decreases to 5% if the book is used as a premium. The average advance against royalties offered by the major book clubs (Book of the Month Club and Literary Guild) for a main selection is between $65,000 and $12,000. For featured alternates, the advance will be around $25,000; and for other alternates, advances can range from $4,000 to $10,000. The smaller book clubs usually offer an advance of half the royalties expected to be earned based on the club's initial press run or purchase.

The term for most book club contracts is two to three years, during which time the book club has the right to distribute the book to its members as they see fit. Generally, the major book club licenses require exclusive book club rights. Most smaller ones do not require such exclusivity.

When submitting books to various book clubs for consideration, don't pass by a book club just because it has never offered a similar book in the past. If you believe that their members would be in one of your titles, send them a copy. Don't rule out any club; let them make the selections. For example, M. Evans sold Rodale's Prevention Book Club (which normally features health and nutrition books) Julia Grice's *How to Find Romance After 40*. Although the book is clearly not a health book, it still has a natural appeal to the club's members, most of whom are over 40.

Below is a list of various categories of book clubs. For a complete list of book clubs, their addresses, phone numbers, and interests, see *Book Marketing Opportunities: A Directory*.

- General-interest hardcover book clubs: Book of the Month Club and Literary Guild are the two major ones.

- General-interest paperback book clubs: Quality Paperback Book Club, a subsidiary of Book of the Month Club, is the major paperback book club.

- Book Condensations—Reader's Digest Condensed Books are the leaders in this field. While book abridgements and condensations are not technically book club sales, we list them here because in most ways they are very similar. Reader's Digest recently paid $40,000 to abridge Howard Goldfluss's *The Judgment*.

- Professional book clubs—McGraw-Hill, Prentice-Hall, and Macmillan all offer a number of different specialized book clubs for professionals, from engineers to doctors, architects to computer programmers.

- Special interest book clubs—There are a good number of special interest book clubs offering books for almost any interest including writing (Writer's Digest Book Club), science fiction (Science Fiction Book Club), cooking (Cookery Book Club as well as the cookbook division of Book of the Month Club), and military (Military Book Club).

- Children's book clubs—Field Publications (with their Weekly Reader, Buddy Books, Discovering Books, and other book clubs), Scholastic (with their Arrow, See-Saw, and Teen Age Book Clubs), and Grolier (with their Beginning Readers' Program and Disney's Wonderful World of Reading) are the major companies in this field.
- Religious book clubs—There are a good number of book clubs in this field—for Catholics, Protestants, Evangelicals, and Jews.
- Small press book clubs—The major book club in this area is the one offered by Dustbooks as part of their *Small Press Review.*
- Subscription book clubs—Franklin Mint, for example, offers a fifty-volume series on Great American Fiction. The Easton Press offers a limited edition collection of the Masterpieces of Science Fiction.

16:11 Motion Picture Rights

Except for mass-market reprint rights, sales of movie and TV screenplay rights probably generate more excitement than any other sale—primarily because they usually involve more money. Options can go for anywhere from $500 to $100,000, with an average of about $5000. Pickup rights go for anywhere from $25,000 to $2.5 million (that's how much United Artists paid for rights to Gay Talese's *Thy Neighbor's Wife*). The average pickup prices for movie rights are between $50,000 and $75,000.

Options allow movie producers to gain exclusive rights to a book while they arrange for financing of the movie, assemble the necessary talent (screenwriters, directors, actors, and other necessary personnel), and explore the feasibility of making a movie based on the book. The term of most options varies from 90 days to 1 year. Option payments are non-refundable. That means that the author and/or publisher keeps the money whether the option is or is not exercised (i.e., the movie is not produced). If the option is exercised, the option payment is applied to the movie purchase price.

Besides the pickup or purchase price, "brand name" authors are also usually able to get a percentage of the profits after the pickup price has been accounted for. In any movie or TV rights contract, there should be a provision allowing for the reversion of rights to the author if the movie or TV series is not produced within so many years (for instance, five years).

While most books are optioned for movies as the result of sustained publicity efforts by the books's publishers and the work of special TV/movie agents (most of whom are based in California), happenchance also often plays a role in which books are chosen for production as movies. For example, Calvin Floyd of Producers Enterprises Ltd. recently optioned Judith Richards's 1978 novel *Summer Lightning* after his Swedish-born wife happened to pick up a Swedish translation of the novel while they were visiting in Stockholm.

- Novelizations and movie tie-ins—In recent years, there has been a turnabout in book/movie rights. Now, not only do movie producers buy screenplay rights to books, but publishers buy novelization rights to screenplays. Novelizations of *Rocky*, *Return of the Jedi*, *Raiders of the Lost Ark*, and *E.T.* have all become best sellers as a result of their tie-ins to the original movies. On the other side, previously published novels such as William Styron's *Sophie's Choice*, Tom Wolfe's *The Right Stuff*, and Isak Dinesen's *Out of Africa* have all become best sellers for a second time after the release of a movie by the same name. Because the one media helps to spur sales in the other media and vice versa, both book publishers and movie producers benefit from the sales of such rights.

- Sequel rights—If the movie producer decides to produce a second movie based on the book, the purchase price is usually about 1/2 of the pickup price for the original movie.

- Remakes—Payments for remakes are usually less than the payment for the original version (unless, of course, the original version was made many years ago). The 1960's musical movie *Shangrila* was a remake of the 1930's movie *Lost Horizons* based on a novel by James Hilton.

16:12 Television Rights

Often TV rights are sold at the same time or in lieu of motion picture rights. In general, the option and pickup prices for prime time TV movies are about the same as those for movies. However, while TV movie rights might sell for anywhere from $25,000 to $75,000, miniseries rights sell for about $20,000 to $40,000 per two-hour segment. The other terms of the contract are basically the same as for movies and other subsidiary rights.

Besides rights to adapt a book to a TV movie or miniseries, there are several other rights which can be sold to television:

- Specials—Rights can be sold to produce a special based on a book. For example, Motown has bought rights to produce a show about weight loss and fitness based on Harvey and Marilyn Diamond's *Fit for Life*.

- Series—The ABC series *Spencer: For Hire* is based on Robert B. Parker's series of novels about a detective named Spencer. Rights for a television series go for about $1000 per episode for a half-hour show and about $1500 or more per episode for a full hour show.

- Reruns—Reruns pay about 20% of the fee for the original show.

- Cable TV—Rodale Press has begun producing special shows on gardening and other how-to subjects for distribution to cable TV stations. Since cable is still a rather new field, no standards have been set for payment, terms, or other conditions of sale.

- Cable networks—Home Box Office (HBO), other movie channels, and specialized cable networks are all potential buyers of TV rights to books. At the same time, a number of best sellers have come out of original HBO programming. For instance, Rich Hall's best selling trade paperbacks, *Sniglets* and *More Sniglets*, came out of HBO's *Not Necessarily the News*. Similarly, Xerox sold over 50,000 copies of an activity book tied into HBO's *Brain Games* series created by Jim Henson of Muppet fame.

- Videotapes—Probably the fastest growing area of TV rights sales at the present time is the area of video rights (book rights for videotapes). MGM/UA Home Video recently paid a $50,000 advance against a 20% royalty for video rights to Stuart Berger's *Dr. Berger's Immune Power Diet*. Many book publishers have begun forming their own videotape publishing departments to take advantage of this growing trend. By 1995, it is estimated that 85% of all American homes will own a videotape player. Again, since this is such a new market, no standard terms have been set.

Videotapes have had a secondary effect on the sale of movie tie-ins and novelizations. Since videotapes usually do not go on sale until after the original run of the movie (and often not for a year or two after the original movie), they can create a secondary burst of sales for tie-in books. Scholastic didn't even publish its novelization of *The Karate Kid* until after the film, yet the book sold so well that they are considering publishing a sequel. Tor has recently published a novelization by Richard Mueller of the movie *Ghostbusters*—two years after the movie; yet, because the videotape is still selling well, they expect to do quite well with the book.

When selling movie and TV rights, don't overlook nonfiction books. Certainly biographies, histories, current events stories such as *All the President's Men* are all adaptable to the screen. Plus feature films and TV movies have been made of such prosaic titles as *How to Succeed in Business Without Really Trying*, *Everything You Always Wanted to Know about Sex*, and *Sex and the Single Girl*. Plus, of course, some of the biggest selling videotapes have been nonfiction titles such as *Jane Fonda's Workout*.

16:13 Other Subsidiary Rights

There are any number of other subsidiary rights that you can sell, everything from merchandising rights to dramatic rights to other print rights. Indeed, you can sell rights from books for almost any product or service that uses words or illustrations. Just use your imagination. Here, though, are a few of the other major subsidiary rights that are regularly sold:

- Audio rights—Besides those already mentioned, these rights are the most important and can bring in significant royalties. For instance, Nightingale-

Conant paid an advance in the high five figures for George Burn's two best sellers, *How to Live to Be 100 or More* and *Dr. Burns' Prescription for Happiness*. Audio or recording rights can be sold separately for audiotapes, records, and the new compact discs. The standard royalty is around 10%. The term of such rights is usually two years with automatic renewals until one or the other party serves notice.

- Radio rights—The right to broadcast a recording of a book via radio can be licensed separately. There are a number of such programs currently run on both public and commercial networks. Among other books, Jeffrey Archer's *Kane and Abel* and a number of James Herriott's books have been broadcast on radio.

- Dramatic rights—Books are sometimes made into stage plays before or even after they have been made into movies. These dramatic rights may be for amateur or professional productions, on Broadway or off, for serious drama or musical comedies.

- Ballet or Opera—Although such rights are rarely sold, choreographer John Butler is currently preparing a ballet trilogy based on books or stories by Southern authors. The ballet was commissioned by the Jackson, Mississippi public television station and will be aired sometime in 1987.

- Film strips, microfiche, microfilm, transparencies—These rights rarely bring in much money. Such rights are used primarily in preparing educational support material for schools, government programs, and business training programs.

- Computer software—These rights could develop into a significant source of income for book publishers as home computers develop more and more capability at less and less cost. Random House currently licenses its dictionary and thesaurus to be used in the computer spelling check programs of Reference Desk and Borland's Turbo Lightning.

- Electronic database—A number of publishers have already sold rights to reference books to be used on electronic databases available from such computer services as the Source, CompuServe, and NewsNet. This field has yet to develop a strong market and may well be usurped by the new laser discs now becoming available for computers. Meanwhile, if you publish reference books, these rights could be a significant source of additional income.

- Interactive novels—Spinnaker currently publishes a series of interactive crime detective novels for home computers. Recently Spinnaker paid a five figure advance against royalties for the right to adapt an Ellery Queen novel to this format.

- Computer games—Software rights can also be sold for computer games. For example, Roger Zelazny's *Nine Princes of Amber* has been licensed to

Telarium Corporation for its role-playing game available on the Apple, Commodore and IBM computers.

- Board and role-playing games—Victory Games has bought rights to produce a role-playing game based on the James Bond books by Ian Fleming. A number of other books, especially in the fantasy and science fiction fields, have been licensed for such games.

- Merchandising rights—Also known as licensing rights, these rights can cover any commercial reproduction of words, illustrations, or characters from a book (or movie, or whatever). Almost any product can be—and has been—licensed, from T-shirts to coffee mugs, from greeting cards to rubber stamps, from dolls to toys.

- Permissions—If another publisher wants to use a short section, chapter, or larger unit of one of your books in one of their books, they will have to request permission from you to reprint. You will then have to decide how much to charge for such permission. Permission rates range from token charges for shorter quotes to charges comparable to second serial rights for anthology selections.

- Limited editions—It is possible to sell rights to another publisher to produce limited editions of your books. For example, both Phantasia Press and Underwood-Miller publish autographed, numbered and slipcased editions of books by wellknown science fiction authors (such as a $50.00 autographed edition of Roger Zelazny's *Trumps of Doom* or a $40.00 autographed edition of C. J. Cherryh's *Cuckoo's Egg*). These higher priced editions rarely compete with standard hardcover or paperback editions since they are issued in limited runs of 250 to 1000 and are sold primarily to collectors.

- Library editions—Some publishers like Gregg Press specialize in publishing library editions of books whose hardcover editions have gone out of print.

CHAPTER 17

Selling Your Books Overseas

For a smaller publisher with a limited list of titles, the best way to sell books overseas is to sell the translation rights rather than the books themselves. Translation rights require no shipping, warehousing, distribution, or customs clearance. Even then, translation rights sales are not likely to make you rich. Not only do translation rights usually sell for less than a $5000 advance, but your payment can also be reduced by agent fees, taxes, changing exchange rates, shared translation costs, and the author's share of the sale (usually 75%).

Besides translations rights, there are a number of other ways to arrange distribution of your books overseas. This chapter will outline these strategies in brief.

For more information on selling your books overseas, see *Marketing Books and Journals to Western Europe* by Pamela Spence Richards (published by Oryx Press). Or subscribe to the *International Publishing Newsletter* which reports on worldwide book trade news, foreign exchange rates, international copyright concerns, and other matters of interest to publishers. For subscription information, write to the International Publishing Newsletter, 80 S. Early Street, Alexandria, VA 22304.

17:01 Two Kinds of Foreign Rights

You have two basic options when you sell foreign rights: You can sell reprint rights (e.g., British Commonwealth rights) or translation rights (e.g., French language rights). In each case you can divvy up these rights into certain territories. For example, you can sell English language reprint rights to the entire British Commonwealth or to Great Britain only (thus allowing you to sell separate reprint rights to Australia, India, and other countries which publish in English).

Reprint rights allow a foreign publisher to reprint the English language edition of the book and market it in certain territories. The most common English language reprint rights are for British Commonwealth rights (exclusive of Canada), Canadian rights, and Australian rights.

Translation rights permit a publisher to translate the book into another language and then sell that book in any country speaking that language. Because of the cost of making good translations, translation rights are rarely divvied up into smaller territories. For instance, the buyer of Spanish language rights may sell the translation not only in Spain, but also in most Latin American countries.

17:02 Advantages of Selling Foreign Rights

When you sell foreign rights, you give away most of your control over how your books are to be packaged and marketed. Nonetheless, if you are careful in your selection of which publishers you sell rights to, the advantages to selling foreign rights far outweigh the disadvantages. Here's a few of the advantages:

• You don't have to deal with the vagaries of selling your books in a foreign country. Foreign publishers are much better prepared to deal with the laws, customs, and changing tastes of their own countries.

• With the sale of foreign rights, you don't have to arrange customs clearances, shipping, distribution, and fulfillment.

• You receive payment for the rights up front.

• You can draw on the experience of these publishers to sell not only to the direct market, but to a number of related countries. For example, by selling British Commonwealth rights to a British publisher, you not only get distribution in Great Britain, but also in Australia, New Zealand, India, South Africa, and other members of the British Commonwealth. In most cases the British publisher will also handle distribution of English language books to other European countries, Africa, and Asia.

• Sales of a translated edition can also spur sales of the English language edition, especially among libraries and scholars.

17:03 How to Sell Foreign Rights

Out of almost 52,000 titles published by West German publishers in 1984, slightly over 4000 (or about 8%) were translations from English. Similarly, out of over 32,000 titles published by Spanish publishers in 1982, almost 4000 (or about 12%) were translations from English, while 10% of Italy's book production of 20,000 plus titles for that year were translations from English. In general, then, if we allow for duplication, anywhere from 5000 to 8000 English language titles are bought for translation each year. Since as many as half of these titles were originally published in Great Britain, the total annual market for translation rights of American books is probably about 3500 titles, or about 8% of all titles produced each year.

What all this means is that each new book has about one chance in twelve of selling any translation rights. Since a good number of the books produced in the United States have a limited foreign market, your chances of selling translation rights to your books increases even more. Your chances, then, of selling foreign rights are much greater than your chances of selling mass-market reprint rights or any dramatic rights.

To help you in arranging a sale, here's a few tips and suggestions for working with foreign publishers:

• The most important thing you can do to sell foreign rights is to get reviews and distribution in this country. If the book sells well here and has a potential market overseas, you'll be contacted.

• You have a choice to 1) contact foreign publishers on your own, or 2) hire an agent such as Lynn Franklin who specializes in foreign rights sales, or 3) commission foreign agents who handle English language rights sales in their own country. For a list of such agents, see *Literary Market Place*. The main advantage of using agents when you are first starting out is that they know the market better than you could possibly get to know it without devoting full time to the project. Agents are well worth the 10% to 20% fee that they charge.

• If you do hire agents, keep them up to date on what you are publishing. Send them copies of your major titles, support material, and copies of any major reviews. Work with them the same way you'd work with any key contact.

• While it is possible to find an agent or to sell rights direct to publishers via phone calls and letters, the most practical way to make the necessary contacts is to attend the major international book fairs. While some contacts can be made at the annual ABA convention, the major international trade event of the year is the Frankfurt Book Fair, held every year around the beginning of October in Frankfurt, West Germany. Almost 200,000 people representing about 6000 different firms from around the world attend this fair every year. Other major international book fairs of importance to general trade publishers are the Bologna Children's Book Fair held in early April in Bologna, Italy and the London Book Fair held in midApril. Other fairs are held either annually or biennially in Jerusalem, Barcelona, Cairo, Quebec, Mexico City, Brussels, Stockholm, Belgrade, Warsaw, Moscow, and New Delhi, among other cities.

• If you cannot afford to display your books on your own, you can join one of the cooperative exhibits put on by USA-Book Expo, Independent

Publishers Services, and others. Last year the Literature Program of the National Endowment for the Arts sponsored a pilot project to represent small press literary titles in Barcelona and Frankfurt. Some wholesalers, among them Baker & Taylor and Bookpeople, have also mounted group exhibits at international book fairs.

- Whether you have your own display or participate in a cooperative exhibit, you should definitely attend one of these book fairs yourself if you are at all serious about pursuing overseas sales of your books. Attending such fairs, especially the Frankfurt fair, will enable you to make invaluable contacts, learn firsthand how foreign rights are sold, and perhaps even buy some translation rights from others (to expand your own list of titles here in the U.S.).

- Before you go, write letters and send your catalog to those publishers or agents you'd like to meet (use the *International Literary Market Place* to locate their names and addresses). Try to make appointments beforehand. Because the Frankfurt fair is spread over six buildings and thousands of exhibits, it is almost impossible to meet with anyone unless you have already made an appointment prior to the fair.

- When you send out information to prospective rights buyers, include a fact sheet which describes the book, its author, its audience, and what rights are available. This rights sheet should provide all the information a rights buyer would want to know in a clear and concise format.

- Be persistent. If the first publisher you approach is not interested in your books, ask them what publishers they think would be interested in your line of books. These references can be the most valuable leads you will receive.

- And remember the bandwagon effect. Once you make one foreign rights sale, publishers from other countries are more likely to jump on the bandwagon as well. It is not uncommon to find that one rights sale leads to another which leads to another until you've signed up five or six or more countries.

- When selling rights, don't just take the first offer or the highest advance; look for the publisher who can best market the book. Check out the publisher. What other titles do they offer? How are their sales? What is their reputation in their market? Look for publishers you'd like to work with. Try to establish long-lasting working relationships.

- Don't overlook the third world countries. While they might not have that much money to spend, they can be a continuing source of sales for your other titles. The third world is still a wide open market, hungry for knowledge.

- To reach the Spanish language market, try advertising in *CONTACTO*, a Spanish language newsletter that is sent to over 500 editors and publishers in Spain and Latin America. The cost to advertise one title is $40.00. In previous editions, Harper & Row has advertised *Macroeconomics* and *The*

Complete Postpartum Guide, while Holt, Rinehart and Winston has advertised *China: 100 Years of Revolution*. Hence, judging from the titles advertised by these major publishers, the range of titles that might appeal to the Spanish language market is quite wide. For more information, write to CONTACTO, Rafael Domingo, Cervantes International, 1708 11th Avenue, Brooklyn, NY 11218; (718) 768-0755.

17:04 Other Ways to Sell Overseas

While selling translation rights may be the quickest and easiest way to get your books distributed abroad, it is not always the most financially rewarding. Plus you do lose control over the presentation and marketing of your books. If you decide you'd rather market the books yourself, there are a number of arrangements you can make. The rest of the chapter will outline these ways: direct sales, co-publishing, export sales agents, agency arrangements, bookselling distributors, U.S. exporting distributors, and subsidiaries.

17:05 Selling Direct to Overseas Customers

In 1982, U.S. publishers exported $641.3 million worth of books, which represents a little over 8% of all U.S. book sales for that year. These figures indicate that foreign markets represent a significant market for English language books. For direct sales, the best selling American titles are in the fields of business, science, technology, and reference books.

- The major markets for direct sales of American books are Great Britain, continental Europe, Japan, and Australia. Smaller markets for more technical titles exist in almost every country.

- Mailing lists to reach these overseas markets are available from IBIS Information Services, 215 Park Avenue S., New York, NY 10003-1603; (212) 505-7620. Lists area also available from Mailing List Marketing, Medical Economics Company, 680 Kinderkamack Road, Oradell, NJ 07649; (201) 262-3030.

- IBIS Informations Services also provides a number of international co-op mailing opportunities for publishers. Write to the above address to find out about these services.

- Another source of targeted mailing lists of international book buyers are the foreign subscribers of U.S. magazines. For example, the *Harvard Business Review* has over 30,000 foreign subscribers. Foreign members of professional associations would also be prime prospects for books in their areas of interest.

- Besides direct mail promotions, you could test advertisements in leading overseas journals. Check *Ulrich's International Periodicals Directory* (available in most libraries) for periodicals that might appeal to the same audience as your books.

- The main advantage of direct sales is that you are in total control; the main disadvantages are the expenses of mailing promotions overseas and the problems with collecting payments with changing foreign currency rates. The best way to avoid the second problem is to request payment in U.S. dollars.

- To cut your costs for mailing promotional literature and packages overseas, look into using the U.S. Postal Service's International Surface Air Lift (ISAL). To use this service, you must have enough volume to be able to ship in bulk. Plus, you need to be near an ISAL airport (New York, Chicago, Boston, Philadelphia, Washington, Los Angeles, San Francisco, Houston, and Dallas). Write to the U.S. Postal Service, Customer Service Department, Room 5520, 475 L'Enfant Plaza, Washington, DC 20260-6342; (202) 245-5757.

- If you are not near such an airport or do not mail in sufficient volume, you may want to use the services of Expediters of the Printed Word who will consolidate your shipments with those of other publishers, fill out the necessary postal forms, and ship through ISAL for you. For more information about their services, write to Expediters of the Printed Word, 527 Madison Avenue, New York, NY 10022; (212) 838-1364.

- To learn more about the international direct mail market, subscribe to the *Publisher's Multinational Direct* newsletter (12 issues for $195.00). This newsletter covers everything from how to find the best international advertising media to the least expensive ways of mailing, plus it provides many tips for working with companies in other countries. For more information, write to Publisher's Multinational Direct, 150 East 74th Street, New York, NY 10021-3528; (212) 861-4188.

17:06 Co-Publishing

When two publishers agree to share the costs of acquiring, producing, and marketing a book, this arrangement is known as co-publishing. Such co-publishing arrangements are usually made between two English-language publishers since the main benefit of co-publishing is the savings in typesetting and production costs. Co-publishing offers a number of advantages to smaller publishers:

- The two publishers can share the costs of production. Sometimes one publisher simply joins the print run of the other publisher so each gains from the reduced costs of a larger print run. In other cases, the originating publisher provides camera-ready copy to the other publisher, thereby eliminating duplicate typesetting and preparation costs.

- They can often share marketing costs as well, especially when exhibiting the book at international book fairs and when selling translation rights.

- Promotional efforts by one of the publishers will often spill over into the other publisher's marketing area. For example, advertisements or reviews in *Publishers Weekly* or the *New York Times Book Review* will benefit other English language publishers of the same book since many international buyers read these publications.

17:07 Export Sales Agencies

Export sales agencies are U.S. organizations which act as distributors of books by American publishers in overseas book markets. They function in much the same way as an American distributor: 1) They represent the titles of a number of different publishers (anywhere from ten to one hundred publishers), 2) Their sales representatives call on the book trade (booksellers, libraries, and schools) in each country they serve, 3) They handle all distribution and collections, and 4) They handle most of the promotion of the titles they carry in the markets they serve.

If you are a smaller publisher who wants to avoid all the hassles of marketing to the book trade overseas and would rather not have to worry about the details of distribution, fulfillment, and collection, an export sales agency will serve you well. On the other hand, if the overseas market is a significant source of sales for your books and you'd like to market your books more aggressively, you would probably be better off seeking other arrangements. Since an exports sales agency may be serving as many as a hundred different publishers, you can't expect your books to get the royal treatment.

Export sales agencies expect a discount and commission structure similar to many U.S. distributors (40% to 45% discount with a 15% commission). They pay quickly with checks drawn on U.S. banks. Most export sales agencies do not warehouse books, but rather place orders as they receive orders through their sales visits and other promotions in the countries they serve.

Here are a few of the major export sales agencies in the U.S.:

- AIMS International Marketing Services, 629 Market Street, P.O. Box 890, Troy, OH 45373; (513) 339-2600. Territories served: Europe and Latin America.

- Feffer & Simons, 100 Park Avenue, New York, NY 10017; (212) 686-0888. A subsidiary of Doubleday and the largest export sales agency in the U.S., they represent all countries except the U.S. and Canada. They have offices in England, India, Australia, Japan, Mexico, Switzerland, and the Netherlands.

- International Educational Representatives, P.O. Box 1118, Concord, MA 01742; (617) 369-1905. Exports to most black African countries.

- Kaimon & Polon, 2175 Lemoine Avenue, Fort Lee, NJ 07024; (201) 944-0500. They have offices in England, Australia, Israel, Japan, South Africa, and Switzerland.
- Worldwide Media Service, 386 Park Avenue S., New York, NY 10016; (212) 686-1520. Exports to most countries.

17:08 Agency Arrangements

An agency is a company (either another publisher or a sales representative) which stocks books, fulfill orders, and handles billing and collection for other publishers. Some agencies will also handle marketing functions, including sending out review copies, mailing promotions, advertising in journals, exhibiting at conferences and book fairs, and visiting stores and jobbers. Exactly what services they offer is determined at the time you sign a contract with them. Their services can be either exclusive or non-exclusive.

The main advantage of agencies is that they stock books in the countries they represent. Hence, you can refer orders from overseas customers direct to a distributor in their own country. This saves them time and money, as well as saving you the hassle of handling such orders. Plus the agencies know the markets and media in the countries they represent and can therefore often do a better job than you could in promoting your books in these countries.

The disadvantages of such agencies are: 1) Agencies may be not be able to offer the kind of marketing service you'd like because they are representing too many other companies. 2) Since they take books on consignment, they may tie up stock that you could be selling. 3) They may not cover all areas of their market territory as well as you or another agent might do. 4) They are expensive. As a rule of thumb, you should have at least $50,000 in sales to those countries served by the agency in order to justify the expense of such arrangements (especially the cost of shipping the books to them on consignment).

The actual terms for such arrangements vary depending on the services provided and the territories covered. As a general rule, agencies expect a discount between 45% and 55%. They handle all costs of shipping, insurance, warehousing, trade discounts, fulfillment, and promotion.

The best place to make agency arrangements is at an international book fair such as Frankfurt or London. If that is not possible, then locate another publisher who works through an agency and see if their agency would be willing to take your line on as well. The overseas subsidiaries of John Wiley and Harper & Row both act as agents for a number of smaller U.S. publishers. General Publishing of Toronto acts as an agent for U.S. publishers in Canada.

17:09 Bookselling Distributors

You can also distribute your titles overseas by using library jobbers, booksellers who also act as distributors, and academic booksellers (such as Blackwell's). Most such distribution arrangements, like those with library jobbers in the U.S., are non-exclusive. Such distributors will usually stock your books, take orders, bill, and distribute for a 20% to 30% discount. If these distributors also to major advertising and promotion, the discount would go up to 40% or 50%.

17:10 U.S. Exporting Distributors

A number of U.S. library jobbers and wholesalers also offer export services to other countries. Among these are Baker & Taylor (which exports to all areas of the world including the Soviet Union and the People's Republic of China), Ballen Booksellers International, and Key Book Service. You may want to check with these companies to see if they'd like to participate in any joint promotions of your titles.

17:11 Establishing Your Own Subsidiary

One final way to distribute your books in other countries is to establish your own subsidiary in that country to not only distribute your books but to acquire and publish original editions in that country. Such arrangements are not for small companies. To justify the costs of establishing a subsidiary, you would have to have a million dollar a year market potential in the area served by the subsidiary.

While a number of U.S. publishers have Canadian subsidiaries, only a few have established subsidiaries elsewhere. The prime other market area for U.S. subsidiaries is Great Britain. Among U.S. publishers, John Wiley has established subsidiaries in Canada, Great Britain, Singapore, and Latin America. Harper & Row has offices in Great Britain, the Netherlands, Australia, Mexico, and Brazil. Bantam, itself a subsidiary of the giant Bertelsmann Group of West Germany, has subsidiaries in Canada, England, Australia, and New Zealand. McGraw-Hill has subsidiaries in Australia, Brazil, Canada, Colombia, France, Great Britain, India, Japan, Mexico, New Zealand, Panama, Portugal, Singapore, South Africa, Spain, and West Germany.

17:12 Selling Books to Mainland China

As part of its modernization effort, China is rapidly becoming a major market for English language books (English is already the second most popular language in China). Over 30,000 book buyers were attracted to China's first international book fair held in Shanghai. The market is wide open to small publishers as well as large publishers. Here are a few pointers on how to get your books distributed in China:

• Several national book import agencies are currently very active in seeking out new titles from American and Canadian publishers. Send them your catalog on a regular basis. Also let them know about your new titles as they are published. Since they are more likely to respond to publishers whose names they recognize, make sure you keep sending them material on a regular basis.

• When the import agencies receive your catalog, they review the catalog very thoroughly, select those titles which would most interest Chinese readers, clip out the information from the catalog, publish a collection of these clippings grouped by subject, and send the resulting catalog to bookstores, libraries, and universities around the country. A network of foreign-language bookstores receive the orders from these institutions, send them on to the import agencies who then order the books from the appropriate American or Canadian publisher.

• The first and largest of these import agencies is the China National Publications Import and Export Corporation. They buy books from every category. Send your catalogs and other correspondence to China National Import and Export Corporation, Box 88, Beijing, People's Republic of China (cable: PUBLIMEX BEIJING; telex: 22313 CPC CN). They also have a subsidiary in the U.S. for handling shipping of the books to China. Their address is Beijing Book Company, 701 E. Linden Avenue, Linden, NJ 07036; (201) 862-0909.

• The other major agency handles only books in the humanities and social sciences. Write to China Book Import Centre, Box 399, Beijing, People's Republic of China (cable: CIBTC BEIJING; telex: 22496 CIBTC CN). They also have a subsidiary to handle fulfillment. Write to Cypress Book Company, Paramus Place #225, 205 Robin Road, Paramus, NJ 07652; (201) 967-7820.

• A relative newcomer is Shanghai Book Traders, which acts as both an importer and a distributor (through it chain of Shanghai Foreign Language Bookstores). They request that you send your offer of terms (discount schedule, payment requirements, freight arrangements) along with your catalogs for review. If they feel your titles are appropriate for their audience, they will ask you to send sufficient catalogs and other promotional material on a regular basis so they can, in turn, distribute them to their prospective book buyers. Shanghai Book Traders currently only distribute in the immediate region around Shanghai. Their address is Shanghai Book Traders, Box 234, Shanghai, People's Republic of China (cable: SHANBOT; telex: 33355 SBT CN).

- A mailing list of 2500 institutional book buyers of scientific and scholarly books in China is available from James Chan, a consultant on selling books to China. The list costs one dollar per entry. For more information, write to James Chan, P.O. Box 30338, Philadelphia, PA 19103.
- Finally, Baker & Taylor has recently established a bookselling program in China. Write to them for details.

CHAPTER 18

Special Sales: Special Opportunities

Special sales are those sales made outside the normal book trade and retail channels. Some standard special sales outlets include corporate sales, premium uses, catalog items, fundraisers, and remainders. Nonetheless, you need not be limited to these outlets. Because books both inform and entertain, they can fulfill almost any need and appeal to almost any audience. Hence, in reality, the range or extent of your special sales are limited only by your imagination.

The great incentive for pursuing special sales is the real possibility of making high volume sales in a single stroke. It is not unusual for a single key contact to result in sales of thousands, sometimes even millions of copies of a book.

The other great advantage of special sales for smaller publishers is that the major publishers do not—and cannot—have a stranglehold on the distribution and sales network (since, in fact, there is no such network). Hence, it is possible for a small unknown publisher to compete for even the biggest sales in this area.

18:01 How to Make Special Sales

Since special sales are—as their name implies—special, there are no standardized channels for making such book sales. Nonetheless, there are certain steps you can take. Here are a few of them:

- Work directly with people, not titles. When you contact a company to make a sale to their sales division or personnel division, get the name of the sales manager (or personnel manager) and then call them direct. If they seem interested, then send a sample book and appropriate sales information. As with most key contacts, follow up with a phone call within a few weeks after sending out the book.

- Again, as with other key contacts, keep in touch. Cultivate a lasting relationship with these people. Even if they do not buy your first book, or second, or whatever, continue to approach them. Sooner or later, if you have done your research and your books do meet their needs, they will place an order with you.

- In the case of most special sales (especially catalog and premium sales), be prepared to wait as long as six months or more before any final decision is made. Even then, it may be another three to six months before you receive the order. Most catalogs, for instance, work with at least a nine-month lead time.

- When approaching these special contacts, make a clear and direct connection between your book and their needs. Don't assume they'll make the connection. Point out the benefits of your book to their targeted audience (whether it be consumers, salesmen, buyers, or whatever).

- Prepare a merchandise data sheet or other fact sheet which provides all the details about your book at a glance. Refer to page 145 of *Book Marketing Made Easier* for a standard data sheet that provides all the information these buyers would want to know.

- If the deal has the potential of being really big (25,000 or more unit sales), offer them exclusive use of the book within their market.

- Some special markets will insist on a discount as high as 60% or 70% (sometimes even more). If you are not prepared to give a discount that high, then you should reconsider whether you want to invest the time and money to enter this market. Note, however, that you should not offer such a high discount unless they, in turn, are prepared to order a large quantity. Arrange your discount schedule so that higher discounts are available to them if they order sufficient quantities to make it worth your while.

- Most special markets will require some sort of assurance that you can fulfill their order. This means that you must be able to prove to them that you either have the manufacturing capacity, stock on hand, or reputation to be able to handle whatever volume they require.

- For some special markets, there are sales representatives, consultants, or distributors who can do most of your selling for you. For example, the premium/incentive field has premium rep groups and wholesaler suppliers who provide many businesses with prearranged premium programs. The premium field also has sales organizations such as Sales Aides International (7425 Old York Road, Melrose Park, PA 19126; 215-782-9090) who specialize in bringing together suppliers and potential buyers.

- You can also exhibit at appropriate conventions such as the annual Premium/ Incentive Show or the Licensing Show. If nothing else, you should attend such shows to learn more about the industry. Plus, of course, they provide great opportunities to make connections with sales reps, wholesalers, distributors, and buyers. A number of publishers, such as Viking Penguin and Warner Books, have exhibited at the New York Premium Incentive Show. For example, at the 1986 show, Viking exhibited *The Essential Wine Book*, *Lyn St. James' Car Owners Manual for Women*, and *Fitness after 50*—all superb candidates for incentive programs.

• In some cases you can also advertise in appropriate magazines. Again, in the case of premium sales, you could advertise in *Premium/Incentive Business* or *Potentials in Marketing*. In the past year, I've seen advertisements by Warner Books, Addison-Wesley, Hammond, Viking Penguin, Random House, Time-Life Books, Western Publishing, and Rand McNally, among others. You could also advertise in other sales and marketing magazines (if you are offering a book as a sales incentive) or in personnel or training magazines (if you are offering a book for training programs).

• Use consultants. Crisp Productions has been successful approaching personnel consultants to sell their *Retirement Planning Book*. The advantages of using such consultants are that 1) they already have established clients, 2) they know the needs of their clients, and 3) their clients will usually have confidence in their recommendations. For the consultants, such sales offer two benefits: 1) they are able to provide an additional service to their clients, and 2) they are paid a commission on the sale. One consultant working with Crisp Productions sold 800 copies of their *Retirement Planning Guide* to Monsanto.

18:02 Premium and Incentive Sales

In 1985, American businesses spent over $18.8 billion dollars on premiums and incentives. Of that amount over 50% was spent on incentives (20.8% for dealer incentives and 30.8% for sales incentives). Business gifts made up 13.2%, self-liquidators another 11.5%, continuity programs another 9.2%, and all other programs the remaining 15%.

Of the $18.8 billion dollars in premium sales, about half a billion was spent on books. Books can be used in any of the above ways as either premiums or incentives. You should be aware of these different ways so you can adapt your promotional literature so it clearly addresses the needs of companies and other organizations who buy premiums.

Books have a number of advantages over other premiums. The premium buyer does not have to worry about styles, colors, sizes, breakage during shipping, or service problems afterward. Plus, books are available to suit almost any need, for any audience, at any price range. Finally, of course, books can be imprinted with almost any message.

Here, now, are just a few of the ways that companies might use your books as premiums:

- Dealer incentives—Such incentives reward retailers and other dealers for displaying a manufacturer's wares prominently and/or for selling a significant amount of those wares. While most dealer incentives are for larger gifts such as trips, appliances, and gift certificates, books can supplement or augment other dealer promotions. For instance, Coors Beer bought 100,000 of *The Colorado Scenic Calendar* from Westcliffe Publishers to give to their distributors who, in turn, gave them to their retail accounts. While these calendars were a small gift, the calendars did help to keep Coors's name in front of their key accounts.

- Sales incentives—To encourage salespeople to better their previous sales records, companies often give them prizes (the greater their sales, the larger the prize). Again, most sales incentives involve higher priced prizes such as trips or appliances. Nonetheless, books could be used to spur the salespeople along during the middle of a sales competition. For example, a travel guide book for France could be offered to any salespeople meeting a minimum sales goal. Not only would such a prize give a boost to their sales enthusiasm during the middle of a contest, but it could also be tied into a grand prize trip to Paris and, thus, as the salespeople read the guidebook, they would be inspired to work that much harder to win the trip.

- Employee incentives—Such incentives are given to employees who meet certain goals (other than sales goals), for example, increasing production. For example, *In Search of Excellence* by Tom Peters and Robert Waterman or another business best seller such as Lee Iacocca's biography would make a suitable incentive for employees who come up with suggestions that save time or make the business environment a better place in which to work.

- Business gifts—To show their appreciation to their major customers, businesses often give gifts during the holiday season. While in many cases, these gifts involve food for the body, there is no reason such gifts could not involve food for the mind. Why not encourage businesses to give holiday best sellers instead of food? Or a beautiful coffee-table book that employees could enjoy for years to come.

- Company celebrations—Upjohn celebrated its 100th anniversary by having the Benjamin Company prepare a history of its first 100 years, which it gave to its employees and customers. To celebrate its 100th anniversary, Pet Foods offered consumers a cookbook using recipes from Pet products. The book, *Celebration of Cooking in America*, sold for $8.95.

- Opening celebrations—A Santa Barbara bank celebrating the opening of a new branch gave away 5000 copies of Judy Dugan's self-published book *Santa Barbara Highlights and History* to every customer that came in during the first week.

- Giveaways—One small publisher sold a book on dental care to the American Dental Association which, in turn, provided the book to its members.

- Publicity—The Benjamin Company produced a *Consumer's Buying Guide* for a number of Better Business Bureaus who, in turn, sold to various utilities and banks to be use in their public relations programs. The Benjamin Company produced a similar book for banks on *How to Manage Your Money*.

- Increase name recognition—As part of its continuing promotion to the youth market, Coors bought the exclusive rights to distribute Edward J. Rogers's *Getting Hired: Everything You Need to Know about Resumes, Interviews and Job Hunting Strategies* free to the college market. This spring Coors distributed 165,000 copies of the book on college campuses. The man who put this deal together, Jeff Herman, notes that such a promotion need not be a one-time thing since every year there is an entirely new crop of graduating seniors.

- Increase store traffic—Bamberger's department store chain gave away 50,000 copies of Hammond's *A Taste of German Cooking* to promote its restaurant during its Octoberfest celebration.

- Attention-getters—To reinforce its image as an air cargo service, United Airlines shipped a book case, magnifying glass, and *Doubleday Dictionary* to 1700 freight forwarders and commercial shippers. Later, they also sent copies of the *Hammond Almanac*, *Guinness Book of Records*, and *Hammond World Atlas*. Each book had a specially printed jacket outlining United's services. For example, the Guinness book carried the following legend: "Who holds the record for serving the commercial shipper? United Airlines Cargo."

- Bonus premiums—To encourage subscriptions to its magazine, *Working Woman* gave away copies of *Boss Lady*, the autobiography of advertising executive, Jo Foxworth, as a bonus to new subscribers. The response rate to their direct mail promotions increased by 25% as compared to other giveaways they had been using.

- Self-liquidators—Many cereals and other food products offer special items for sale at wholesale with a small payment plus proof of purchase. Life cereals offered a *Rand McNally Road Atlas* for $3.50 and two UPC symbols. Post Grape Nuts, to reinforce its natural image, offered a free copy of a *Rand McNally Nature Guide* for three box tops or one box top and $2.00. Total cereal offered a *Reader's Digest Do-It-Yourself Manual* for $1.30 and two UPC symbols. Gerber baby foods offered a Rand McNally *Travel with Baby* manual for 50 cents and 24 UPC symbols.

Grosset & Dunlap sold over a million Nancy Drew and Hardy Boys books when they were offered as a self-liquidating premium on over 20 million boxes of Post Raisin Bran cereal. Not only do such on-pack offers sell a lot of books, but they also provide incredible exposure to your books. Additional copies of the Nancy Drew and Hardy Boy titles were sold in retail bookstores during this same promotional period.

- Educational promotions—Dorsey Laboratories in cooperation with Random House developed a children's book, *The Care Bears Help Chase Colds* to help promote the sale of their Triaminic cold care product. Not only did this promotion help them to sell 2 million units of Triaminic (each with a free book), but it also helped them to get better display space in stores.

- Introduce new products—When OM Scott introduced its new line of lawn care products, it decided to use a book that would appeal to the same audience as its products. Hence, it offered a free copy of *How to Watch Pro Football on TV* prepared by The Benjamin Company. During their promotion, they gave away almost one and a half million copies of the book.

- Promote product use—Meredith Publishing prepared a special *Best You Can Bake Chocolate Desserts* cookbook for Nestle. This 32-page booklet was given away free to 2 million people who bought Nestle's tollhouse morsels. Western Publishing put together an even fancier cookbook for Hershey's chocolates called *Hershey's Chocolate Treasures*.

- Sweepstakes prizes—Any company offering a grand prize of a trip in a sweepstakes promotion could use a travel guide to the trip's destination as one of the lower priced prizes to be given away at the same time. Since sweepstakes tend to work better when there are more prizes to be awarded, such low-cost yet valuable prizes (which books are) can add considerably to the perceived value of the sweepstakes.

You won't have to look far for companies interested in premiums and incentives. They are all around you. To help get you started, here's a "short" list of some of Hammond's premium clients:

Allied Chemical, American Cyanamid, American Express, Amoco Oil, AT&T, Audubon Society, Avis, Avon, Award Lines, Bank of the South, Barclays Visa, Bell of Pennsylvania, Bendix Corporation, Bloomfield State Bank, BMW, Book of the Month Club, BristolMyers, Burger King, Britches of Georgetown, Byron Broadcasting, Cadillac, Chemical Bank, Citibank, Coca-Cola, Contadina Foods, Crown Life Insurance, Diamond Shamrock, Doubleday, ESPN, Exxon, Farmers & Merchants Bank, Farrell Lines, Firestone, Fortune Magazine, Ford, GAF, Gallo Winery, General Motors, GEO Magazine, Glendale Federal S&L, Goya, Green Giant Company, Gulf, Honda, IBM, Indiana University Alumni Association, Ingersoll-Rand, International Playtex, J. C. Penney Life Insurance, Johnson & Johnson, J. P. Stevens, Kavco Marketing, Kawasaki, Keystone Automobile Club, KLM, Korea Shipping, Leathersmith of London, L'eggs, Lever Brothers, Liberty National Life Insurance, Lumbermans Mutual Insurance, Mazda, Media Networks, Mercedes Benz, Merrill-Lynch, Mister Doughnut, Money Magazine, Morris County Savings, Mother's Trucking, Myron Manufacturing, Nabisco, New York Life, Paine Webber, Parents Magazine, Parke-Davis; Peugeot, Pfizer, Pitney Bowes Credit, Pontiac, Prudential, RCA, Reader's Digest, Royal Crown Cola, Sandoz, Seagrams, Sea-Land Service, Shell Chemical, Standard

Commercial Tobacco, Stanley Tools, Sunshine Specialties, Texaco, Time Magazine, Travel Masters, Truckstops of America, TWA, Union Pacific, United Technologies, U.S. Air Force Academy, U.S. Golf Association, Volkswagen, Volvo, Warner Brothers, and Warner Lauren.

18:03 Other Corporate Sales

Besides premiums and sales incentive uses, corporations and other organizations can use books to aid their other departments. Here are just a few of the other approaches you can use to sell your books to corporations:

- Training programs—Corporations and governmental units spent $60 billion in 1984 to train their employees. Addison-Wesley has a separate sales force that calls only on businesses. One of their trade best sellers, *Born to Win*, originated in a Bank of America training program. Since expanding that book to the trade market, they have sold almost two million copies (plus sold the mass-market reprint rights for just over $1 million).

  Roger Von Oech sold many copies of his self-published book, *A Whack on the Side of the Head* to corporations who used them in training their creative staffs. IBM bought 2000 copies, Hewlett Packard 700 copies, and Control Data 600 copies.

- Health care programs—In order to promote the health and well-being of their employees, many companies have established health care programs. To support these programs, companies often buy books to give their employees to help them understand how to take better care of themselves. Over the years, Addison-Wesley has sold 3 million copies of D. M. Vickery and J. F. Fries's *Take Care of Yourself*. 450,000 copies of the book were sold in 1985 alone, yet the book never showed up on the bestseller lists because over 90% of those copies were sold to corporate health care programs.

  To promote employee health awareness, the Texas Medical Association and the University of Texas have offered copies of *The American Medical Association Family Medical Guide* to their employees. Random House reports some companies buying as many as 75,000 copies of the book at $7.25 each—that's a half a million dollar sale!

- Retirement planning—As mentioned previously, Monsanto bought 800 copies of Crisp Production's *Retirement Planning Guide* to give its employees.

- Sponsorships—As part of their public relations programs, some companies will sponsor worthy causes and special publishing projects. Many banks, for example, have sponsored giveaway books like *How to Manage Your Money* produced by the Benjamin Company.

  Collins has used corporate sponsors to help underwrite the costs of producing their Day in the Life series of books. Sponsors have included Kodak, Canon, American Express, Apple Computers as well as many hotels and airlines, plus some nonprofit associations and governmental agencies. Every sponsor is given credit in the front of each book. One of the corporate sponsors, Petro Canada, offered a free copy of *A Day in the Life of Canada Road Atlas* to patrons of its gas stations just prior to the publication of the larger book *A Day in the Life of Canada*. Not only did this provide income for Collins from the sale of the atlas, but it also provided some of the best prepublication promotion the book received.

- Public service—DC Comics produced a Supergirl comic promoting car safety for Honda who, in turn, gave the comic away free to driver's education classes around the country.

- Bundling—Apple Computer bundles Addison-Wesley's two books about the PostScript programming language along with every LaserWriter it sells. A number of other laser printers have also begun bundling the books with their machines as well.

  Wham-O bundles Para Publishing's *Frisbee Player's Handbook* with many of its frisbees. Minolta is offering Lowen Publishing's *Office Purchasing Guide* with its office machines. And Hayes Microcomputer bundles St. Martin's *The Complete Handbook of Personal Computer Communications* with its modems.

- Examples of their work—McNaughton & Gunn, printers of Dan Poynter's third edition of *The Self-Publishing Manual*, gives a free copy of the book to each new publisher who requests a quotation from them. Delta Lithograph does the same thing with Dan's *Business Letters for Publishers* which they printed. And, finally, Xerox bought 1000 copies of Dan's *Word Processors & Information Processing* book for which they did the typesetting—again, to show as samples of their work.

- Company connections—When Prentice-Hall published Eddie Rickenbacker's autobiography, they offered to print a special edition for Eastern Airlines (Rickenbacker had been chairman of Eastern's board of directors). Eastern bought 15,000 copies of the special edition.

- Editorial mentions—You may recall that in section 6:03 I recommended that you edit your books for promotional clout. As an example, I suggested that if you were editing a book on gardening, why not list specific seed and tool companies as resources in the appendix? Not only do such lists benefit the reader, but they also provide you with potential premium sales.

  That's what Warner Books did with the resource directory in the back of Howard Ruff's best-selling book, *How to Prosper During the Coming Bad Years*. They mailed a copy of the directory to each company on the list with a short note suggesting that they might want to offer the book to their customers. They received many orders as a result of this promotion. One dehydrated food company began ordering over 1000 copies each month.

When they published *The Best of Everything*, St. Martin's Press did a similar promotion. As a result, they sold a premium edition of the book to Sylvania, whose nineteen-inch color TV had been voted the best in the field.

* Corporate libraries—Many corporations have business or technical libraries to support their administrative, marketing, or research personnel. Some of your initial contacts with corporations could result in orders trickling in from these libraries even if you don't make a direct premium or corporate sale.

18:04 Sales to Fundraisers

Schools, churches, clubs, associations, and other organizations often sell books as a means of raising money to support their activities. For example, schools sponsor book fairs to raise money for their libraries. Churches often have book sales tables where they sell books after church services. To reach groups which might be interested in using books as fundraisers, advertise in appropriate media (such as a magazine for church leaders or a journal aimed at faculty advisors of school clubs). You might also use direct mail aimed at such church leaders or faculty advisors.

When you do approach these leaders, be sure to emphasize the educational value of your books as well as their sales value. Books are far more likely to tie in with the group's purposes and activities than are other standard fundraising items such as cookies, candy, or magazines. Indeed, some books might actually be used in their educational activities.

The standard discount schedule for such sales is a 30% to 40% discount on sales of 25 or more books.

New Society Publishers has sold their books on social change to the Seneca Women's Peace Encampment, the San Diego Peace Resource Center, New England Greenpeace, the Resource Center for Nonviolence, the Maine Nuclear Freeze Campaign, the National Fellowship of Reconciliation, and the Women's Division of the Methodist Board of Global Ministries. These associations have used the books for both educational and fundraising work.

18:05 Sales to Mail Order Catalogs

While the major mail order catalogs drive a hard bargain—requiring as much as an 80% discount—they can move a lot of books. Not only that, but the exposure they give your books to all their customers will often result in spillover sales through bookstores. Where else could you find outlets who are willing to pay you so they can advertise your books to as many as 5,000,000 people?

Irena Chalmers Cookbooks has sold over 250,000 books through the Lillian Vernon catalog, which is mailed to over five million people. They have also sold many cookbooks through Jessica's Biscuit, another mail order cookbook catalog which is mailed to almost a million people. Indeed, they have found catalogs to be far more productive than book clubs.

To sell to catalogs, first research those catalogs which target the same audience as your book. If possible, get a sample copy of their catalog and review it to see if they offer any other books. Then send a finished copy of your book to those catalogs which you think would do the best job of presenting and selling your book. At the same time, enclose a merchandise data sheet (see page 145 of *Book Marketing Made Easier*) which provides all the details about your book, from its shipping weight and size to its potential markets.

Catalogs can be broken down into a number of different categories as follows:

- General catalogs—Spencers, Sunset House, Lillian Vernon, Hanover House, Miles Kimball, Potpourri, Walter Drake, Harriet Carter.

- High-ticket catalogs—Horchow, Neiman-Marcus, Charles Keath, Joan Cook, Adam York, Pennsylvania Station, Unicorn Gallery, FHI Folio.

- Hi-tech catalogs—Edmund's Scientific, Sharper Image, DAK, JSA, Aztech, Features, New Horizons, On the Run, Russell's, Video Playground, Synchronics.

- Children's catalogs—Toys to Grow On, Childcraft, Giggletree, A Child's Collection, Children's Book and Music Center, Just for Kids, KidsRight, My Child's Destiny.

- Games catalogs—Game Room, Games, Fun House, Johnson Smith, Whole Mirth, FAO Schwarz, Constructive Playthings.

- Cooking catalogs—Jessica's Biscuits, Kitchen Arts and Letters, Wine and Food Library.

- Business catalogs—Quill, Small Business Success, Whole Work Catalog, Drawing Board Computer Supply, Lotus Computers.

- Remainder and general book catalogs—Publishers Central Bureau, Edward R. Hamilton, Daedelus, Barnes & Noble.

- Specialized catalogs—Brookstone and Tools for Living (tools); Lee Ward, Dick Blick, and Boycan's (crafts); Dance Mart (dance); Genealogist's Bookshelf (genealogy); J.C. Whitney (auto); Traveller's Checklist (travel); Especially Maine (regional).

For complete addresses of these and many more catalogs, see *Book Marketing Opportunities: A Directory* or one of the following directories: *Mail Order Business Directory*, B. Klèin Publications, P.O. Box 8503, Coral Springs, FL 33065; *The Great Catalog Guide*, Direct Marketing Association, 6 East 43rd Street, New York, NY 10017; or *The Directory of Mail Order Catalogs*, Grey House Publishing, Two Colonial Bank Building, Sharon, CT 06069.

18:06 Sales through Other Mail Order Dealers

Besides catalogs, there are a number of other ways to market your books through mail order book sellers. Here's a few of them:

• If you publish books on diet, health, exercise, crafts, or other subjects that would interest the readership of the large circulation Sunday magazines such as *Parade* and *USA Weekend*, contact National Syndication. This company buys up remnant ad space in these magazines to advertise books which they buy from publishers at discounts of 65% to 70%. If they decide one of your books might appeal to their audience, they will test the ad. If it tests well, they will continue placing ads for the book. Depending on the title, they can move anywhere from 5000 to 100,000 copies in a year. For more information, write to Jess Joseph or Kathleen Ryan, National Syndications, 230 Fifth Avenue #2010, New York, NY 10001; (212) 686-8680.

• There are a good number of smaller enterprises which sell books by mail. Many of these mail order book dealers obtain their stock from one or two major sources (at discounts ranging from 50% to 70%) and then resell to their own customers. If your book appeals to the opportunity seeker, you should contact these major sources to see if they'd be interested in stocking your books. Since they require a discount of 60% to 80%, you shouldn't contact them unless you can afford to give such discounts. Two of the major mail order book dealer sources are: Premier Publishers, Attn: Neal Michaels, P.O. Box 330309, Fort Worth, TX 76163-0309; (817) 293-7030, and Insiders Publications, P.O. Box 879, New Hyde Park, NY 11040. These prime sources can sell anywhere from a few hundred to a few thousand of your books for you each year.

• If you'd rather sell directly to the mail order book dealers, you can advertise in *BookDealers World*, *Income Opportunities*, *Opportunity Magazine*, *Moneysworth*, or in other magazines where people read the classifieds to find money-making opportunities. Wilshire Books and George Sterne's Profit Ideas are two publishers who have been using such mail order dealers for many years—and selling books as a result.

• When you sign up these independent dealers, you can offer them 50% to 70% terms depending on the quantity they order. These discounts are justified since all sales should be prepaid with no returns allowed (these are the standard terms). As an alternative, you can offer to dropship books for these dealers at a 50% discount plus a $1.00 for postage and handling. Under these arrangements, they only need to send you a check for the appropriate amount plus a label already made out to their customer. Then all you have to do is stuff the book into a shipping bag, attach the label and appropriate postage, and mail.

18:07 Multi-Level Marketing of Books

A few attempts have been made to market books through multi-level marketing. I haven't seen any such plans that were anything more than a variation on chain letter schemes. While multi-level plans apparently work for some consumable products such as vitamins, beauty care products, and cleansers, they are not really feasible for non-consumable items such as books.

The only success story I am aware of involves Charles Paul Cohn's book, *The Possible Dream*, which was written about the Amway multi-level distribution network and which sold thousands of copies through that network.

18:08 Bartering for Books and Other Services

As long as I am exploring all possibilities, it is quite possible to use your books as exchange items for other services. I know of a number of poets who have bartered their poetry books for goods or services from family and friends.

When I published the third edition of my *Directory of Short-Run Book Printers*, I exchanged several hundred copies of the second edition of the *Directory* for books from other publishers. They, in turn, distributed the books to their customers or friends. In this way I ensured that the outdated books were distributed rather than trashed.

18:09 Sell Advertisements in Your Books

To increase the income from your books, you might consider selling advertisements for related products in the back pages of your books. Though some people would question whether such advertising would corrupt the editorial integrity of books, advertisements have not interfered with the quality of most magazines which carry advertising nor with the many directories (such as *Literary Market Place* and the *Thomas Register*) which also carry advertising.

Indeed, I see advertisements as being a service to readers, especially for users of directories. When we published the second and third editions of my *Directory of Short-Run Book Printers*, we accepted ads from book printers listed in the *Directory* as well as from typographers and binders who were not. Not only did the ads bring in extra money (enough, in fact, to pay for the entire editorial and production costs of the book), but the ads also allowed readers to catch a glimpse of how the printers viewed themselves—a glimpse I could not have provided in the actual listings. I believe that giving printers the opportunity to tell their story their way is an integral part of any really useful directory.

But why stop with advertising in directories? Why couldn't other books carry advertising as well? Recently, I saw an ad for a new quarterly fantasy magazine in a trade paperback fantasy novel. Such advertising might be the only feasible way for a quality magazine to reach the target audience for its editorial content. Why not give readers an opportunity to learn about related products or services?

Of course, you could also accept just about any advertising which targets the same market as your books. For example, romance novels could carry ads for soaps, beauty aids, and diet plans while westerns could carry ads for chewing tobacco or Marlboro cigarettes. Such ads may be getting too commercial, but they could help to hold the line on rising prices for massmarket paperbacks and, for that matter, hardcovers as well. Perhaps there could be some selection criteria which would limit ads to certain clearly defined commercial products that you feel would be compatible with the book's content and style and which would actually be a service to the reader.

18:10 Remainder Sales: The Final Frontier

At some point in the life of a book, no matter how committed you are to keeping your books in print, you must consider whether or not to sell out any remaining stock to remainder dealers. Sometimes you'll have to remainder a book simply because it is outdated or because the author wants to do another edition, but the major reason most books are remaindered is that the book is no longer selling enough copies to justify the costs of warehousing it. Remaindering is actually just another way to keep a book alive rather than, as many publishers think, a way to bury a book. John Fielder of Westcliffe Publishers, which produces many fancy photo books, actually welcomes remaindering. It is, he says, a way to reach an entirely new market. When you cut the price of a book by half or more, you make your book affordable to a whole new group of book buyers. Indeed, a number of publishers are now actually publishing books for the remainder market. They don't really expect the books to sell that well in a bookstore at a high price, but they do expect them to sell quite well when they are marked down to the remaindered retail price.

True remainders are not damaged or returned copies which have been sitting on some bookseller's shelves for year; rather, true remainders are actual publishers' overstocks which have never been distributed. Most books are bought by remainder dealers at or below the publisher's actual productions costs (between 5% and 15% of the list price, or at a cost 1/3 that of the retail price the remainder will carry when sold in stores).

There are two basic ways to sell your books for remaindering:

1. You can offer a packaged deal to one or more remainder dealers. Send them a copy of the titles you want to remainder, along with inventory information for each title. Once the dealers have had a chance to review the books, you can negotiate a price with them either over the phone or by mail. This is a quick and easy method to remainder a few titles.

2. You can offer a larger list of titles on a bid-list basis. Send the list to all remainder dealers who might be interested in bidding on the books. The list should include the following information about each book: title of book, name of author, other biographical details about the author that might encourage them to stock the book, the copyright date, original retail price, and remaining inventory. Offer review copies of any title they might be interested in reviewing more closely. In your cover letter, indicate a closing date for receiving bids, the terms of payment you expect, and information about how (and where) the books are stored. Under this method, the remainder dealer who offers the lowest price for each book gets all the inventory for that book.

The major remainder dealers are Outlet Book Company (which, with $80 million in sales, does about half of all remainder business), Book Sales Inc. (with annual sales of $15 million), Book Thrift ($12 million in annual sales), and Sunflower Books ($10 million in annual sales). Their addresses are as follows (for the addresses of other remainder dealers, see *Book Marketing Opportunities: A Directory*):

* Outlet Book Company, 225 Park Avenue S., New York, NY 10003; (212) 532-9200.

* Book Sales Inc., 110 Enterprise Avenue, Secaucus, NJ 07094; (201) 864-6341.

* Bookthrift, 45 West 36th Street, New York, NY 10018; (212) 947-0909.

* Sunflower Books, W. H. Smith Publishers, 112 Madison Avenue, New York, NY 10016; (212) 532-6600.

Note that the major chains (B. Dalton and Waldenbooks) have begun buying remainders as well.

CHAPTER 19

Book Spinoffs (For Publishers and Authors)

If you consider yourself a provider of information, entertainment, and/or enlightenment, then you don't have to limit your activities simply to publishing books. In most cases you can take the same contents that are in your books and create new products—products that can help you to reach markets you could not reach in any other way. Almost any book—whether fiction or nonfiction, whether illustrated or text only, whether a best seller or only an also-ran—can be adapted to other media.

Indeed, there are so many possibilities that the real question is not whether you can do it but whether you want to do it. You must decide if adapting your books to other media is worth your time and effort—time and effort that will be taken away from your book publishing activities, time and effort that might be better spent promoting your current titles or creating new ones.

If you do decide to adapt your books, you have three basic options:

1. You can design, produce, and market the adaptations yourself.

2. You can license the rights to another company, as many book publishers and authors already do when they sell subsidiary rights.

3. You can work with another company. This joint project could be organized as a separate venture where each participating company provided a proportionate amount of money and personnel. Or it could be arranged so that one company was responsible for design and production while the other company was responsible for marketing and fulfillment. Or it could be some combination or permutation of these two possibilities.

In the rest of this chapter I will be describing many of the different ways you can adapt your books. I will not, however, be going into detail on how you should go about adapting and marketing your books under these different conditions (that would be a whole new book just by itself). For now just review the possibilities. If you decide that you'd like to pursue some of the different options, then begin by studying that field in greater detail (subscribe to the trade magazines covering that field; talk to retail shop owners; attend exhibitions). Look before you leap.

19:01 Books into Books into Books

Once you've written and/or published a book, don't sit on your laurels. Rather, look for ways to change the format of your book so it will attract new audiences. Publishers already do this when they publish books in hardcover format, then trade paperback format, and then mass-market paperback format. At each change in format (and price), a new audience is reached. But you don't have to settle for three printed formats. A book can be adapted to a good number of other printed formats as well. Here's just a few of them:

- New size—Westcliff publishes their big coffee-table books in a smaller size as well which they've trademarked by the title of Littlebooks. These Littlebooks sell for half what the bigger books cost and, thus, open up a new market for their titles.

- Excerpts—Most of the Littlebooks do not reproduce the entire text of the original but rather excerpt only a portion of the bigger book—aiming to reach a specific market. Hence, a photography book on Colorado might be broken up into separate editions for each area or city. Westcliff publishes separate titles for *Aspen*, *Vail*, and *Steamboat Springs*.

   Ten Speed Press excerpted *The New Quick Job-Hunting Map* from Richard Bolles's best-selling *What Color Is Your Parachute?*. This excerpt is regularly updated with new editions to supplement the original book. While the original book has sold over 3,000,000 copies, the smaller 64-page *Map* has sold over 500,000 copies in all editions.

- Anthologies and collections—Why not publish an anthology using selected excerpts from some of your best books? Not only could such a collection sell quite a few copies on its own (if it were well edited), but it could also help to sell many of your other titles by providing readers with a sample of the other books. Such collections need not be limited to fiction titles (though I believe they would work best for fiction). Why not a selection from each of your travel guides? Or cookbooks?

- Change titles—While a rose by any other name would smell as sweet, title changes can help to increase sales of a book. For example, NAL changed the title of Maharishi Mahesh Yogi's *The Science of Being and Art of Living* to *Transcendental Meditation* right at the peak of interest in the TM program.

As a result, they sold many more copies than they would have with the original title.

When St. Martins published Jack and Lois Johnstad's self-published book, *Attaining Financial Peace of Mind*, they changed the title to *The Power of Prosperous Thinking* (perhaps to draw a connection between that book and Norman Vincent Peale's *The Power of Positive Thinking*). Many paperback publishers will change the titles of books when they bring them out for the mass market.

• Dress it up—Irena Chalmers once described how a department store took one of her $5.95 cookbooks and dressed it up by tying a scarlet ribbon and some cinnamon sticks around it—and then charging ten dollars for the book! At Christmas time, such dressed-up books make perfect gifts.

• Loose-leaf binders—Loose-leaf publishing was originated by Richard Ettinger (one of the founders of Prentice-Hall) when one of his books became outdated by a change in the tax laws just as the book was coming off the press. To solve the problem, he tore off the covers of the books, removed the obsolete chapter, replaced it with the new information, and then published the new book in a loose-leaf binder. Loose-leaf publishing is especially useful for publications which need continual updating or for collections of forms and other illustrations which need to be duplicated with a copier.

• Kits—Dan Poynter of Para Publishing collected many forms and applications needed by beginning publishers (such as the ABI and copyright forms) and put them into a folder to supplement his *Self-Publishing Manual*. This new kit of *Publishing Forms* allows beginners to make necessary applications and to send in submissions to distributors and reviewers without having to first write to the appropriate companies for the proper forms and procedures.

• Directories—Susi Torre-Bueno of Rainbow Designs first self-published her own needlework design books. Then, finding no national directory of such needlework books, she published such a directory, *The Index of Counted Thread*, to connect the thousands of craft shops with the 5000 publishers in this field (most of them home-based businesswomen just like her).

When I first outlined the proposal for this book, I had intended to include listings of all the various book marketing channels in the appropriate chapters. But as I began to collect the listing information together, I realized that I couldn't possibly list all the resources without making this book too cumbersome to use (and too susceptible to becoming outdated very quickly). Hence, I decided to publish a separate directory. Since that time *Book Marketing Opportunities: A Directory* has taken on a life of its own, becoming about three times larger than I had originally envisioned.

• Manuals and workbooks—Many textbook publishers already provide workbooks and/or teacher's manuals to supplement their textbooks. Yet, why couldn't other publishers of nonfiction do the same? For example, a publisher of business books could well profit from providing the necessary forms to supplement a guide on direct marketing or personnel management or whatever. Ad-Lib published *FormAides for Direct Response Marketing: Mail Order Selling Made Easy* because no other publisher of books on mail order marketing had published a collection of forms to make it easier to apply the principles and practices outlined in their books.

To supplement its best-selling book on *Hang-Gliding*, Para Publishing published its *Hang Gliding Manual with Log*. Now in its seventh edition, the *Log* has sold over 75,000 copies while the original book has sold over 130,000 copies.

- Purse books—When Marilyn Ross self-published her book on genealogy, *Discover Your Roots*, she also contacted Dell about publishing excerpts from the book in their purse book series sold in supermarkets. While Dell rejected that proposal, they did contract to have her produce a new book on the same subject. Since her original book sold to bookstores, libraries, and schools, she was able to reach an entirely new audience through the purse books.

- Large print books—Over 400 large print titles are now produced each year. Among the leaders in this field are G. K. Hall and Doubleday (which has just recently formed a separate book club for large print editions, the Large Print Home Library). Large print editions allow you to market your books to readers with deteriorating eyesight, thus reaching an audience otherwise ignored by the traditional market. If your titles appeal to older people, you should consider issuing a separate large print edition.

- Diaries—Harper & Row has recently published *The Little House Diary* based on the novels by Laura Ingalls Wilder.

- Address books—Bo-Tree Productions has produced a number of address books including one on *Words of Women*.

- Activity and coloring books—Western Publishing produces many activity and coloring books based on licensed characters as well as some storybook characters.

- Comics—Various classics, from *Swiss Family Robinson* to *Huckleberry Finn*, have been published in comic format. Recently, a number of newer books have also been reproduced as comics and/or graphic novels.

- Literary magazines—Penguin Books has introduced an English literary magazine, *Granta*, into this country in paperback format.

19:02 Audio/Video Adaptations

Though printed books should be around for some time to come, more and more people are choosing to get their information and entertainment through other media, especially audio and video formats. To meet their desire for a more lively format, publishers have begun to adapt books into a number of different audio and video formats including movies, TV programs, TV series, videotape format, read-aloud or dramatized audiotapes, records, and filmstrips.

- Movies, TV programs, and TV series—While few book publishers are currently producing movies or TV programming, several major publishers are connected to larger entertainment companies. Simon & Schuster is a subsidiary of Gulf & Western Industries which also owns Paramount. Warner Books is part of the Warner Communications conglomerate. Time-Life Books owns Home Box Office which produces many of its own shows.

  Most authors and publishers license movie/TV rights to experienced movie producers and production companies rather than attempt to produce such shows themselves.

- Videotapes—Many book publishers have begun to jump on the videotape bandwagon. Currently there are over 40,000 videotape titles divided as follows: 13,000 general interest and educational; 10,000 health and science; 9,000 movies and entertainment; and 2,000 each of fine arts, children's programming, sports and recreation, and how-to titles. According to one study, by 1995 over 85% of all U.S. households will own a videotape player—and they will be spending $14 billion a year for tapes.

  Videotapes are already cheaper than books in some cases. Family Home Entertainment offers several $14.95 videotapes by T. Berry Brazelton which cost less that his books on the same subject (pediatrics).

  Karl-Lorimar has sold over 1,000,000 copies of Jane Fonda's *Workout* video. Alfred Knopf has a best-selling series of videotapes featuring Julia Child.

  To learn more about this expanding field, write to the National Video Clearinghouse, 100 Lafayette Drive, Syosset, NY 11791. Their *Video Source Book* provides data on the 40,000 plus video titles now on the market.

- Audiotapes—One buyer at the Scribner's bookstores has said that the demand for books on cassettes is so large that each time they reorder, they order twice as many as the last time. Recognizing this greater demand for books on tape, many book publishers (including Bantam and Simon & Schuster) have begun pushing their editors to obtain audio rights at the same time they buy book rights. Audiotapes have one great advantage over books: They can be listened to while driving. Tapes make a perfect companion during rush hour traffic.

  As further signs of the importance of audio cassettes in the book trade, Bowker has just brought out its first edition of *On Cassette*, a bibliography of spoken word audio cassettes. Meanwhile, Newman has sold over 100,000 copies of a 4-cassette package of Garrison Keillor's *News from Lake Wobegon*—more copies than many hardcover best sellers.

- Book/cassette packs—Book and cassette packages are especially popular among producers of children's books and tapes because they allow children to read along with the tape. Harper & Row has published an entire series of "I Can Read" book/cassette packs. Other major producers of book/cassette packs include Kidstuff Books, Price/Stern/Sloan, and Yellow Moon Press.

  Other cassette packages are also being made available. Warner Audio Publishing offers travel tapes from Stephen Birnbaum covering the major European cities. Each tape comes with a city map and a bonus travel tips cassette.

- Records—While records are rapidly being replaced by audiotapes, some companies are still producing records featuring the spoken word. The best known company in this field, of course, is Caedmon who has been producing such records for many years, especially records of poetry, short stories, and plays for educational use. Nonetheless, because records do not have the portability of cassette tapes and because compact discs are beginning to replace records, records are not likely to play a large role in future book adaptations.

- Filmstrips—Filmstrips are produced primarily for the school market. As more and more schools obtain videotape players, however, filmstrips will be used less and less.

19:03 Computer Related Adaptations

While many publishers have not done well with computer software or books in the past few years, computer adaptations still offer great possibilities for further expansion. Here's just a few examples of how books can be adapted for computers:

- Software for computers users—Simon & Schuster has published *The Fully Powered PC*, a combination of a book and software disc making an IBM-PC easier to use for nontechnical users.

- Educational software—Simon & Schuster's *Typing Tutor III* has sold over 100,000 copies.

- Business software and databases—When we published the third edition of my *Directory of Short-Run Book Printers*, we also decided to publish a mailmerge version of the *Directory* to make it easier for users to contact only those book printers who could provide the services they wanted. Similarly, we have also produced a computer database version of *Book Marketing Opportunities*, which will enable users to target only those sources which are interested in a particular subject (such as crafts, children's books, travel, science fiction, or poetry).

- Home software—CDA Electronic Publishing has published cookbooks, wine collector's books, and even the *Mr. Boston Bartender Guide* on discs. Simon and Schuster adapted *The Great International Paper Airplane Construction Kit* to the Macintosh computer.

- Novels on disc—Addison-Wesley sold 50,000 copies of *The Hobbit*. Other interactive novels have been published by Bantam (*Sherlock Holmes in Another Bow*) and Simon & Schuster (*Star Trek, The Kobayshi Alternative*).

- Electronic publishing—Lee Foster published his travel book, *West Coast Travel*, on the CompuServe bulletin board. He is following that up with a disc version to be sold in bookstores.

- CD ROM—The compact disc technology is opening an entirely new set of possibilities for publishers. Grolier has already published its *Academic American Encyclopedia* in CD ROM format. Since the CD-Interactive standard allows for audio, video, text, and data interaction, CD ROM products will eventually go beyond simple reference texts to fancier how-to and fiction texts for home use and entertainment.

19:04 Toys and Games Adapted from Books

Books have been used for years as a means of both educating and entertaining children. Since the book that combines play value with content has the better chance of attracting and keeping a child's attention, book publishers have been creating pop-ups, board books, washable books, coloring books, and other activity books to bridge the gap between the ordinary book and toys in general.

There are now books created as toys for adults, books such as the paper airplane construction kits and the new Make Your Own Working Paper series from Harper & Row (including *Make Your Own Working Paper Clock* by James Rudolph and *Make Your Own Working Paper Steam Engine* by Kyle Wickware).

Books have also inspired new games and toys. Here's just a few examples:

- Toy/book packages—Klutz Press has built its business by packaging a toy with a book describing how to use the toy. Klutz has done books on juggling (packaged with three small balls), kicking a hacky sack (with a hacky sack), throwing a boomerang (with a boomerang), and playing an harmonica (with an harmonica).

- Toys—WJ Fantasy has produced the Illustrators Collection of packaged toys which usually include paper toys, stickers, punch out figures, and other items centered around one theme such as *A Child's Chanukah Festival*. Each package is designed and illustrated by a prominent children's book artists.

A few years ago I designed and wrote a book for Dover Publications on kinetic optical illusions. This book packaged together a number of cut-out patterns that would create illusions when the patterns were moved in a certain way. The book included an old-time movie carrousel, a Fechner-Benham disc, several flip books, four thaumatropes, the Ames window illusion, and a number of other wonderful toy illusions that kids could color, cut out, and assemble for themselves. Someday, as soon as I finish all my other projects, I hope to create another optical illusion kit featuring nonkinetic illusions.

- Board games—Milton Bradley manufactures a board game based on J. R. R. Tolkein's *The Hobbit*. Mayfair Games, distributed by Berkley Publishing Group, offers board games based on Anne McCaffrey's *Dragonriders of Pern* and Barbara Cartland's romance novels. And Victory Games has produced a game based on Dr. Ruth's nonfiction books called *Dr. Ruth's Game of Good Sex*.

- Role-playing games—Role-playing games have been produced based on the James Bond and Sherlock Holmes books as well as many science fiction and fantasy novels, including Iron Crown's Middle Earth games based on Tolkein's *Lord of the Rings*.

- Jigsaw puzzles—International Polygonics has manufactured puzzles based on *The Wind in the Willows*, *Treasure Island*, *Midsummer Night's Dream*, and *Peter Pan*. Similarly, American Publishing has produced jigsaw puzzles featuring characters from the Sesame Street TV show and Tolkein's *The Hobbit*.

- Other puzzles—Perigee Books has recently distributed a new puzzle, Mental Blocks (aka Pandora's Blocks) created by artists Jacklyn Lambert and Jeffrey Samborski. The set of sixteen cubes can be manipulated into 96 different illustrations (and more than a million other combinations).

- Model kits—The Globe Playhouse, U.S. Capitol, and the House of Seven Gables are just a few of the buildings which can be created by the model kits from Kenilworth Publishing.

- Card decks—Western Publishing produces baseball trivia cards. Wingbow Press publishes a tarot deck to accompany *The Motherpeace Tarot Playbook* by Vicki Noble and Jonathan Tenney.

- Dolls—A Ramona Quimby doll based on the heroine of eight novels by Beverly Cleary has recently been offered by Morrow. Tide-Rider has produced a number of collectible dolls based on fictional characters (including Sherlock Holmes and Doc Watson).

- Doll/book sets—Harper & Row offered a doll/book set featuring a copy of Maurice Sendak's *Where the Wild Things Are* and a doll based on a character from the book.

- Paper dolls—Dover Publications has published a good number of paper doll books over the years. Recently Green Tiger Press published a *Spirit of the Flowers* paper doll box.

- Plush—Eden Toys produces stuffed animals and toys to coordinate with books featuring such characters as Babar, Paddington Bear, and Beatrix Potter's Peter Rabbit.

- Plush/book sets—Alfred Knopf packaged a stuffed Velveteen Rabbit to accompany the hardcover edition of Margery William's classic *The Velveteen Rabbit*. For $15.95 E. P. Dutton put together two Very First Books by Rosemary Wells with a plush version of Max, the rabbit featured in this series.

- Other possibilities—Balloons, buttons, pins, kites, windsocks, hobby kits, doll houses, action figures, and so on.

19:05 Posters and Calendars From Books

More publishers have probably adapted their books to posters and calendars than to any other format. Because publishers are already comfortable working with printed products and because they already have all the artwork ready to go, they can easily produce calendars and posters. Furthermore, calendars and posters are readily accepted into bookstores—the one market most publishers already serve through their distribution network.

Here, again, are just a few examples of how publishers are adapting their books to these formats:

- Posters—Posters can be made from original paintings, storybook illustrations, book covers, commemorative posters, fine art reproductions, old engravings, movie posters, photographs, and even words.

  Art 101, for example, has produced an entire series of Thousand Words posters featuring quotes by and about women, dance, Shakespeare, and other topics.

  Dover Publications regularly produces posters from public domain sources—including old advertising posters by Mucha and others.

  Fairfax Prints has produced fantasy art prints by Frank Frazetta, a number of which were originally painted for book covers.

  Peaceable Kingdom Press offers posters from a good number of children's books, including *Goodnight Moon*, *The Runaway Bunny*, *The Story of Babar*, and *Where the Wild Things Are*.

- Art prints—Art prints are reproductions of fine art in sizes ranging from postcards to posters. Many of the same companies that produce posters also produce art prints. For book publishers, one of the advantages of smaller art prints is that that can be shipped more easily than posters which must be shipped flat or in rolled cartons. Few publishers are currently set up to handle the shipping of large flat posters.

- Maps—Hammond, Rand McNally, and the American Map Company specialize in publishing maps, atlases, and globes. Only a few other publishers have done much with maps. Bradt Enterprises, for instance, has published maps to supplement its hiking guides. Warner Audio Publishing includes a free city map with each of its Stephen Birnbaum European Tour travel cassettes. To be honest, I'm surprised that more travel guide publishers have not produced large-size maps to accompany their books. Such maps would seem to be a natural add-on sale. I know that I've always wished for a larger map when I've used travel guides.

- Globes—Rand McNally offers a world globe featuring Sesame Street characters. Sunstone Publications has produced a 3-D astrodome map of the night sky.

- Wall calendars—The most popular kind of calendar to produce is the wall calendar. There have been calendars featuring children's book illustrations, B. Kliban cat calendars, Tolkein calendars, and many, many others.

- Desk calendars—The Crossing Press publishes the *Women Writers Desk Calendar*. Price/Stern/Sloan has adapted their best-selling book on Murphy's Laws to a desk calendar format.

- Engagement calendars—Galison Books produces the *Library of Congress Engagement Calendar* and the *National Gallery Book of Days*. Main Street Press produces the *Gay Engagement Calendar* and the *Mystery and Suspense Engagement Calendar.*

- Page-a-day calendars—Antioch and Workman both produce lines of page-a-day calendars. Andrews, McMeel & Parker recently introduced a *Sniglet-a-day* calendar to supplement the bestselling *Sniglet* books.

19:06 Stationery and Other Paper Goods

Like posters and calendars, stationery and other paper goods are printed products which make it easy to adapt books to their formats. Hence, many book publishers have expanded their lines to include a variety of paper goods as well. Here's just a few examples to stimulate your own thinking:

- Stationery—C. R. Gibson offers stationery and accessories based on books by Beatrix Potter and Roger Tory Peterson. Quillmark, a division of Random House, also offers a wide variety of stationery items, including social stationery, invitations, address books, diaries, blank books, note cards, and thank you cards.

- Note cards—SRM Editions publishes a line of note cards based on illustrations from Paul Goble's books, *The Girl Who Loved Wild Horses*, *Star Boy*, *Gift of the Sacred Dog*, and others. Fotofolio specializes in notecards taken from images produced by well-known photographers and artists, from Edward Hopper to Jill Krementz.

- Note pads—Quillmark produces notepads and note cubes featuring B. Kliban cats. Besides the *Sniglet-a-day* calendars, Andrews, McMeel & Parker also produce *Sniglet* note cards, greeting cards, and Post-it notes.

- Note and memo boards—Noteboards featuring Tolkein's *The Hobbit* and *Lord of the Rings* are available from Allen & Unwin. Cheers Workshop offers a wipe-off board illustrated with bear paws from Dennis Kyte's *The Last Elegant Bear.*

- Postcards—Dover Publications publishers a wide variety of postcard books featuring everything from photographs of New York to Mucha postcards to photos taken from Eadweard Muybridge's *Human Figures in Motion.* The *New York Review of Books* sells postcards featuring caricatures by David Levine of such literary notables as Marcel Proust and Virginia Woolf.

- Greeting cards—There are greeting cards for almost any occasion, from Christmas to Easter, from birthdays to graduations, from get well to farewell, from weddings to Mother's Day, and for about everything in between.

Abingdon Press has published three full-color Christmas card/booklets with poems and verses from the Bible.

Redbird Productions has established a line of greeting cards based on illustrations from their self-published book, *Cream and Bread*, about growing up in a Scandinavian-Lutheran small town.

Susan Polis Schutz began Blue Mountain Arts by publishing a book of her poetry illustrated by her husband, Steven Polis. She is now one of the best-selling poets of all time, and the greeting cards based on their works are among the major lines of independent greeting cards.

Golden Turtle Press has published a line greeting cards illustrated by Mollie Katzen, author/illustrator of the *Moosewood Cookbook*. Each card features a recipe inside.

- Party invitations—Dennis Kyte's *The Last Elegant Bear* is the basis for a line of party invitations produced by Cheers Workshop.

- Gift wrap—Harry N. Abrams is currently offering *Giftwraps by Artists*, a series of wrapping-paper books created by noted artists, designers and craftspeople. Each book contains sixteen large sheets of wrapping paper plus an introduction discussing the history and art of the particular patterns featured inside.

- Gift tags—Dover Publications, as part of its series of books featuring postcards, labels, stickers, and other stationery items, also publishes several books of gift tags.

- Party goods—Irena Chalmers Cookbooks has licensed her logo to C. R. Gibson which will imprint her logo on a line of party goods, including paper plates, napkins, and gift tags. Chalmers then plans to package some of these items with her cookbooks, thus giving her an opening into the gift and houseware departments of major department stores.

- Labels, stickers, and decals—Again, Dover publishes a number of sticker and label books featuring images from the public domain such as Thomas Nast's Santa Claus and illustrations from *Alice in Wonderland*.

  Worcester Art Museum has a whole line of kitchen labels drawing upon designs by such illustrators as George Cruikshank and Francois Millet.

  Broadman has published a sticker book called *The Birth of Jesus* which includes 55 full-color reusable vinyl stickers.

- Rubber stamps—Inkadinkado manufacturers rubber stamps featuring illustrations by Edward Gorey. Kidstamps offers rubber stamps taken from children's book illustrations by Tomi DiPaola, Bill Peet, Sandra Boynton, and many others.

- Bookmarks and bookplates—Antioch Publishing has built its business on its bookmarks featuring many licensed characters as well as storybook characters.

- Book bags and totes—Ars Longa Productions has produced a collection of silkscreened book bags featuring images from primitive and popular art.

- Miscellaneous paper items—C. R. Gibson produces many paper goods featuring Beatrix Potter and Roger Tory Peterson (among others). These paper goods include photo albums, baby books, scrapbooks, diaries, notes, enclosures, gift wrap, and stationery.

  In the Little Gourmet series from Workman Publishing are included such kits as the *Cookbook Lover's Kit* (with bookplates, recipe sheets, and helpers), the *Kitchen Organizer* (a vinyl binder with stationery and note sheets), and the *Recipe Collector's Notebook*. Workman also offers *My First Travel Book* which features a drawing pad, construction paper, and crayons.

19:07 Gifts and Accessories

While few publishers have ever manufactured gifts and accessories based on their books, some have licensed the rights to produce gifts to other companies. Here are some of the gift items that have been produced from books:

- Mugs—Andrews, McMeel & Parker currently markets *Sniglets* mugs through their Oz division. One of the mugs features the definition for "mugluk"—the stuff that collects in the bottom of coffee mugs that are not in use (i.e., peach pits, coins, old stamps, paper clips, etc.).

- Figurines—Royal Doulton produces china figurines, including a number of them based on characters from Beatrix Potter's books.

- Jewelry—Winnie the Pooh scrimshaw is available from Briarcliff Studios.

- Music boxes—Besides dishes, mugs, and figurines, Gorham also produces music boxes featuring the Sesame Street characters and Paddington Bear.

- Recipe boxes—Cheers Workshop offers a recipe box decorated with illustrations from Dennis Kyte's *The Last Elegant Bear*. A Bear Paws cookie recipe is included inside the box.

- Giftware—Pelican Publishing offers Cajun Night giftware.

- Miscellaneous items—Butterfly Originals and Aviva Enterprises both offer many licensed products (Muppets, Garfield, Berenstein Bears, Snoopy), everything from sunglasses to banks, from pencil cases to erasers, from mirrors to small purses.

19:08 Clothing Related Items

T-shirts are the major clothing category that has been traditionally adapted from books. Dallas Alice offers screenprinted T-shirts featuring Babar, The Far Side, Bialosky and Friends, Beatrix Potter, and many other licensed characters as well as definitions from Workman's *Well-Defined Dictionary*. Art 101 offers Thousand Words T-shirts. Fairfax Prints markets Frank Frazetta T-shirt transfers.

But why should T-shirts be the only clothing adaptations? How about a "Fit for Life" exercise outfit? Or Stephen Birnbaum or Baedecker designer luggage? *Moosewood Kitchen* aprons? *The Cat in the Hat* hats? *Ball Four* baseball caps? *Paper Lion* football jerseys?

19:09 Food Related Items

With so many cookbooks published every year, why have there been so few cookbook related foods put on the market? The only one I am aware of is Cajun Magic Seasonings by Chef Paul Prudhomme. Are there any others? If not, why not? Certainly there should be some other gourmet foods that could tie into cookbooks. Or how about candies? Cookies? Breads? Other prepared food?

19:10 CMG Skin Care: An Example

Here's one final example of how a product can grow out of a line of books. Marjorie Ainsborough Decker, the Christian Mother Goose, has written a number of books Christianizing basic fairy tales. Among her books are *Humpty Dumpty's Together Tales* about the togetherness of faith, *Nothing-Im-possible Possum Stories* about the positive power of faith, and *Grandpa Mole and Cousin Mole's Journeys* about the journey of faith.

Recently, in partnership with Ebenezer Toys, her press has produced and marketed seven plush animals based on characters in her books. Finally, she has also formulated three skin care products to ensure that "our precious children can have happysoft skin." The three CMG Skin Care products include a body soap, a lotion, and an oil.

The moral of this story? Don't limit your vision. Almost anything can be related to your books if you take the time to make the connections that are most important to you (as either author or publisher). Take time to consider why you wrote or published a particular book. Then look to see if there are any other products, services, or ways of marketing that will help you to bring your message, idea, entertainment, or whatever to the attention of more people. Finally, decide whether you want to spend your time marketing this new product or service or you want to spend it writing and/or publishing a new book.

CHAPTER 20

Expansion Options for Publishers

As a publishing company grows, it begins to accumulate other resources besides its backlist of books and other knowledge besides its skill at editing and marketing books. Rather than let these other resources go to waste, you could make them an integral part of your publishing and marketing plans.

In Chapter 19, I have already described a number of different ways that book publishers can make use of their editing and marketing know-how to create and distribute related products. In this chapter, I'd like to describe a few other ways that book publishers can expand on the basis of resources they accumulate as part of the publishing process.

20:01 Getting the Most from Your Mailing Lists

Time-Life Books's mailing list is reportedly worth more than a million dollars in list rental income each year. That's about a dollar per name per year. What is your house list worth? Figure it out: At $50.00 per thousand, one name is worth five cents each time it is rented out. If you rent your house list twice a month (for a total of 24 times per year), your rental income would be $1.20 per name per year. Multiply that by the number of names on your house list, and you have a good estimate of what your house list could be worth.

You can, of course, rent your list for $60.00 or more per thousand. And you can rent it more than twice a month. A good list, in fact, can be rented three to four times a month with comparative ease, though most mail order experts would caution against renting your list out more often than that. Because you will want to mail your own offers to your list, you don't want your list to get swamped with too much mail from other sources. Hence, about the maximum income you can expect to obtain from your house list is about $2.88 per name per year (at a cost of six cents per name, rented four times per month).

How do you go about renting your lists to other companies? There are two basic ways: 1) Handle it yourself, or 2) Let a list management company handle the maintenance and rental of your lists. Here's how a few major publishers have chosen to handle their house lists:

- Time-Life Books has recently assigned its combined lists of over a million names to Woodruff-Stevens, a list management company which also handles lists for *Newsweek*, *McCall's*, Avon Fashions, Ideals Publishing Company, and Prentice-Hall.

- Doubleday handles its own lists of over half a million book club members.

- Dartnell sells its own list of 120,000 active executive buyers. Its buyers have paid anywhere from $55.00 for a handbook to $635.00 for a training film. They update their list every day.

- Meredith Corporation has a separate division, Meredith List Marketing, which is responsible for maintaining and marketing their various house lists: 695,000 buyers of Frank Cawood health books, 15,000 active subscribers of *Prescription Drug News*, 220,000 buyers of the *Better Homes and Gardens Dieter's Cook Book*, and many other lists.

- Random House has assigned its lists of book buyers to The Kleid Company, including over 22,000 buyers of Times Books (cookbooks, crossword puzzles, etc.), over 180,000 buyers of the *AMA Family Medical Guide*, and 24,000 buyers of the Audobon Society's *Encyclopedia of North American Birds*. The Kleid Company also handles the Simon & Schuster J.K. Lasser lists consisting of over half a million names.

- The Southwestern Company has assigned its 315,000 1985 book buyers to Rubin Response Management Services. Southwestern's lists consists primarily of women who have purchased high quality books (religion, reference, cooking and children's books), with an average order of $60.00.

- Better Health Publications has given Prescott List Management responsibility to manage its list of men who have bought a book on sexual nutrition. Their list consists of 4,092 names of men over 50 years of age.

- Rodale offers its complete list of almost 8 million names through CompuName. Prices for their lists range from $55.00 per thousand for the total list to $60.00 per thousand for its subscriber lists to $75.00 per thousand for its multi-buyer lists.

- Enterprise Publishing has formed a separate division, Enterprise Lists, to handle list rentals and the production of a quarterly card deck. Its list consists of 215,000 book buyers and newsletter subscribers, all mail order generated buyers with an average purchase price of $44.00 (cash with order). They clean their list quarterly. They've rented their lists to *U.S. News and*

World Report, Prentice-Hall, Xerox Corporation, *Boardroom Reports, Inc* magazine, and New England Business Services, among others.

- Ad-Lib Publications maintains and markets our own lists. Indeed, we sell both ways. We sell our list of book printers to book publishers via our *Directory of Short-Run Book Printers* and the mailmerge version of that *Directory*. At the same time, we rent our list of buyers of the *Directory* to book printers. Since buyers of the *Directory* are clearly interested in buying book printing services, our list is the most targeted list in the industry for book printers to use. Currently, without any advertising at all, we rent our list about three times a month. We feel that the rental of our list is a service to our book buyers since it puts them in touch with book printers who are actively seeking short-run work from smaller publishers.

20:02 How to Market Your House Lists

If you turn over management of your lists to an outside list management service, they do all the marketing and promotion of the list, handle the updating of the list, and do all the fulfillment. You have only two responsibilities under such an arrangement: 1) to provide them with new and updated names on a regular basis (usually once or twice a month), and 2) to approve the rental of your lists to any users (which means you have the responsibility to screen out any direct competitors or other companies who would like to make what you feel are inappropriate offers to your lists).

Since many list management companies will not take on a list unless it has at least 50,000 names (or the potential to generate 50,000 names within a reasonable amount of time), you may have no choice but to handle your own lists. Even if your lists contain enough names, you may still prefer to keep your lists in house. In such cases, here are some tips and suggestions on how to go about marketing your lists:

- Write letters directly to marketing managers at those companies which you feel would be most interested in using your lists. When describing your list or lists, you should provide the following information if available: number of names, whether buyers or inquirers or both (with percentages), what kind of offer did they responded to, average size of purchase, dates of purchases (i.e., whether recent, within the past three months, within the past year, within the last two years, or whatever), frequency of purchases (how many are multi-buyers, and can these be rented separately), plus any information you have on the personal characteristics of the names (age, sex, occupation, median income).

  Finally, let them know in what format the list is available (4-up cheshire, 2-up pressure sensitive, or whatever), in what ways the list can be sorted (by zip code, recency of purchase, multi-buyers, sex, income, or whatever), the cost per thousand, shipping charges, how payment is to be made, whether you guarantee accuracy of addresses (most lists guarantee a delivery rate of at least 95%), how often your list is cleaned, the minimum number of names which may be ordered at one time. To get a better idea of what information to provide and in what format, write away for the media kits of several list owners and review how they describe their lists.

- Mail news releases describing your list to the major direct marketing and advertising magazines: *Direct Marketing*, *DM News*, *Zip Target Marketing*, *Catalog Age*, *Business Marketing*, and *Advertising Age*, among others.

- Advertise in these same magazines. Most of the major list owners and list brokers advertise regularly in these magazines. They wouldn't continue to advertise in these magazines if they were not getting a profitable response.

- Write to Standard Rate & Data for information on how to get listed in their directory, *Direct Mail List Rates and Data*. This directory, which describes over 55,000 different lists, is updated six times a year. Write to Standard Rate & Data Service, 3004 Glenview Road, Wilmette, IL 60091; (312) 256-8333.

- Inform major list brokers of the availability of your lists. List brokers are companies who act as intermediaries between list owners or managers and companies wanting to rent a list. While some brokers are also list managers, most are independent agents who make their money on the commission they receive from the list owner. The standard commission is 20% of the rental fee—a small price to pay for rentals you would not otherwise receive. You can find lists of such brokers in the major direct marketing magazines as well as in SRDS's *Direct Mail List Rates and Data*.

- When you do send out your list for rental, be sure to seed your list with a few decoy names so you can track the usage of your list (to verify that the list renter only uses the list the one time, that the renter mails to the list within the time period stated in your contract, and to see that no unauthorized compiling of your lists occurs). These decoy names should be real people (friends, relatives, or associates) who can monitor their mail for any letters addressed to the code you have assigned them. Have them note the date they received the letter before they send it on to you. If you'd rather not rely on friends or associates, there are companies which provide a similar service for a small annual fee plus a minimum charge per piece returned. Two such companies are U.S. Monitor Service, 86 Maple Avenue, New York, NY 10956; (914) 634-1331, and National List Protection System, 116 Byron Place, Livingston, NJ 07039; (201) 992-6606.

20:03 Start Your Own Card Deck

As an adjunct to the rental of your mailing list and as an additional opportunity to promote your books, you could start your own card deck. Not only could you reserve as much as half the deck for your own titles, but you could also pay for the costs of the entire mailing by selling the remaining cards to non-competing companies.

While you could start a card deck with as few as 10,000 names if the list is highly targeted, most such decks mail to at least 50,000 names. To publish a deck of 50 cards with a circulation of 50,000 would cost you between $20,000 and $30,000, depending on your in-house costs for marketing and administering the deck. Since each card you sell will bring in between $800.00 and $1000.00, you could pay for the entire deck by selling 25 to 30 cards.

To market your card deck, follow procedures similar to the steps listed above for marketing your mailing lists. Note, however, that your card deck should be listed in SRDS's *Business Publication Rates and Data* directory (which currently lists almost 600 card decks) rather than in its direct marketing directory.

To learn more about starting up your own card deck, write to Solar Press for a copy of its booklet, *How to Publish a Direct Response Card Publication*. Solar Press is one of a number of card deck manufacturers:

- Solar Press, 5 S. 550 Frontenac Road, Naperville, IL 60566; (312) 357-0100.
- Preiss Printing Company, 265 Bethpage-Spagnoli Road, Melville, NY 11747; (800) 645-9588 or (516) 752-7100.
- Scoville Press, 14505 - 27th Avenue N., Plymouth, MN 55441; (612) 553-1400.
- Rose Printing Company, 2503 Jackson Bluff, P. O. Box 5078, Tallahassee, FL 32314; (904) 576-4151.

Here's a list of a few book publishers with notes on how they handle the card decks they publish:

- John Wiley & Sons publishes three card decks which they market on their own: Engineers Action Cards (100,000 for $1,700), Financial Executive Action Cards (75,000 for $1,275), and Business/Computer Action Cards (100,000 for $1,700).
- Enterprise Publishing offers the Enterprise Action Pack with a circulation of 100,000 for $1695 per card. Enterprise markets the deck on its own and also through Media Organization, a broker.
- Matthew Bender & Company markets its own card decks aimed at lawyers and accountants.
- Caddylak Systems markets its card deck of 100,000 book buyers through Direct Media List Management.
- Prentice-Hall offers four different card decks through Venture Communications. The four decks are: Prentice-Hall Business Management (100,000 circulation), Prentice-Hall Law (40,000), Prentice-Hall Tax (70,000), and Prentice-Hall Educators (100,000).

- McGraw-Hill offers its Business Leaders Direct Response Deck of 100,000 circulation through the management of Abelow Response. It also offers its Active Investor, Marketing Management, and Human Resources card packs through BRC Inc., another card pack management company.

20:04 Publish a Mail Order Catalog

If you are a smaller publisher with a limited number of titles of your own, you might consider organizing a catalog that includes related titles from other publishers. Keep the catalog focussed on a specific topic, such as health care, real estate, or child development. Start small, with perhaps only five or ten other titles, and expand as the demand requires. Besides using the catalog as a bounceback offer to your mail order customers, you might also offer it to targeted lists outside your own.

Here's a few examples of how other publishers are using catalogs to increase their income:

- Here at Ad-Lib, when we fulfill orders for our own books, we also enclose a 4-page brochure describing other books about printing, publishing, direct marketing, publicity, and advertising. We offer these books to help fill out our own line of books. Hence, even though we only receive several thousand dollars a month in sales from this brochure, we still continue it because we feel it is a service to our customers.

- Midwest Financial Publications, to supplement its own list of real estate books, began offering a catalog of other titles as well. The catalog has since become a major profit center for them.

- JLA Associates have put together a Small Business Success catalog which offers about thirty books and newsletters to help individuals start up and manage their own businesses. Currently, all orders received from the catalog are dropshipped direct from the original publisher. JLA stocks none of the books themselves.

- Twenty First Century Publications advertises their catalog of new age and health-related titles in various national magazines. Along with their own titles, they also sell about 100 other titles from a number of different publishers. Since they also operate a bookstore, the books for the catalog do double duty as backup stock for the bookstore as well.

20:05 Other Mail Order Options

If you publish directories and other information resources, here's a few suggestions to help you to expand your services to those companies who are listed in your directories (or who advertise in your directories). These suggestions are taken from Russell Perkins's *Directory Publishing: A Practical Guide* (a superb guide to publishing directories).

- Offer literature fulfillment services. To make it easier for users of your directory to request information from different companies, you could offer to handle multiple requests for information. In such a case, you could fulfill all the requests yourself (by stocking appropriate literature from each participating company) or you could pass on the requests for information as they come in (just as many magazines now pass on requests for information via bingo cards inserted into the magazine). In either case, you would charge the companies for each request you fulfilled or passed on. The companies benefit by not having to add on extra staff to handle literature requests, and the users benefit by not having to write to many different sources.

- Offer sample pack promotions. Arrange to mail product samples from a number of different companies to all buyers of your directory. Under such an arrangement, each participating company would supply you with enough product samples (preferably small and unbreakable) to cover your user base. You would then mail out these samples with orders for the directory or as a separate mailing.

- Include package inserts in all your outgoing mail. While some companies might not want to advertise in your directory, they might be willing to pay you to stuff their promotional literature in with each outgoing order for your directory. They would provide you with sufficient inserts and pay you $40.00 or more per thousand inserts. If your directory has an annual circulation of 5,000 or more copies, a package insert broker could help you to locate interested companies. Here's the addresses of two well-known package insert brokers: Leon Henry Inc., 455 Central Avenue, Scarsdale, NY 10583; (914) 723-3176, and Larry Tucker Inc., 607 Palisade Avenue, Englewood Cliffs, NJ 07632; (201) 569-8888.

- Print discount coupons inside your directory. For example, one publisher of an on-line database directory offers discount coupons for various database services. Not only are discount coupons an excellent way for advertisers to attract attention to their services, but they are also a bonus value for users of your directory (hence, they are an additional benefit that you can feature when advertising the directory). Here, again, you can use brokers to help you sell discount coupons. Russell Perkins recommends Directory Discounts, 2200 Union Center, Los Angeles, CA 90036.

20:06 Organize a Book Club

In 1982, book clubs sold over $560 million worth of books. Of the approximately 200 book clubs now in existence, the majority are run as subsidiaries of book publishers, including the two biggest (Literary Guild and Book-of-the-Month Club). Here's a few examples:

- Macmillian operates fifteen different clubs. They have separate clubs for architects, astronomers, psychologists, grade school teachers, electrical engineers, business executives, computer specialists, scientists, special education teachers, natural scientists, nurses, civil engineers, mechanical engineers, owners of personal computers, and teachers.

- Prentice-Hall also operates fifteen different clubs, including ones for psychologists, accountants, builders, coaches, data processors, educators, electronic engineers, health enthusiasts, lawyers, managers, music educators, personal achievement, real estate specialists, salespeople, and speakers.

- McGraw-Hill operates seven different clubs, including ones for architects, personal computer owners, chemical engineers, civil engineers, electronics engineers, general engineers, and mechanical engineers.

- Doubleday owns Literary Guild, Doubleday Book Club, Fireside Theater, International Collectors Library, Military Book Club, Science Fiction and Fantasy Book Club, Mystery Guild, and the Large Print Home Library. They also operate the Junior Literary Guild whose membership is made up only of school and children's librarians.

- Time-Life Books owns Book-of-the-Month Club, Cooking and Crafts Book Club, Dolphin Book Club, Fortune Book Club, and Quality Paperback Book Club.

- Watson-Guptil operates book clubs for artists, designers, and photographers.

- TAB Books operates the Aviator Guild, Computer Book Club, Electronics Book Club, and the How-to Book Club.

- Rodale offers the Self-Sufficiency Book Club, Prevention Book Club, Organic Gardening Book Club, and the Practical Homeowner's Book Club.

- Other publishers offer clubs on dance (Princeton Book Company), ecology (Devin-Adair), history (Harcourt Brace Jovanovich), nostalgia (Crown), jewelers (Chilton), mystic arts (Lyle Stuart), writing and art (Writers Digest Books), small press literature (Dustbooks), and religion (Word Books).

While book clubs would seem to be a natural extension of a book publishing program, there are many possible pitfalls to running a successful book club program. I don't have room here to go into all the potential problems. I would recommend that you talk to a book club consultant. Irvin Haas, a consultant who specializes in book clubs, has organized 27 book clubs over the last 30 years, including clubs for photographers, horse lovers, and family health. The other consultants listed below will consult on book club operations as well as many other phases of book publishing and direct marketing.

- Irvin Haas, Book Club Consultant, 65 Diana's Trail, Roslyn Estate, NY 11576; (516) 621-1807.
- Book Publishers Projects, 115 Fifth Avenue, New York, NY 10003; (212) 586-6950.
- Fenvessy & Schwab, 645 Madison Avenue, New York, NY 10022; (212) 758-6800.
- Immergut and Siolek Associates, 2 Sidney Place, Brooklyn, NY 11201; (718) 625-1364. Their specialty is professional and technical books.
- Andrew Svenson Company, 1950 Landings Boulevard #202, Sarasota, FL 33581; (813) 923-1465.

20:07 Become a Distributor

I know of quite a few smaller book publishers who have become distributors simply because they wanted to get better distribution for their own titles, especially outside the ordinary book trade channels. Since it usually doesn't cost any more to distribute fifty titles as does to distribute five titles, the publishers began to take on titles from other publishers as well. Similarly, some major publishers have agreed to distribute the books of smaller publishers to help cover their costs in setting up their own network of house sales representatives.

Should you become a distributor? That all depends on how much time you want to devote to working with other publishers to bring their books before the markets you are already approaching. To justify the expense and additional work load, you will probably need at least a 55% to 65% discount. Remember that you will not only have the costs of marketing the books, but you will have to pay warehousing, fulfillment, and accounting costs as well.

To give you an idea of the variety of approaches publishers have taken in distributing books, here's a few examples:

- 101 Productions set up a network of 40 commissioned sales representatives to promote their line of cookbooks to 2000 cookware shops and houseware departments in stores around the country. Since they had the network already set up, they decided to take on the books of other publishers as well. They now serve as distributors to these nontraditional outlets for even some of the largest publishers such as Macmillan and its subsidiary the Scribner Book Companies.

- Gryphon House distributes children's books from over 80 publishers (16 of which are distributed under an exclusive arrangement). They use no sales reps, but rather distribute all books through mail order (via catalogs, book club programs, and book fairs). Gryphon sells to the library market, early childhood centers, and elementary schools.

- Samuel Weiser distributes books on metaphysics, astrology, the occult, health, and other subjects for over 200 different publishers. Most books are distributed on a nonexclusive basis to bookstores, other retail accounts, and individual book buyers.

- Lowen Publishing has begun the Business Books Marketing Group to promote business books to corporate libraries. Since they have also set up a network of office supply sales reps to market their *Office Purchasing Guide*, they are starting to accept other publisher's business titles for distribution to these outlets as well.

- In section 12:10 earlier in this book, we also listed the names of a number of major publishers who distribute books from smaller publishers to the book trade. In most cases, these major publishers use their own in-house reps to promote the titles of other publishers as well. Among these major publishers are Harper & Row, Random House, W. W. Norton, Farrar Straus Giroux, and Simon & Schuster.

20:08 Operate Bookstores

In the early days of American publishing, publishers and bookstores were essentially one and the same. The bookstores published books which they then sold. Few other publishers even existed. Nowadays, few publishers own bookstores. I'm not even sure if the following publishers still own the bookstores which carry their names: McGraw-Hill Book Stores, Doubleday Bookshops, Harcourt Brace Jovanovich, and Barnes & Noble. Yet operating a bookstore would seem to be a natural outgrowth of some publishers's activities. For instance, Dover Publications operates a bookstore at their publishing headquarters in downtown New York. Because they publish so many titles themselves, the bookstore only features their own books.

On the other side of the coin, in order to serve their local clientele and to fill gaps they see in the books now produced by publishers, a number of bookstores have begun publishing books. I remember reading about one bookstore in Kentucky or Tennessee who published their own regional title which sold quite well. And, of course, Waldenbooks now publishes a number of books under its own special imprint.

Here's a few examples of bookstores operated by book publishers:

- Penguin operates seven company-owned stores in England and has recently franchised its first U.S. bookshop in Cambridge, Massachusetts. I would expect more Penguin franchised bookstores to come out of Penguin's promotion of its bookstore boutiques.

- Twenty First Century Publications operates a local bookstore here in Fairfield, Iowa. The bookstore grew out of their mail order catalog business. Since they were already stocking a wide variety of books for their catalog business, they decided to open a retail outlet as well.

* Llewellyn Publications has operated a bookstore in downtown Saint Paul, Minnesota for a good number of years. Llewellyn also offers a mail order catalog featuring books on astrology and the occult, including titles from other publishers.

* Besides publishing their own books and a regional arts newspaper called *Uncle Jam*, Fragments West also operates The Cobblestone Gallery, a book and card shop. In this case I'm not sure which came first, the publisher or the bookstore.

20:09 Publish a Newsletter or Magazine

Many book publishers also publish magazines (or newsletters, or newspapers), and many magazine publishers also publish books. Here's just a few of them: Time-Life Books, Atlantic Monthly Press, McGraw-Hill, Chilton Books, Rodale Press, Fragments West, Prentice-Hall, Reader's Digest Books, Field Publications, R. R. Bowker, Modern Handcraft, Motorbooks International, Dustbooks, Our Sunday Visitor, Parents Magazine Press, Warren Gorham & Lamont, Watson-Guptill, Williams & Wilkins, H. W. Wilson, Enterprise Publishing, Beckley Group, Verbatim Books, Consumer Guide Books, Matthew Bender, and Writers Digest Books.

One of the advantages of publishing newsletters and magazines is that they can provide you with material for new books. Not only can you create books by collecting articles together under a general theme, but you can also develop books out of major articles in your magazine. Magazines also put you into contact with some of the best writers in the subjects you specialize in publishing. Hence, you have a means to draw upon the best talent for your books.

Magazines and newsletters also give you a strong promotional base for marketing any new books you publish. Certainly Writers Digest Books makes good use of its connection with the magazine. McGraw-Hill also makes good use of the magazines it publishes, including *BYTE* and *Popular Computing*, to promote its new computer books. At the very least, you can use any unsold ad space to advertise your books.

Howard J. Ruff sent $2.00 discount coupons to the readers of his newsletter, *Financial Success Report*, to promote one of his new books. The coupons, though, were only good if the readers bought the book at one of the major chain stores such as B. Dalton or Waldenbooks. As a result of this promotion, his book soon rose to the top of the chains's best-seller lists. Once on these lists, it didn't take long for the book to also appear on other major best-seller lists including the *New York Times* list.

20:10 Miscellaneous Businesses

Here's a list of a few other businesses that publishers have gone into at one time or another. You might find that some of them will fit well into your own expansion plans.

- **Advertising agency**—Some publishers have formed advertising agencies only to take advantage of the standard 15 % agency discount for placing ads. Ad-Lib Publications, on the other hand, grew out of Ad-Lib Consultants, which was a consulting service specializing in the design, development, and promotion of toys and gifts. While the consulting part of our business is now only a small part of our operation, it still functions as our advertising agency (as well as serving a few other smaller companies).

  If I'm correct, the major advertising agency serving book publishers, the Franklin Spier Agency, was once a division of Doubleday. It is now a subsidiary of BBDO International.

- **Export representatives**—Feffer and Simons, one of the major export representatives for books, is a subsidiary of Doubleday. Both Harper & Row and John Wiley & Sons have international subsidiaries which function as foreign agents for a number of other publishers.

- **Telemarketing services**—Grolier has a subsidiary, Grolier Telemarketing, which offers inbound and outbound telemarketing services to other companies.

- **List management services**—Meredith Corporation has a division, Meredith List Marketing, which not only handles the management and marketing of its own list but also manages a variety of independently owned lists. Business Mailers Inc., a major supplier of lists of medical professionals, is a subsidiary of Macmillan.

- **Printing**—Thomas Nelson owns Interstate Book Manufacturers. Acropolis Books also operates Colortone Press, a high quality four-color printing company. Williams & Wilkins is a division of Waverly Press, another book printer. Offset Paperback Book Manufacturers is a division of the same company that owns Bantam. Eerdmans Publishing, Naturegraph Publishers, Westview Press, and Rand McNally are among the publishers who also print books for other publishers. If you own a printing press and are not using it fully for the production of your own books, it makes sense to use the unfilled time to produce books for other publishers.

- **Real estate agencies**—Meredith Corporation, publishers of *Better Homes and Gardens*, has franchised BH&G real estate agencies all over the country.

As you read the next chapter, you might also come up with some other ideas for new products and services that your company can develop. For example, how about giving seminars? Offering consulting services? Establishing an institute (such as the Writers Digest Writing School)? Hence, even though the next chapter is directed primarily at authors, book publishers should also find it interesting. Read on.

CHAPTER 21

Authors: How to Capitalize on Your Books

My advice is not to create something totally different from what you are now selling until you have pursued every means of marketing your existing information. The best strategy is to repackage your bestselling, proven products and market them to a brand new audience. . . . Don't be shy about selling your repackaged information for a higher price. People want your information but may not have the time or desire to read a book. They will gladly pay more to get the same information presented in a convenient form. That's why you see the exact same information sold as a $10 book, a $25 cassette series, a $40 non-credit course, a $75 videotape, a $100 newsletter, a $150 per hour consultation, a $250 seminar, etc.

—Mark Nolan, *Information Marketing Newsletter*

No other publication establishes the credentials of an author the way the publication of a book does. Until you've written a book and had it published, you will always be an incomplete writer in the eyes of many people. Why is this? I don't know. Perhaps it's because books are more substantial, more impressive. Maybe it's because the book stands or falls on your work alone. Whatever the reason, you should be ready to capitalize on the increase recognition that publication of a book gives your work.

This chapter lists some of the ways that you can use your new-found recognition to expand the audience for your creative endeavors—and make more money in the process. While some of these opportunities will come your way unasked, don't wait for them to happen. Instead, envision what you really want, and then create it on your own.

21:01 Sell Your Writing Skills

Once you've demonstrated that you can write a book that merits publishing, you'll find that many new opportunities begin to open up for you in the writing field. Here's just a few of them:

- You'll finally be able to convince a literary agent to take on your work. Few agents will represent authors who only produce short pieces simply because there's not enough money in selling articles and short stories. The agents have to be able to justify the time and money they spend on representing their clients. Selling one book is more cost-effective for them than trying to sell dozens of articles to generate the same amount of income.

- Magazine editors will take you more seriously since you've demonstrated that you can produce major works. Also, by getting your book published, you've passed a screening test far more rigorous than any magazine writer. Your book is one out of 35,000 new titles, while a magazine article is only one out of half a million or more features.

- With the publication of your book, you become an instant expert. Again, I'm not sure why this is the case, but it is a fact of life. People will seek you out for advice. Editors will pay more attention to your article proposals, especially those having to do with your area of expertise (as indicated by your book). You might even find yourself teaching PhD candidates even though you have nothing more than a B.A. or high school diploma.

- You'll also find more doors open to you in the business world and other areas where your knowledge and/or writing skill (again, as evidenced by your book) are needed. You could well be offered job opportunities that are much more in line with what you really like to do.

- A published book will increase your chances of obtaining grants to continue developing your skills as a poet or fiction writer. Foundations and other organizations are more willing to support authors who have demonstrated that they can produce a significant amount of work.

21:02 One Book Two Ways

Once you've established your reputation as an expert on one subject, why not write another book on the same subject. Not only is it easier to write another book on the same subject, but you will be able to use many of the same contacts to promote, market, and distribute your new book. Just as a publisher benefits from specializing in specific areas, so can a writer.

Here's a few examples of how other writers have drawn upon their previous books to create new books:

- Sheldon Gerstenfeld, a veterinarian, wrote one book on *Taking Care of Your Cat*. Then, using much of the same information and advice, he wrote another book on *Taking Care of Your Dog*. Both books used the same cover design, format, and style (thus saving the publisher time and money in designing and producing the books). Later, Gerstenfeld wrote still another book, *The Bird Care Book*, which incorporated much of the same information and made use of the same book design.

- Archie Satterfield and Eddie Bauer put together three books for Addison-Wesley, all using the same format and design. The first book, *The Eddie Bauer Guide to Cross-Country Skiing*, was followed by two other books aimed at a more general audience, *The Eddie Bauer Guide to Family Camping* and *The Eddie Bauer Guide to Backpacking*.

- When Durk Pearson and Sandy Shaw wrote their book on *Life Extension*, they filled it with many complicated and technical articles, which made the book difficult for the average reader to follow. Nonetheless, the book sold over a million copies. To make the information in the book more accessible to the average person, they wrote a second book, *The Life Extension Companion*, which used less technical language to make the same points as the first book. Recently, they've written a third book, *The Life Extension Weight Loss Program*, to reach an even greater audience.

- This book you're now reading could easily be adapted to address two new markets. If I ever get the time and incentive to follow up on the idea, I'd like to write a second book aimed at small businesses, to be titled *101 Ways to Sell Almost Anything*, and a third book aimed at consultants and other professionals, to be titled *101 Ways to Sell Yourself (and Your Services)*. Though each book would be organized in the same way and draw upon much of the same information, the detailed resources and examples would be different. While any business or professional could gain many insights and ideas from reading this book, they'd gain even more from reading a book aimed directly at them.

- It's possible to write one book aimed, for instance, at doctors and another one aimed at patients. Both books could contain much of the same information; only the angle of approach would be different. For instance, in my *Directory of Short-Run Book Printers* I included several special sections giving publishers pointers on how to select a book printer and work with that printer to produce a high quality yet inexpensive book. Recently I've taken that same information and adapted it to a report aimed at printers who want to develop more short-run business. The report, *How to Sell Your Short-Run Production Services to Smaller Publishers*, shows book printers how to adapt their advertising and actual capabilities to better serve the short-run needs of smaller publishers.

- Peter McWilliams essentially wrote the same book three different times. First he wrote *The Word Processing Book*, then *The Personal Computer Book*, and then *The Personal Computer in Business Book*. While each book contained much of the same information, each was aimed at a different market. Each, in turn, became a national best seller. He even followed up the word processing book with another book, *Questions and Answers on Word Processing*, based on questions readers has asked him to answer. More recently, he published a special edition of the word processing book for the IBM computer, *Word Processing on the IBM*.

21:03 Self-Publishing Successes

For those of you who are thinking of self-publishing your own book, here's a few examples of other writers who have done so successfully—and then sold their book to a major publisher in order to gain even wider distribution.

- Norman Dacey self-published *How to Avoid Probate* and sold 10,000 copies on his own before the book was picked up by Crown, who then went on to sell over a million copies of the book.

- After having triple bypass surgery at the age of 32, Joseph Piscatella was forced to change his eating habits. As a result, he and his wife developed 400 recipes for foods low in salt, sugar, and fat. In the spring of 1983, he self-published 5,000 copies of *Don't Eat Your Heart Out*. Within a month the entire edition had sold out. Later that fall Workman Publishing published the book, printing 30,000 copies in their first edition. Since that time, they've sold 170,000 copies of the book at the rate of about 6,000 copies per month.

- Mildred Newman and Bernard Berkowitz self-published *How to Be Your Own Best Friend*. The book sold so well in their own local area (the West Coast) that Random House paid them a $60,000 advance for the rights to publish the book nationally.

- When Jim Everroad lost his job as a high school athletic coach, he decided to become a sportswriter. The first job he tackled was to write an article describing the exercises he had developed to tighten his pot belly. After selling the article to a newspaper, he expanded it into a full book (6,000 words plus several dozen photographs) and printed a first edition of 3,000 copies. That edition sold so quickly that he ordered another edition of 50,000 copies, which he sold primarily in his own region (Indiana). Later the book was discovered by Price/Stern/Sloan who published a new national edition of the book. The book has since sold over 2,000,000 copies.

- Spencer Johnson and Kenneth Blanchard originally self-published *The One Minute Manager* because they wanted to sell their book at a $15.00 cover price (a price few major publishers would have dared set for such a slim book). After they'd sold over 20,000 copies of the book in a very short time, seventeen publishers bid for the rights to republish the book. Since then, the book has sold millions of copies and been on the best-sellers list for both hardcover and trade paperback.

21:04 How to Make Money on Remainders

Unless your book becomes a steady backlist seller, your book will sooner or later be dropped by your publisher. You then have the choice to let the book die at a remainder house or to buy up the remainder copies yourself and try to promote them on your own. If you do decide to promote them on your own, you will become, in effect, your own publisher. You can then use many of the tips and suggestions in this book to help you market the book.

One other option you have is to get your book listed in the Buckley-Little Catalogue. This catalogue was started by William F. Buckley and Stuart W. Little to help keep out-of-print titles available to the public. The catalogue currently lists over 1000 such titles, all available through their authors. While the first two editions of the catalogue were distributed free to the first thousand libraries and bookstores who requested them, the new 1986 edition sells for $12.50. If you'd like to have your book listed in this catalogue, write to The Buckley-Little Catalogue, P. O. Box 512, Canal Street Station, New York, NY 10013; (212) 982-9357.

21:05 Syndicating Your Expertise

Having a book published establishes your credentials both as a writer and as an expert. You can use both these credentials to syndicate your knowledge via radio stations and newspapers or to obtain a position as a commentator on a radio or TV show. Here's a few examples of what other authors are doing:

- **Syndicated newspaper columns**—Mary Ellen Pinkham, author of a number of books on helpful hints, writes a syndicated column that is carried by over 125 newspapers with a combined circulation of well over ten million readers.

  Peter McWilliams, author/publisher of a number of computer books, writes a weekly column on personal computers for the Universal Press Syndicate; the column is carried by over 75 newspapers with a circulation of ten million, making him one of the most widely read computer journalists in the country.

  Tom Peters, co-author of *In Search of Excellence*, writes a weekly syndicated newspaper column on business management for the Tribune Company.

- **Television features**—Besides the weekly newspaper column, Tom Peters also appears weekly on the cable TV show, *Business Times*.

After publishing her books on helpful hints, Mary Ellen Pinkham joined *Good Morning America* for two years as a commentator on helpful hints for the home.

- **Syndicated television show**—Howard Ruff, author of *How to Prosper During the Coming Bad Years*, had a nationally syndicated TV show, *Ruff Times*.
- **Syndicated radio series**—Beverly Nye, self-publisher of *A Family Raised on Sunshine*, syndicated her own series of shows on homemaking tips to radio stations across the country. Not only did the radio stations pay her royalties for airing the show, but she was able to use the show to plug her own books.
- **Magazine columnist**—Herschell Gordon Lewis, author of *Direct Mail Copy That Sells* and *More Than You Ever Wanted to Know about Mail Order Advertising*, writes a regular column for *Direct Marketing* magazine. At the end of each column, the magazine prints a short biography which plugs his books and his copywriting services.
- **Newsletter columnist**—I write a regular column about book marketing for the COSMEP newsletter. Although I receive no compensation for this column, I do receive a short plug for my books. I am also on the editorial board for the *Information Marketing* newsletter and submit regular features for it as well.

21:06 Publish Your Own Newsletter

Once you've established your expertise, you might consider publishing a newsletter, especially if your expertise is in a rapidly changing field. Newsletters can command high prices and, because they are shorter than books, can be easier to produce. The major drawback to newsletters is that they do require a long-haul commitment to meeting deadlines (whether monthly, bimonthly, or quarterly). It's not worth publishing a newsletter if you don't intend to continue publishing it for at least two years.

For more information on publishing newsletters, write to the Newsletter Association, 1341 "G" Street NW #700, Washington, DC 20005; (202) 347-5220, and the Newsletter Clearinghouse, 44 West Market Street, Rhinebeck, NY 12572; (914) 876-2081 (publishers of the *Newsletter on Newsletters*).

- Howard Ruff's *Financial Success Report* currently has 115,000 subscribers paying $109.00 per year (that works out to over $12 million per year in subscription income).
- Pam Young and Peggy Jones, authors of *Sidetracked Home Executives*, publish a bimonthly newsletter, *S.H.E.s On Track*, which helps to promote their other books, cassette tapes, and Home Executive Kit.

- For several years Robert Ringer, author/publisher of *Winning Through Intimidation* and *Restoring the American Dream*, published a newsletter, *The Tortoise Report*, which was essentially an expression of his personal philosophy. Several hundred thousand subscribers paid $59.00 per year for the monthly newsletter.

- To supplement his $300.00 home study course, *The No-Downpayment Seminar*, Ed Beckley publishes a monthly newsletter called *The Beckley Report*. The newsletter, which costs $77.00 per year, details changes in the real estate and tax laws that would affect individual investors. It also, of course, contains the latest information on Beckley seminars, other courses, tapes, and books.

21:07 Speaking Out Your Knowledge

As the author of a book, you will often be asked to speak before groups. At some point you will have to decide if you will charge for your speaking services or continue to offer them gratis. To be honest, the lecture circuit could provide you with more income than your writing. For instance, Mary Cunningham, author of *Powerplay*, commands $10,000 per speaking engagement. Angela Davis, Betty Friedan, Jane Fonda, and Joan Mondale all get $5,000 per talk.

To learn more about earning money as a speaker, read Jeffrey Lant's book, *Money Talks*. If you decide to get serious about a career as a speaker, join the National Speakers Association (4323 N. Twelfth Street #103, Phoenix, AZ 85014) and subscribe to Dottie Walter's newsletter, *Sharing Ideas Among Professional Speakers* (18825 Hicrest Road, Glendora, CA 91740; 800-438-1242).

Here are a number of ways to earn money as a speaker:

- Engage a lecture agent to represent you. Like other agents, they work on a commission (usually anywhere from 15% to 30%). For a list of such agents, see the appendix of Jeffrey Lant's *Unabashed Self-Promoter's Guide* or Richard Weiner's *Professional's Guide to Public Relations Services*.

- Register with speakers bureaus who work on a nonexclusive basis. Speakers bureaus assist organizations looking for speakers to address their meetings and conventions. One such bureau is operated by Dottie Walters of *Sharing Ideas* (see address above).

- The possibilities for speaking are almost endless. Not only can you speak at local club meetings, but you can also speak for sales meetings, seminars, conventions, association meetings, company training programs, on board cruise ships, and anywhere else that people go to find useful information. Almost every company and association has need of speakers at least once a year (for their annual conference or meeting) and many require speakers more often than that (for monthly sales meetings, training programs, and other educational seminars).

- Once you've had some experience as a speaker, you might consider setting up your own seminars, such as the "Implementing In Search of Excellence" seminars (informally known as skunkcamps) put on by Tom Peters. The skunkcamps are only one of five services offered by the Tom Peters Group; the other four are consulting, research, publishing, and audio/video products.
- You could also offer specific workshops such as those offered by Dan Poynter, author of *The Self-Publishing Manual* and a number of other books about book publishing. Dan and Mindy Bingham of Advocacy Press host quarterly workshops on book marketing at Dan's hilltop home outside Santa Barbara. The charge for a weekend workshop is $250.00 and, according to all reports, they are well worth the small fee.
- Finally, you might consider organizing your own conventions. That's what Howard Ruff did. In the late 1970's he organized a number of Ruff Times National Conventions featuring well-known political and business figures giving advice on how to survive in the coming hard times. The cost for the full three-day convention in 1979 was $95.00.

21:08 Making Money as a Teacher

While speaking before large groups might pay more, teaching classes can often be more fulfilling. Teaching is an especially good way to gain experience talking before groups, and it is possible to arrange the classes you teach so you are well compensated for your time. Here are a number of possibilities:

- Teach continuing education classes for adults. Most high schools and colleges offer evening and weekend courses for adults who are not able to attend classes during the day. These continuing education courses are usually non-credit courses, so even if you don't have a teaching certificate, you may still teach these classes. Indeed, as an author, you are probably more experienced and qualified than many of the other people teaching such courses.

  Since most schools charge students a fee (anywhere from $20 to $50) for a three to ten hour course. Usually the teacher gets paid a portion of the course fees collected (anywhere from 30% to 60%). Hence, if 30 students were to take one of your courses, you could well make $500 or more for a five hour course (a $35 fee at 50% equals $525). Plus, you can assign your book as the textbook for the course and gross another $300 or more. Since you will undoubtedly be teaching a course related to your book, it is certainly reasonable to draw upon your book as the course text.

  Another bonus benefit of teaching continuing education classes is that your course (and book) will be publicized before as many as a million potential customers (as could happen when a large university system picks up your course to offer in its continuing education program and sends out catalogs announcing its course schedule to an entire metropolitan community).

- You could also teach correspondence courses similar to the ones offered by the Writer's Digest School.

- If you wrote a cooking, craft, or other how-to book, you could arrange to teach classes at local stores, community centers, or shopping centers.

- You could even open your own school. For example, if you write cookbooks, why not open a cooking school. Not only could the school bring in additional money, but it could also give you a place to test new recipes or cooking techniques.

One thing I've learned in all the years I've taught classes and spoken before groups: The teacher always learns more than the student. This, perhaps, is the strongest argument that can be made for teaching at least a few classes a year. You will always come away from such classes with renewed enthusiasm for your subject, renewed interest and, if my experience is any indication, a mind bursting with ideas for new books.

21:09 Making Money as a Consultant

If you are not comfortable speaking before large groups, you can still put your expertise to work as a consultant. No matter what your subject area, somewhere at sometime someone is going to need your expertise—and be willing to pay well for your services.

To learn more about setting yourself up as a consultant, read Jeffrey Lant's book, *The Consultant's Kit*, or Herman Holtz's *How to Succeed as an Independent Consultant*, or Kate Kelly's *How to Set Your Fees and Get Them*. All three books are superb. You might also want to subscribe to the *Consulting Opportunities Journal* (P.O. Box 1277, Leesburg, VA 22075; 304-725-8726).

- **Become a consultant**—Sheilah Kaufman, author of 11 cookbooks including *Sheilah's Fearless Fussless Cooking*, does consulting for gourmet food, gift, and houseware companies. She also travels around the country teaching cooking classes.

- **Offer consulting services via the mail**—Herschell Gordon Lewis, author of a number of books on direct marketing, has his own business called Communicomp, which offers direct mail copywriting for a wide variety of companies and organizations including the UN Children's Fund, Grolier Enterprises, Heritage House, and American Bankers Insurance Company. All his business is conducted through the mail and by phone.

- **Offer consulting services via the phone**—The Beckley Group offers their Million Dollar Advisory Service via a toll-free phone number to all subscribers of their Beckley Report newsletter. Any subscriber can call at any time to get advice from one of their trained real estate advisors.

- **Franchise your consulting services**—Carole Jackson, author of multi-million copy best seller, *Color Me Beautiful*, has franchised Color Me Beautiful consultants all over the country. When Acropolis Books came out with a new book, *Always in Style with Color Me Beautiful* by Doris Pooser, their 30-city publicity campaign was fully supported by Color Me Beautiful consultants in each of those cities.

- **Establish an institute**—John Naisbitt, author of the best-selling book, *Megatrends*, has organized an institute to study trends. The institute offers consulting services, a newsletter, and seminars, plus a number of annual reports. One of Tom Peter's five businesses, as noted above, is a research institute. The research institute provides data and other information to support the other businesses in his group.

- **Establish a center**—Jed Diamond, author of *Inside Out: Becoming My Own Man*, and Carlin Diamond, author of *Love It, Don't Label It*, have organized the Center for Prospering Relationships to help promote the principles and practices they believe in. Both books were self-published by their own press, Fifth Wave Press.

- **Form an association**—Chase Revel formed the American Entrepreneur's Association to promote his line of business start-up manuals. Through the association's *Entrepreneur* magazine and other services, it actually provides much support for business newcomers.

The Business Books Marketing Group was formed by myself and Tod Snodgrass of Lowen Publishing because we were looking for ways to increase the distribution of our books in the business world. The association has just mailed its first co-op mailing to corporate libraries, and Tod is now working to provide other services for publishers of business books. For more information, please contact Tod (not me). Write to Lowen Publishing, Attn: BBMG, P.O. Box 6870, Torrance, CA 90504-0870.

21:10 Become a Legal Expert Witness

A number of authors have found a lucrative sideline income from appearing as expert witnesses for various legal questions. As a legal expert, you may be called upon to investigate cases, testify at trials, give depositions, counsel attorneys, or provide other advice either by mail or over the phone. The standard fee for such work is around $100 or more an hour. If you have to go out of town to do on-site investigations or testify at a trial, the standard fee is anywhere from $500 to a $1000 per day, plus expenses.

How do you become an expert witness? Well, first, of course, you need to be an expert. While writing a book on a particular subject will authenticate your expertise, you should also have a lot of experience in that subject because you will have to stand up to cross examinations in court. Being an expert witness can be hard work since you must do your homework for each case, so if you are not enthusiastic about studying or learning more about your subject, you should not get into this field.

If you do decide to become a legal expert, visit your local law library (at the county courthouse or local law school) and ask to see the directories of legal experts. Review these directories to see if your area of expertise is listed. If so, write to the various directories and request an application to be listed. According to Dan Poynter, a expert witness in cases, there are five major legal expert directories:

- Expert Witness Directory, National Forensic Center, 17 Temple Terrace, Lawrenceville, NJ 08648; (609) 883-0550.
- Experts Unlimited, 1212 N. Lakeshore Drive, Chicago, IL 60610.
- Lawyers Desk Reference, 409 Griswold, Detroit, MI 48226; (313) 496-1330.
- National Medical Advisory Service, 7315 Wisconsin Avenue, Bethesda, MD 20814.
- Technical Advisory Service for Attorneys, 428 Pennsylvania Avenue, Fort Washington, PA 19034; (215) 643-5252.

Among author/publishers who are working as legal experts are Dan Poynter, author of *The Parachuting Manual* and *Parachuting, The Skydiver's Handbook* (who also spent seven years as an skydiving instructor and active member of several parachuting associations) and Dick Murdock, a former railroad engineer and author of a number of books about the old days of railroading in northern California. As a side benefit to his legal expert work, Dick recently sold 1000 copies of one of his railroading books to a law firm which specializes in railroad cases (and for whom Dick has often done consulting).

21:11 A Couple Unusual Spinoffs

Jim Everroad, author of the two million copy best seller, *How to Flatten Your Stomach*, now endorses and markets the Belly Burner, an exercise device. Commercials for this product appear on TV all over the country. A copy of his book is enclosed as a bonus with every order for the Belly Burner.

Chef Paul Prudhomme, author of *Louisiana Kitchen*, has just published a catalog featuring cast-iron skillets and other cookware necessary for preparing Cajun foods, plus his own brand of herbs and seasonings, Cajun Magic Seasonings, and several Cajun delicacies known as Tasso Ham and Andouille sausage (both of which are prepared in his manufacturing plant in Melville, Louisiana).

He distributes these catalogs through his three Louisiana Kitchen restaurants in New Orleans, New York, and San Francisco, as well as to people who have written in asking for more information. Recently he has also begun direct mail advertising for the catalog in *The New Yorker* and *Cook's Magazine* as well as on the Owen Spann syndicated radio show.

21:12 Fringe Benefits

One of the fringe benefits of being a writer is that you are often sent free products to review. I know of a number of cookbook writers, for instance, who have received dozens of blenders or microwaves to test while they were preparing cookbooks featuring those machines.

When writing his book on word processing, Dan Poynter received a free Xerox word processor to review. Similarly, when Peter McWilliams was producing all his books on computers and word processing, he would receive a new machine to review almost every month. He had machines sitting in his hallways, kitchen, even his bathroom.

While preparing the my books on book publishing, I've received a good number of complimentary review copies of books on publishing and marketing (all of which I've reviewed in my *Independent Publisher's Bookshelf*). Also, when I began looking for a database program to form the functional heart of my new *Book Marketing Opportunities: A Database*, I was sent a number of different database programs to review. As it happened, the best one I've found was developed by a local programmer, which means that I'll be able to have the program customized to better serve the users of the database.

When you are preparing a new book, don't overlook the possibility of receiving complimentary review copies of materials that you require in your research. It never hurts to ask for such review copies. Remember, if you feature anything in your book, you'll be giving it publicity that no amount of advertising could possibly buy.

These fringe benefits may not amount to much, but they do help you to cut down your upfront costs in producing a book. So don't be shy about making an honest request for review material needed for your book.

CHAPTER 22

What to Do Next

This book, as I noted in the introduction, was designed to be a potpourri of ideas, examples, tips, and suggestions to encourage you to explore new ways to market your books. I hope the book has achieved this purpose for you. To be honest, I'd be surprised if you didn't come away from this book with at least one new promotional possibility for your books. As a caution, however, I'd like to repeat what I said in the introduction. Don't get so excited about all the possibilities for marketing your book that you try to do everything at once. It won't work. Instead, focus your attention on those markets and promotional methods that offer the best possible return for your time and money. Remember the old 80/20 rule. Put your attention on your prime markets first because those markets are the ones that are going to produce the vast majority of your sales and profits.

22:01 The Ad-Lib Book Marketing Library

As you undoubtedly noticed, I've referred a good number of times to two other books that I have written: *Book Marketing Made Easier* and *Book Marketing Opportunities: A Directory*. This book plus those two books were designed to be used as a unit. Each complements and supplements the others.

Book Marketing Made Easier provides all the forms and records any publisher would need to prepare and carry out an effective marketing program to the book trade (bookstores, libraries, and schools). Every step is covered— from preparing a marketing strategy, forecasting sales, and planning budgets to researching the media, sending out press releases, and obtaining reviews; everything from getting distribution and working with bookstores to exhibiting books and granting subsidiary rights. This book, in short, takes a lot of the fuss and bother out of organizing an effective marketing program, thus allowing you more time to do the actual marketing.

On the other hand, *Book Marketing Opportunities: A Directory* lists almost 5000 key contacts for the major book marketing channels: wholesalers. . . distributors. . .sales representatives. . .chain stores. . .book clubs. . .catalogs. . . card decks. . .mailing lists. . .book fairs. . .foreign rights representatives. . . remainder dealers. . .publicity services. . .marketing co-ops. . .and a number of other marketing services. Plus it includes a select list of book reviewers (about 400 newspapers, 500 magazines, 800 radio shows, 600 TV shows, and 200 syndicates). Each listing includes names, addresses, phone numbers, topics of interest, and other applicable information. This directory will help you to tailor your promotional campaigns to fit each new book you publish.

As you can see, all three books were designed to work together as a unit. I do hope you will read all three of them. If you'd like copies of the other two books, ask your bookstore to order them. Or, if the books are not available locally, you may order them direct from Ad-Lib Publications, P.O. Box 1102, Fairfield, IA 52556-1102; (800) 624-5893 or (515) 472-6617.

22:02 Book Marketing Opportunities: A Database

Book Marketing Opportunities comes in two formats: as a printed directory and as a database for use on any IBM-PC or compatible. You must have an IBM-PC with a minimum 256K RAM. Alternatively, the database files are also available as comma-delimited ASCII files which may be formatted for use on a Macintosh or almost any CPM computer. To use these comma-delimited files, you will have to have a database program that can import such files. If you have an IBM-PC or any other MS-DOS computer, you won't have to worry about those details. The program will work with your computer as is.

Besides the data files, *Book Marketing Opportunities: A Database* also includes a software program to allow you to add, delete, edit, or update any records. You can create instant reports on screen or to the printer, with fast sorts for almost any combination of fields, operators, and conditions you could ever want to use. The database includes report formats for labels, media activity worksheets, and media response records. The program is incredibly fast.

All this for only $150.00. For less than it would cost you to rent a portion of this database list just once, you can own the entire database and use it as often as you like.

Semi-annual updates will also be available for the database so you won't have to spend a fortune trying to keep your own lists up to date. With each such update we will be improving the database—adding new information, new listings, and new categories. For instance, a list of specialty bookstores will be added by the end of this year (1986).

22:03 Other Books

I have written three other books which also supplement the material in the Ad-Lib Book Marketing Library. For instance, if you are serious about marketing your books by mail, you should definitely have a copy of my *FormAides for Direct Response Marketing: Mail Order Selling Made Easy*. This book is a collection of forms and procedures for organizing and carrying out a direct marketing program. These forms supplement the forms contained in *Book Marketing Made Easier*.

As mentioned in the introduction to this book, the bibliography for this book is really 80 pages long, since all the books listed in my bibliographic review, *The Independent Publisher's Bookshelf*, contributed to the ideas and examples in this book. The *Bookshelf* reviews over 150 books about publishing, self-publishing, printing, direct marketing, advertising, and publicity. Not only does it contain the basic information about a book (title, author, publisher, publisher's address, ISBN, publication date, price, etc.), but it also includes comments on the strengths and weaknesses of each book. The *Bookshelf* also reviews 25 magazines and newsletters and over 50 publishers' associations in the United States and Canada. It's a superb resource for any publisher.

And then there is my *Directory of Short-Run Book Printers, Third Edition*, which lists almost 400 book printers in the United States, Canada, and abroad. It doesn't matter where you live. With this directory, you can locate a quality book printer who specializes in the quantities, sizes, and bindings you want to use—at a price you can afford. I've had many book publishers call me after using this directory to tell me how much money they saved on their printing bills. I know one publisher who saved $8,000, another who saved over $5,000. Even more important, though, for most publishers are the hassles and delays that they avoided by being able to match their printing job to the printer's capabilities. I think you'll find the book a useful reference tool.

22:04 Other Services

Since I like to practice what I preach, I have been slowly expanding the services that I offer to other publishers and writers. For a number of years now, I've been doing consulting in the design, development, and promotion of toys and books in my local area. Now my consulting services will be available to anyone within reach of a phone.

Starting in July, 1986, I'll be offering a toll-free telephone advisory service for anyone with questions regarding the marketing of their books. Call (800) 624-5893. The charges for this service will be $100.00 per hour, billed by the minute to your credit card number (either MasterCard, VISA, or American Express). The clock doesn't start to tick until you've provided all the appropriate billing information. Of course, the advice won't start flowing until the clock starts ticking.

As an alternative, you may call me at your expense using our regular number (515) 472-6617 and get my advice for free (fifteen minutes maximum). This offer is good only one time and will stand as long as I don't get swamped with callers. Please do not abuse this privilege. Remember, I too have a business to run—and a regular life to live.

I am open to providing other consulting services, either at your facility or mine, but I have to warn you: I won't come cheap. And, to be quite honest, I'm not sure I'd be worth it. I've already put most of what I know in the six books I've written. Nonetheless, if you would like to dredge the bottom of my mind for advice on marketing your books, just give me a call.

Finally, if enough people request it, I'll offer an annual seminar here in beautiful downtown Fairfield. We'll be able to walk through the cornfields together during our lunch breaks. Actually, we have a new deluxe Best Western motel right at the edge of town where the seminar could be held. If you'd be interested in such a seminar, just drop me a note. (There is also a possibility that we could hold such a seminar somewhere else—say, for instance, the Bahamas or Maui or Singapore. Let me know if you'd be interested in other exotic locales other than Iowa.)

About the Author

John Kremer is the president and publisher of Ad-Lib Publications, located in Fairfield, Iowa. He is the author of a number of books on publishing and marketing, including *Book Marketing Made Easier, Book Marketing Opportunities: A Directory, Directory of Short-Run Book Printers, Third Edition*, and *Form-Aides for Direct Response Marketing: Mail Order Made Easy.*

John is currently a member of the board of directors of COSMEP, The International Association of Independent Publishers. He is also a member of Publishers Marketing Association, American Booksellers Association, Upper Midwest Booksellers Association, National Chamber of Prosperity and Progress, and American Society for Information and Inspiration.

He writes a monthly column on book marketing for the COSMEP newsletter. He also serves as a consulting editor for *The Information Marketing Letter.*

Before entering the publishing world, John was a consultant in the design, development, and promotion of toys and gifts. In that capacity he worked with First Impressions rubber stamp company, Economic Foundations, and Great Midwestern Ice Cream Company (makers of America's finest ice cream).

John has also been a newsletter editor, college writing instructor, Transcendental Meditation teacher, editor of workbooks, freelance writer, director of a non-profit organization, library researcher, and copy editor.

In his search for knowledge, John collected two degrees in interdisciplinary studies: a Masters degree from Maharishi International University and a Bachelors degree (with a concentration in anarchy) from Macalester College.

John is single, 37 years old, never been married, highly eligible. Besides being a superb slow-pitch softball pitcher, he also plays volleyball, basketball, and radios. He rides a three-speed bicycle to work.

Bibliography

The following books are the major resources used in writing this book. For a complete bibliography of books, magazines, and other resources used in writing this book, see my 80-page bibliography, *The Independent Publisher's Bookshelf*.

- American Association of University Presses, *One Book/Five Ways* (Los Altos, CA: William Kaufmann, 1978)
- Bodian, Nat G., *Book Marketing Handbook, Volumes One* (New York: R. R. Bowker, 1980)
- Bodian, Nat G., *Book Marketing Handbook, Volume Two* (New York: Bowker, 1983)
- Carter, Robert A., editor, *Trade Book Marketing* (New York: R. R. Bowker, 1983)
- Corwin, Stanley J., *How to Become a Bestselling Author* (Cincinnati: Writer's Digest Books, 1984)
- Glenn, Peggy, *Publicity for Books and Authors* (Huntington Beach, CA: Aames-Allen, 1984)
- Huenefeld, John, *The Huenefeld Guide to Book Publishing, Third Edition* (Bedford: Huenefeld, 1986)
- Kremer, John, *Book Marketing Made Easier* (Fairfield: Ad-Lib Publications, 1986)
- Kremer, John; Marie Kiefer; and Bob McIlvride, *Book Marketing Opportunities: A Directory* (Fairfield: Ad-Lib, 1986)
- Kremer, John, *Book Marketing Opportunities: A Database* (Fairfield: Ad-Lib, 1986)
- Lant, Jeffrey, *The Unabashed Self-Promoter's Guide* (Cambridge, MA: JLA Associates, 1983)
- McHugh, Jack, *McHugh Publishing Reports* (Framingham, MA: McHugh, 198-), various reports (4 pages to 72 pages)
- Parkhurst, William, *How to Get Publicity* (New York: Times Books, 1985)
- Poynter, Dan, *Book Fairs: An Exhibiting Guide for Publishers* (Santa Barbara, CA: Para Publishing, 1986)
- Poynter, Dan, *The Self-Publishing Manual, Third Edition* (Santa Barbara: Para, 1984)
- Richards, Pamela Spence, *Marketing Books and Journals to Western Europe* (Phoenix: Oryx Press, 1985)
- Ross, Marilyn and Tom, *The Complete Guide to Self-Publishing* (Cincinnati: Writer's Digest Books, 1985)

Index

AN UNBEATABLE COMBINATION: SUPERB BOOKS AND
A 30-DAY MONEY-BACK GUARANTEE

Please send me the following books. It is my understanding that if I am not completely satisfied with any book, I may return it within 30 days for a full refund. Thank you.

Quantity	Title of Book	Price	Total Amount
	Book Marketing Made Easier ISBN 0-912411-11-2	$14.95	
	101 Ways to Market Your Books -- For Publishers and Authors ISBN 0-912411-08-2	hc $19.95	
	101 Ways to Market Your Books -- For Publishers and Authors ISBN 0-912411-09-0	pb $14.95	
	Book Marketing Opportunities: A Directory ISBN 0-912411-10-4	$19.95	
	Book Marketing Opportunities: A Database ISBN 0-912411-12-0	$150.00	
	Directory of Short-Run Book Printers, Third Edition ISBN 0-912411-06-6	$12.00	
	Directory of Short-Run Book Printers, MailMerge Edition ISBN 0-912411-06-6	$30.00	
	The Independent Publisher's Bookshelf, Third Edition ISBN 0-912411-07-4	$3.95	
	FormAides for Direct Response Marketing: Mail Order Made Easy ISBN 0-912411-02-3	$9.95	
	TOTAL NUMBER OF BOOKS ORDERED	Subtotal =	

[ ] Check enclosed with order.
[ ] Please charge to my credit card number:
    [ ] American Express [ ] Visa [ ] MasterCard

Postage
$1.00/book

TOTAL ORDER

Number_____

From:_____ To (Exp. Date):_____

Name_____ Signature_____

Address_____ Company Name_____

_____ Phone Number_____

AD-LIB PUBLICATIONS, P.O. BOX 1102, FAIRFIELD, IOWA 52556   (515) 472-6617